Contents

100 Maths Framework Lessons

About the series

100 Maths Framework Lessons is designed to support you with the implementation of the renewed *Primary Framework for Mathematics*. Each title in the series provides clear teaching and appropriate learning challenges for all children within the structure of the renewed Framework. By using the titles in this series, a teacher or school can be sure that they are following the structure and, crucially, embedding the principles and practice identified by the Framework.

About the renewed Framework

The renewed *Primary Framework for Mathematics* has reduced the number of objectives from the original 1999 Framework. Mathematics is divided into seven strands:

- Using and applying mathematics
- Counting and understanding number
- Knowing and using number facts
- Calculating
- Understanding shape
- Measuring
- Handling data.

The focus for teaching is using and applying mathematics, and these objectives are seen as central to success for the children's learning. While the number of objectives is reduced, the teaching programme retains the range of learning contained in the 1999 Framework. There are, though, significant changes in both the structure and content of the objectives in the new Framework and this series of books is designed to help teachers to manage these changes of emphasis in their teaching.

About this book

This book is set out in the five blocks that form the renewed *Primary Framework for Mathematics*. Each block consists of three units. Each unit within a block contains:

- a guide to the objective focus for each lesson within the unit
- links with the objectives from the 1999 objectives
- the 'speaking and listening' objective for the unit
- a list of key aspects of learning, such as problem solving, communication, etc.
- the vocabulary relevant to a group of lessons.

Within each unit the 'using and applying' objectives are clearly stated. They are incorporated within the individual lessons through the teaching and learning approach taken. Sometimes they may be the only focus for a lesson.

Lessons

Each lesson contains:

- A guide to the type of teaching and learning within the lesson, such as Review, Teach, Practise or Apply.
- A starter activity, with a guide to its type, such as Rehearse, Reason, Recall, Read, Refine, Refine and rehearse, or Revisit.
- A main activity, which concentrates on the teaching of the objective(s) for this lesson.
- Group, paired or individual work, which may include the use of an activity sheet from the CD-ROM.
- Clear differentiation, to help you to decide how to help the less confident learners in your group, or how to extend the learning for the more confident. This may also include reference to the differentiated activity sheets found on the CD-ROM.
- Review of the lesson, with guidance for asking questions to assess the children's understanding.

You can choose individual lessons as part of your planning, or whole units as you require.

What's on the CD-ROM?

Each CD-ROM contains a range of printable sheets as follows:

- **Core activity sheets** with answers, where appropriate, that can be toggled by clicking on the 'show' or 'hide' buttons at the bottom of the screen.
- **Differentiated activity sheets** for more or less confident learners where appropriate.
- Blank core activity sheets or **templates** to allow you to make your own differentiated sheets by printing and annotating. 
- **General resource sheets** (such as number grids) designed to support a number of lessons.
- **Editable curriculum grids** (in Word format) to enable you to integrate the lessons into your planning.

In addition, the CD-ROM contains:

- **Interactive whiteboard resources** – a set of supporting resources to be used with the whole class on any interactive whiteboard or on a PC for small group work. These include number grids, money, clocks and so on.
- **Interactive Teaching Programs** – specific ITPs, originally developed for the National Numeracy Strategy, have been included on each CD-ROM.
- **Whiteboard tools** – a set of tools including a 'Pen', 'Highlighter' and 'Eraser', have been included to help you to annotate activity sheets for whole-class lessons. These tools will work on any interactive whiteboard.
- **Diagrams** – copies of all the diagrams included on the lesson pages.

How to use the CD-ROM

System requirements

Minimum specification:

- PC or Mac with a CD-ROM drive and 512 Mb RAM (recommended)
- Windows 98SE or above/Mac OSX.1 or above
- Recommended minimum processor speed: 1 GHz

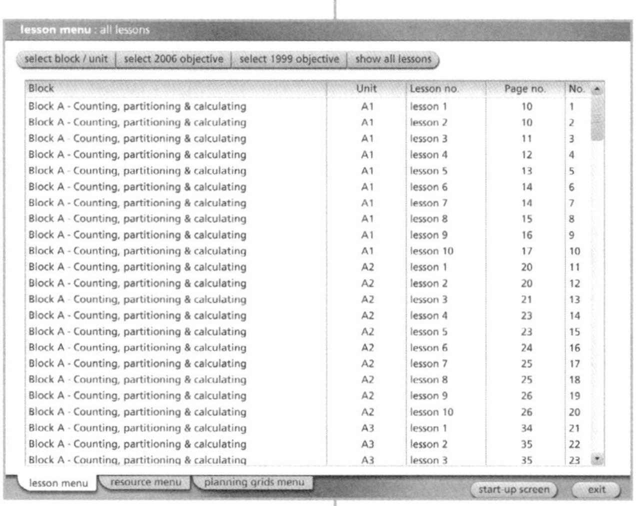

Getting started

The *100 Maths Framework Lessons* CD-ROM should auto run when you insert the CD-ROM into your CD drive. If it does not, use **My Computer** to browse the contents of the CD-ROM and click on the '100 Maths Framework Lessons' icon.

From the start-up screen there are four options: click on **Credits & acknowledgements** to view a list of acknowledgements. You should also view the **Terms and conditions** of use and register the product to receive product updates and special offers. Finally, you can access extensive **How to use this CD-ROM** support notes and (if you agree to the 'Terms and conditions') click on **Start** to move to the main menu.

Each CD-ROM allows you to search for resources by block, unit or lesson. You can also search by Framework objective (both 2006 and 1999 versions) or by resource type (for example, activity sheet, interactive resource or ITP).

Planning

The renewed Framework planning guidance sets out the learning objectives in blocks, and then subdivides these into units. The blocks are entitled:

- **Block A:** Counting, partitioning and calculating
- **Block B:** Securing number facts, understanding shape
- **Block C:** Handling data and measures
- **Block D:** Calculating, measuring and understanding shape
- **Block E:** Securing number facts, relationships and calculating.

Introduction

Within each block there are three progressive units, which set out the learning objectives for a two- or three-week teaching period. Because of the interrelated nature of learning in mathematics, some of the same learning objectives appear in different blocks so that the children have the opportunity to practise and apply their mathematics.

It is recommended that planning for the year takes the blocks and units in the following order:

	Block A: Counting, partitioning and calculating (6 weeks)	**Block B:** Securing number facts, understanding shape (9 weeks)	**Block C:** Handling data and measures (6 weeks)	**Block D:** Calculating, measuring and understanding shape (6 weeks)	**Block E:** Securing number facts, relationships and calculating (9 weeks)
Autumn	Unit A1	Unit B1	Unit C1	Unit D1	Unit E1
Spring	Unit A2	Unit B2	Unit C2	Unit D2	Unit E2
Summer	Unit A3	Unit B3	Unit C3	Unit D3	Unit E3

However, the book has been structured in block order (Block A1, A2, A3 and so on), so that teachers can plan progression across units more effectively, and plan other configurations of lessons where required. You can use the different menus on the CD-ROM to find suitable teaching and learning material to match your planning needs.

In each unit in this book, the 1999 Framework objectives are listed, so that it is possible to use materials from previous planning alongside these lessons. The CD-ROM has a facility, which allows for filtering by 2006 and 1999 learning objectives in order to find suitable lessons.

The blocks and units, taught in the order above, make a comprehensive teaching package which will effectively cover the teaching and learning for this year group.

Differentiation

Each lesson contains three levels of differentiation in order to meet the wide variety of needs within a group of children. There are differentiated activity sheets for many lessons that can be accessed on the CD-ROM (see 'What's on the CD-ROM', above). The units within a block are placed together in this book. This is in order to enable you to make choices about what to teach, when and to which children, in order to encourage more personalised learning.

Assessment

Within this book the guidelines for 'Assessment for learning' from the Framework are followed:

- Assessment questions are provided within each lesson in order to identify children's learning and to provide the children with effective feedback.
- The questions encourage children to be actively involved in their own learning.
- Many activities are undertaken in groups or pairs so that children have the opportunity to plan together and assess the effectiveness of what they have undertaken.
- The assessment outcomes give the teacher the opportunity to adjust teaching to take account of the results of assessment.
- The crucial importance of assessment is recognised, and the profound influence it has on the motivation and self-esteem of children, both of which are essential for learning.
- The assessment questions offer children the opportunity to understand what they know, use and understand and also to understand how to improve.

Counting, partitioning and calculating

Key aspects of learning
- Problem solving
- Communication
- Reasoning

Expected prior learning

Check that children can already:

- talk about how they solve problems, using the vocabulary of addition and subtraction and number sentences to describe and record their work
- count reliably at least 20 objects; estimate a number of objects that can be checked by counting
- read and write numerals from 0 to 20, and order these numbers on a number line
- say the number that is 1 more or less than any given number, and 10 more or less than a multiple of 10
- understand that addition can be done in any order and relate addition to counting
- understand subtraction as 'take away' and counting back, and find a difference by counting up
- recognise the value of coins.

Objectives overview

The text in this diagram identifies the focus of mathematics learning within the block.

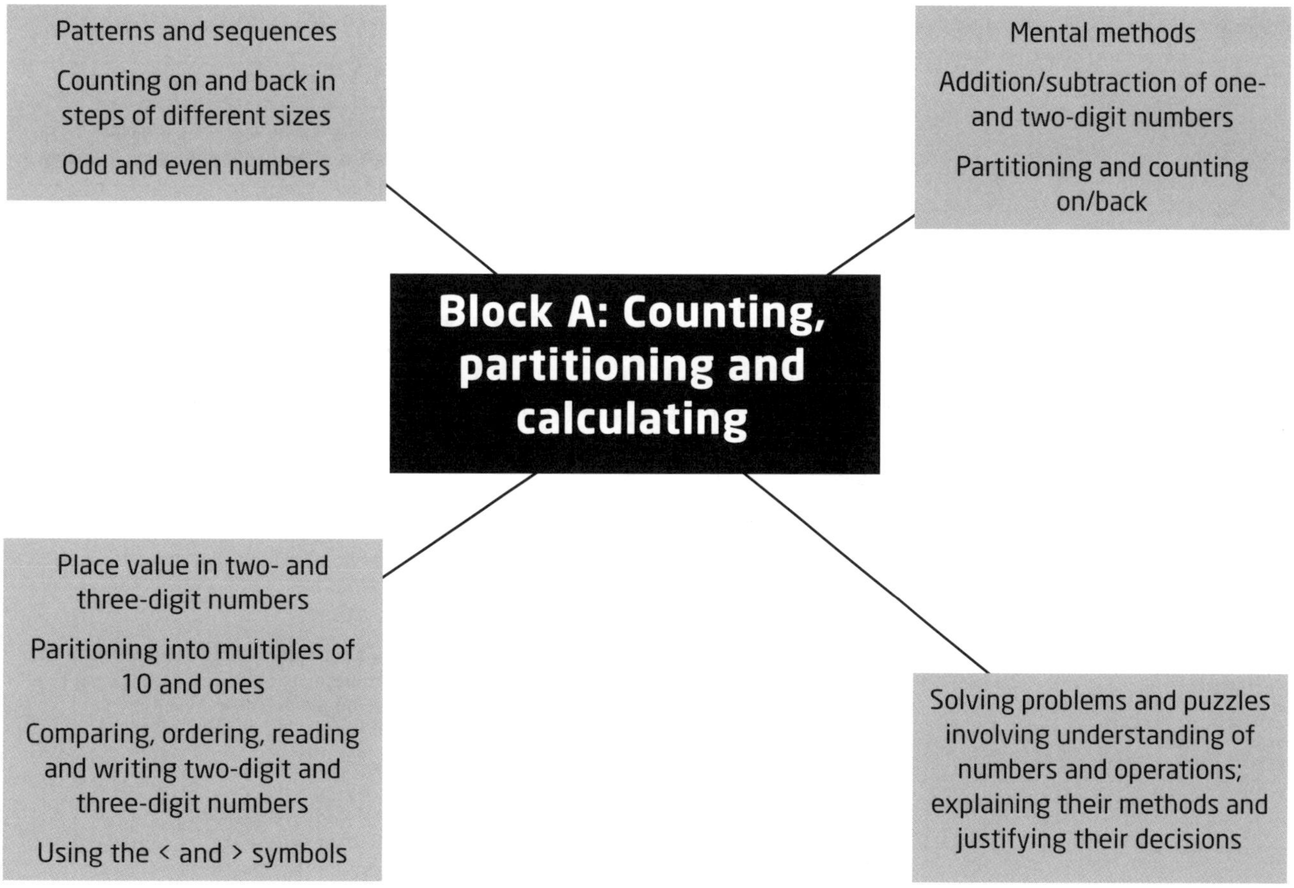

Patterns and sequences
Counting on and back in steps of different sizes
Odd and even numbers

Mental methods
Addition/subtraction of one- and two-digit numbers
Partitioning and counting on/back

Block A: Counting, partitioning and calculating

Place value in two- and three-digit numbers
Paritioning into multiples of 10 and ones
Comparing, ordering, reading and writing two-digit and three-digit numbers
Using the < and > symbols

Solving problems and puzzles involving understanding of numbers and operations; explaining their methods and justifying their decisions

Unit 1 2 weeks

Counting, partitioning and calculating

Speaking and listening objectives

- Speak with clarity and intonation when reading and reciting.
- Respond to presentations by describing characters, repeating some highlights and commenting constructively, choices and solutions to puzzles and problems, orally and in writing, using pictures and diagrams.

Introduction

In this unit there are ten lessons covering elements of the strand Counting, partitioning and calculating. Partitioning, place value, ordering and rounding are important skills and threaded within many of the following lessons are opportunities to rehearse these. The Using and applying mathematics strand is discrete in Lesson 1 but the elements of explaining decisions, methods and results in pictorial, spoken or written form and using mathematical language and number sentences are encouraged in each lesson. At all times, the children should be encouraged to speak and respond in the way highlighted in the speaking and listening objective on the left.

Using and applying mathematics

- Present solutions to puzzles and problems in an organised way; explain decisions, methods and results in pictorial, spoken or written form, using mathematical language and number sentences.

Lesson	Strands	Starter	Main teaching activities
1. Review, teach and practise	Use/apply	• Say the number names in order to at least 100, from and back to zero. • Read and write two-digit and three-digit numbers in figures and words; describe and extend number sequences and recognise odd and even numbers.	Present solutions to puzzles and problems in an organised way; explain decisions, methods and results in pictorial, spoken or written form, using mathematical language and number sentences.
2. Review and practise	Counting	Read and write two-digit and three-digit numbers in figures and words; describe and extend number sequences and recognise odd and even numbers.	• Read and write two-digit and three-digit numbers in figures and words; describe and extend number sequences and recognise odd and even numbers. **• Count up to 100 objects by grouping them and counting in tens, fives or twos; explain what each digit in a two-digit number represents, including numbers where 0 is a place holder; partition two-digit numbers in different ways, including into multiples of 10 and 1.**
3. Teach, practise and evaluate	Counting	As for Lesson 2	As for Lesson 2
4. Teach	Counting	• Say the number names in order to at least 100, from and back to zero. • Recognise odd and even numbers to at least 30.	**• Count up to 100 objects by grouping them and counting in tens, fives or twos; explain what each digit in a two-digit number represents, including numbers where 0 is a place holder.** • Estimate a number of objects; round two-digit numbers to the nearest 10.
5. Review and apply	Counting	As for Lesson 4	As for Lesson 4
6. Teach, practise and evaluate	Counting	Say the number that is 1 or 10 more or less than any given two-digit number.	• As for Lesson 2 and: • Order two-digit numbers and position them on a number line; use the greater than (>) and less than (<) signs.
7. Review and teach	Calculating	Order two-digit numbers and position them on a number line; use the greater than (>) and less than (<) signs.	**Add or subtract mentally a one-digit number or a multiple of 10 to or from any two-digit number; use practical and informal written methods to add/subtract two-digit numbers.**
8. Teach and practise	Calculating	Derive and recall multiplication facts for the 2, 5 and 10 times-tables and the related division facts; recognise multiples of 2, 5 and 10.	As for Lesson 7
9. Teach and practise	Calculating	As for Lesson 8	Understand that subtraction is the inverse of addition and vice versa and use this to derive and record related addition and subtraction number sentences.
10. Practise and evaluate	Calculating	As for Lesson 7	As for Lesson 9

Lesson 1

Preparation
Make a pendulum by threading three Unifix or Multilink cubes onto a string about 1m long.

You will need
Equipment
Number cards 0-9.

Learning objectives

Starter
- Say the number names in order to at least 100, from and back to zero.
- Read and write two-digit and three-digit numbers in figures and words; describe and extend number sequences and recognise odd and even numbers.

Main teaching activities
2006
- Present solutions to puzzles and problems in an organised way; explain decisions, methods and results in pictorial, spoken or written form, using mathematical language and number sentences.

1999
- Explain how a problem was solved orally and, where appropriate, in writing.

Vocabulary
pattern, sequence, continue

Lesson 1 (Review, teach and practise)

Starter
Recall: Tell the children to count on in ones in time to the swing of the pendulum, starting from the number you call out. When you stop swinging the pendulum, say *Backwards* to start the children counting back from that number. Begin with single-digit numbers, and then use numbers such as 23, 56, 67 and 72. Now use a counting stick marked in tens to help the children count on and back in tens from numbers such as 46, 12 and 9. Ask questions such as: *If 12 is at this end, what number will be at the third mark?* (42) ... *the sixth mark?* (72) ... *two more on from here?* (92)

Main teaching activities
Whole class: The aim of this lesson is to review how well the children are able to work systematically. Write the numbers from 0 to 9 on the board. Ask the children to pick two numbers with a total of 15. Ask: *How many possibilities are there?* Next, ask them to pick three numbers with a total of 15, asking the same question. Repeat for four and then five numbers and then ask: *Can we pick six numbers?* (0, 1, 2, 3, 4, 5) *Could we pick seven numbers? Why not?* Once you have established that it is not possible because all the lowest numbers have been used and that choosing a higher number would give a higher answer, look at the ways to record this systematically.
Paired work: The children will explore this further by thinking about how many ways they can use 2, 3, 4, 5 numbers (and so on) to make 20. Encourage them to record systematically as you demonstrated.

Differentiation
Less confident learners: These children should explore ways to make 10. Give them number cards 0-9 so that they can physically put the numbers together and then copy them.
More confident learners: These children could be asked to explore ways to make 200 using tens numbers and then to explain the link to ones numbers during the review.

Review
Take feedback from the activity, asking the children who made 10 to share some of their methods first. Encourage the more confident group to explain the link between totalling ones to make 20 and tens to make 200. Ask questions related to this, for example: *If you know that 7 + 3 = 10, what is 70 + 30? If 10 - 8 = 2, what is 100 - 20?* Ask more general questions relating to using and applying, such as: *How did you know which calculations to do? Could you use a number line to help us understand what you did?*

Unit 1 2 weeks

Lessons 2-3

Preparation

Prepare a set of number cards 10-100 from the CD page '0-100 number cards'. Copy and enlarge a set of 'Arrow cards'. Copy the 'Up the mountain gameboard' onto card, and laminate.

You will need

CD resources
'0-100 number cards', a class set of enlarged 'Arrow cards', 'Up the mountain 1' and 'Up the mountain gameboard' for each group (see General resources); ITP Place Value.
Equipment
An individual whiteboard and pen for each child; counters; a class 100 square.

Learning objectives

Starter

- Read and write two-digit and three-digit numbers in figures and words; describe and extend number sequences and recognise odd and even numbers.

Main teaching activities

2006

- Read and write two-digit and three-digit numbers in figures and words; describe and extend number sequences and recognise odd and even numbers.
- Count up to 100 objects by grouping them and counting in tens, fives or twos; explain what each digit in a two-digit number represents, including numbers where 0 is a place holder; partition two-digit numbers in different ways, including into multiples of 10 and 1.

1999

- Count reliably up to 100 objects by grouping them, eg in tens, then in fives or twos.
- Know what each number in a two-digit number represents, including 0 as a place holder, and partition two-digit numbers into a multiple of ten and ones (TU).

Vocabulary

zero, one, two... to twenty and beyond, units, ones, tens, hundreds, digit, one-, two- or three-digit number, rule, place, place value, stands for, represents

Lesson 2 (Review and practise)

Starter

Reason: Using the counting stick, ask the children to count on and back in ones and then tens from numbers such as 46, 12 and 9. Ask questions such as: *If 12 is at this end, what number will be at the third mark?* (15/42) ... *the sixth mark?* (18/72) ... *two more on from here?* (20/92). Repeat in steps of five and, if appropriate, twos.

Main teaching activities

Whole class: Explain that today the children will be revising how to make numbers over 10 by combining tens and ones. Make sure that the children can read the enlarged 'ones' arrow cards, then the 'tens'. Now hold up one of each (for example, 20 and 5) and ask: *What number can we make if we put these two together?* Show 25. Repeat. Invite two children to come to the front and choose a 'tens' and a 'ones' card respectively. Ask the class to read each card and then say what the number is when the two cards are combined. Ask the two children to demonstrate. Repeat. As an alternative to arrow cards, use the ITP Place Value, selecting the values and clicking on the hundreds, tens and ones to place them on the screen.

Hold up (or display) a 'tens' and a 'ones' card and ask the children to write down what number will be made when the cards are combined. Repeat several times. Show the children how to record this using a number sentence, for example 30 + 6 = 36. Invite some children to write one combination each on the board, then ask everyone to write several combinations on their whiteboards.

Group work: Model the instructions for the first version of the 'Up the mountain 1' game, then let the children play in groups.

Differentiation
Mixed-ability groups would be best for this game so the more confident children can support the less confident.

Review
Invite four or five children to select a 'tens' and a 'ones' card, combine them and say what their new number is. Ask the class to order these children from the lowest number to the highest. *How do you know this is the right order? Which number gives you the clue? How do you know?* Write the order on the board. Repeat.

Lesson 3 (Teach, practise and evaluate)

Starter
Refine and rehearse: Repeat the counting stick part of the Starter from Lesson 1. Now ask the children what number comes after 99. Tell them that they are going to count in steps of 100. Count together up to 900, then ask whether anyone knows what comes next. (1000) Count back to zero.

Main teaching activities
Whole class: Pick a two-digit number card and ask the children to tell you what each digit represents - for example, in 46 the digits represent 4 tens and 6 ones. Demonstrate using the enlarged arrow cards or the ITP Place Value: show the whole number and then reveal the zero of the 40 hidden under the 6. Explain the role of zero as a place holder and what the number would be if it was not present. Write a number sentence: 46 = 40 + 6. Repeat.
Group work: Model the instructions for the second version of the 'Up the mountain 1' game, then let the children play in groups.

Differentiation
Model the instructions for the differentiated versions of the 'Up the mountain' game, then let the children play in groups.

Review
Display eight two-digit number cards. *What do these say?* As they tell you, write them on the board and ask the children to partition them. Show another number and ask: *Which of the eight numbers is the closest to this one? Which is the furthest away?* Draw a number line and write the number you are holding in the middle. Invite volunteers to write the other numbers in the correct places on the line.

Lessons 4-6

Preparation
Make up sets of 'Elephant estimating game' cards by copying onto card, cutting out and laminating.

You will need
Photocopiable pages
'How many pennies?' (page 18) for each child.
CD resources
A set of '0-100 number cards', a set of 'Elephant estimating game' cards and a set of 'Blank number lines' for each pair of children, an enlarged teacher set of 'Elephant estimating game' cards, acetates or A3 copies of 'Dots 1', '2' and '3' for each child (see General resources).

Learning objectives

Starter
- Say the number names in order to at least 100, from and back to zero.
- Recognise odd and even numbers to at least 30.
- Say the number that is 1 or 10 more or less than any given two-digit number.

Main teaching activities
2006
- Count up to 100 objects by grouping them and counting in tens, fives or twos; explain what each digit in a two-digit number represents, including numbers where 0 is a place holder.
- Estimate a number of objects and round two-digit numbers to the nearest 10.
- Order two-digit numbers and position them on a number line; use the greater than (>) and less than (<) signs.

1999
- Count reliably up to 100 objects by grouping them, eg in tens, then in fives or twos.
- Know what each digit in a two-digit number represents, including 0 as a place holder.
- Give a sensible estimate of at least 50 objects.

Unit 1 2 weeks

Equipment
Unifix or Multilink cubes; 1m length of string; counting stick marked in tens; OHP; plastic cup; counters; about £10 worth of pennies; some 10p, 2p and 5p coins; class 100 square; number cards 0-9.

- Round numbers less than 100 to the nearest 10.
- Order whole numbers to at least 100, and position them on a number line and 100 square.
- Use symbols correctly, including less than (<), greater than (>).

Vocabulary
number, zero, one hundred, two hundred... one thousand, count on (from, to), count back (from, to), count in ones, count in tens, multiple of, more, less

Lesson 4 (Teach)

Starter
Recall and reason: Quickly count together in ones from zero to 20 and back, then from any number below 20 for another 20 (for example, 16 to 36). Ask individuals to pick a number from the 10-100 number cards. The children should first say whether it is an odd or an even number and explain how they know. Then say: *Count on until I clap, then start counting backwards.* Clap after every few counts, so that the children keep changing direction. Make sure that the count frequently crosses the tens boundaries, and encourage counting beyond 100.

Main teaching activities
Whole class: Explain to the children that today they will be learning to estimate how many objects there are in a collection, and then finding out how many there actually are by counting them. Place ten cubes on an OHP in twos. Quickly switch the OHP on and off. Ask: *How many cubes did you see? Make an estimate.* Turn on the OHP again: *How could we count the cubes?* Encourage counting in twos. Repeat this with different numbers of cubes less than 30. Group them in different ways to encourage a variety of counting techniques. For example: group 24 as two tens and two twos; group 18 in three fives and three ones. Encourage the children to estimate before counting. When the number of cubes has been found, ask questions about the number that reinforces the place value. Discuss whether it is odd or even and what it would be rounded to, to the nearest ten. When you have counted two or more amounts, compare them using < and > signs.
Paired work: Give each pair a plastic cup containing up to 30 counters, and give each child an 'Elephant estimating card', a pen and paper (or an individual whiteboard). Ask them to take turns to drop a handful of counters on the table. As quickly as possible, both children write down their estimates of how many have been dropped. The first child then counts them in groups onto an Elephant card, grouping them in different ways (not counting them singly).

Review
Drop ten cubes onto the OHP and ask the children to suggest different ways of counting them. Drop on another ten and ask: *How many are there now? How could we count them easily?* Keep adding various numbers of cubes and asking how the total can be counted quickly; discourage counting them all singly. Ask: *If we count in ones or count in tens, will the answer be the same?* Through questioning, check that each child can count by grouping in tens. Assess through questions such as: *What is a quicker way than counting in ones?*

Differentiation
Less confident leaners: This group can use up to 20 counters.
More confident leaners: Give this group up to 40 counters and ask them to drop a minimum of 20; encourage them to explore different ways of counting.

Lesson 5 (Review and apply)

Starter

Read and reason: Quickly count in tens from zero to 100 and back, then from any number below 100 for ten counts (for example, 37 to 137) and back. Ask the children to choose a number that fits certain criteria, such as a two-digit odd number between 30 and 40. Take a suggestion and ask another child to write it on the board and identify whether it is an odd or an even number, explaining how they know. Write 46 and these words on the board, point to each in turn and ask them to find the numbers related to these words: *46 one more... one less... ten more... ten less?* Use the class 100 square to help if needed.

Main teaching activities

Whole class: Recap the meaning of 'estimating'. Put 47 counters on the OHP. Let the children see them briefly, then switch off the OHP. Ask for estimates of the number. Then show the counters again and ask the children to count in the same way as in lesson 4. Ask individuals to demonstrate counting in tens to 40, then fives on to 45, then twos on to 47. Point to the groups and say: *Four tens is 40, add 5 to make 45 and 2 to make 47.* Repeat with another number up to 50.

Show 50 pennies and ask the children to estimate the number, then count. Encourage counting in tens. Demonstrate exchanging each set of ten pennies for a 10p coin, then counting in tens. Repeat with 36p: three tens and six ones. *Can you think of another way to count the six?* If necessary, suggest exchanging five pennies for a 5p coin, or using 2p coins. As in Lesson 4, when the amount has been found, ask questions about the number that reinforces the place value. Discuss whether it is odd or even, what it would be rounded to, to the nearest ten, and compare with other numbers using the < and > signs.

Group work: The children should work in groups of four or five. Demonstrate what to do on the 'How many pennies?' photocopiable page. Give each group up to 50 pennies, ten 10p coins and a few 5p and 2p coins.

Differentiation

Less confident learners: Give this group up to 30 pennies with 10p coins to exchange. Work with these children to help them learn this skill.

More confident learners: Give this group up to 100 pennies with 10p, 5p and 2p coins. Encourage them to use all the coins.

Review

Show the children an OHT or A3 copy of 'Dots 1' (77 dots). Ask them to suggest the best way of counting the dots. Invite children to draw loops around groups of 10. Repeat with 'Dots 2' (72 dots) and 'Dots 3' (90 dots). Assess their understanding by asking: *What is a better way of counting in ones or twos? Why?*

Lesson 6 (Teach, practise and evaluate)

Starter

Read and refresh: Ask the children to give you a selection of two-digit numbers, according to your specific requirements, for example, an odd number between 11 and 24, a multiple of ten, an even multiple of 5. Once you have written five or six of these on the board, point to each one in turn and ask the children to write on their whiteboards the number that is either 1 more or 1 less. Repeat, asking for 10 more or 10 less. For each, check using the class 100 square. For challenge, intersperse some three-digit numbers and ask the same questions.

Main teaching activities

Whole class: Explain that today the children will be concentrating on writing, ordering, comparing and rounding numbers. Write the digits 3, 5 and 8 on the board and ask the children to write on their whiteboards all the two-digit numbers that they can, using these digits: 35, 53, 38, 83, 58, 85. Draw a number line on the board and ask the children to tell you which 'marker' numbers to put on first. (50, 25, 75) They should do this on their boards as well. Ask them to plot the numbers they made onto it. Take

feedback, inviting children to write the numbers on the class line. For each, ask if the class agree on its position. Ask questions about each number: *What would we see if we took the 5 away from 35?(30) What is that 0? Is 35 odd or even? How do you know?* Write the signs < and > and ask the children to tell you what they mean, demonstrate with a number sentence, for example, 35 < 53. Ask the children to make some up using the numbers on the line. Repeat with another set of numbers. Discuss rounding to the nearest 10, explaining that this is a useful skill when estimating.
Individual work: The children's task is consolidation of the main teaching activity. They need the number cards from 1-9. They should pick four and make as many two-digit numbers as they can with them. Then ask them to draw a number line on plain paper and plot the numbers onto it. Then they should make up as many number sentences as they can, using the < and > signs.

Differentiation

Less confident learners: Give these children a pre-prepared number line.
More confident learners: These children could be encouraged to make three-digit numbers.

Review

Take feedback by drawing a number line on the board and asking about 12 children to plot one of their numbers onto it. Ask everyone to write a number sentence on their whiteboards and to explain to a partner what they did and why. Focus on rounding; ask: *What are the 12 numbers rounded to the nearest ten*? Expect them to write the new numbers on their boards.

Lessons 7-10

Preparation

Prepare a set of number cards 0-100 from '0-100 number cards', and a set of 0-9 number cards for each child. Cut out and laminate a character from 'Characters for a number line'. Draw a large number line 0-30 and place it where the children can move the character along it. Copy the relevant photocopiable pages according to ability, one for each child.

You will need

Photocopiable pages
One copy of 'Add and subtract' (page 19) for each child.
CD resources
One set of '0-100 number cards' and a set of 0-9 number cards for each child, a cartoon character from 'Characters for a number line' (see General resources); 'Add and subtract', support, extension and template, 'Arrow sentences', support, extension and template, 'Add 'em up' support and extension, 'Make your own' support and extension.
Equipment
None.

Learning objectives

Starter

- Order two-digit numbers and position them on a number line; use the greater than (>) and less than (<) signs.
- Derive and recall multiplication facts for the 2, 5 and 10 times-tables and the related division facts; recognise multiples of 2, 5 and 10.

Main teaching activities

2006

- Add or subtract mentally a one-digit number or a multiple of 10 to or from any two-digit number; use practical and informal written methods to add and subtract two-digit numbers.
- Understand that subtraction is the inverse of addition and vice versa and use this to derive and record related addition and subtraction number sentences.

1999

- Extend understanding of the operations of addition and subtraction including that subtraction is the inverse of addition.
- Recognise that addition can be done in any order, but not subtraction: for example: 3 + 21 = 21 + 3, but 21 - 3 does not equal 3 - 21.
- Use the +, - and = signs to record mental additions and subtractions in a number sentence, and recognise the use of a symbol to stand for an unknown number.
- Addition strategies: using known facts; partition, then recombine.

Vocabulary

multiple of, odd, even, add, addition, more, plus, +, sum, make, total, altogether, subtract, take away, –, minus, leave, how many are left/left over?, how many less is... than...?, subtraction, one-, two- or three-digit number, place, place value, represents, double, near double, total, addition, sum

Lesson 7 (Review, teach and apply)

Starter

Read and rehearse: Practise reading two- and three-digit numbers. Say: Set out your number cards in order from 0 to 9. Say: *Show me four... seven... one more than 8; ... one less than 4; ... three more than 9; Double it.* Ask the children to put a 3 in front of them, then make the 3 into 53, then make 253. Ask them to swap the 2 and the 5. Ask one of the less confident children to read the digits, then any child to read the actual number. Repeat several times.

Ask the children to make a two-digit number, take six examples and write them on the board. Then ask them to help you order them on a number line with 0, 25, 50, 75 and 100 marked onto it. Pick two numbers and compare using < and >, for example, 45 < 67, 67 > 45. Repeat a few times. Do the same with three-digit numbers on a number line with 0, 250, 500, 750 and 1000 marked.

Main teaching activities

Whole class: Explain that today the children will be adding and subtracting numbers, and finding out whether it matters in which order we do it. Ask: *What does 'add' mean?* Encourage the children to tell you all the 'add' words they can think of. Repeat for 'subtract'.

Make a pile of single-digit number cards and another of two-digit number cards. Invite a child to pick one card from each pile. Write these numbers on the board (for example, 23 and 5). Ask the child to put the cartoon character on the class number line to mark the higher of the two numbers, then add on the other number by counting along the number line with the character (so count on five from 23). Write up the number sentence: 23 + 5 = 28. Now ask the child to put the character on 5 and count on 23. Ask: *Is the answer the same?* Write 5 + 23 = 28 on the board. Try another example.

Repeat with subtraction - for example, counting back 4 from 17 and writing the number sentence: 17 - 4 = 13. Now start at 4 and ask: *If we count back 17, will the answer be the same as before? What will happen?* Encourage the response that 17 cannot be taken away from 4. If someone says the answer will be a negative number, demonstrate by counting back to -13, but don't teach the class this. Repeat several times.

Group work: Explain that the children are going to prove that it doesn't matter which way they add, but it does matter which way they subtract. Give each child a copy of the 'Add and subtract' sheet and talk through the activity with each group.

Differentiation

Less confident learners: Give this group the version of 'Add and subtract' with numbers to 10.
More confident learners: Give this group the version with numbers to 49.

Review

Ask the children whether they proved that addition can be done in any order. Invite a few children to explain. Say: *Can you think of any time when it doesn't matter in which order we subtract numbers?* If they can't answer, prompt them by writing the same number twice on the board.

Lesson 8 (Teach and practise)

Starter

Refine and rehearse: Ask the children to count in twos from zero to 10. Now ask them to count in twos using their fingers: 0 (no fingers), 2 (one finger) and so on to 20 (ten fingers). Repeat, but stop them (for example, at 12) and ask: *How many fingers are you holding up? How many lots of 2 is that?* Write on the board: 2 × 6 = 12.

Main teaching activities

Whole class: Explain that today's lesson is about linking addition and subtraction. Write on the board: 13 + 8 = 21. Ask: *Can you think of another calculation using these numbers?* (8 + 13 = 21) Now ask the children to work out 21 - 13. Draw an arrow diagram to link the addition and the subtraction.

Explain that subtraction is the inverse or opposite of addition. Write the number sentences 13 + 8 = 21 and 21 - 8 = 13. Repeat.
Group work: Give each child a copy of the 'Arrow sentences' activity sheet to complete.

Differentiation

Less confident learners: This group uses the support version of 'Arrow sentences' with totals to 10 and single-digit numbers to add and subtract.
More confident learners: This group can use the extension version with totals to 40 and two-digit numbers to add and subtract.

Review

Ask some children whom you particularly wish to assess to write up an example of their work, using an arrow diagram and number sentences. Now write on the board: 9 + □ = 13 and 13 - □ = 9. Ask the children whether they can use an arrow diagram to find the missing numbers. Encourage them to explain their thinking. Remind them that addition is the opposite or inverse of subtraction.

Write this number sentence: 17 - 9 = 8. Ask: *Write three more sentences using these numbers. How do you know without calculating, that they are correct?*

Lesson 9 (Teach and practise)

Starter

Recall and refresh: Say: *Who can remember what 'multiples' are? What is special about multiples of 2... of 10... of 5?* Count together in ones from any number, asking the children to clap at each multiple of 2. Call out random numbers, asking for the same response. Now play 'Jog and jump'. Start counting slowly from 1. When the children hear you say a multiple of 5, they should jump; for a multiple of 10, they should jog on the spot; for a multiple of both, they should do both. Ask them what they notice. (They never jog without jumping.) Can they explain this?

Main teaching activities

Whole class: Explain that in today's lesson they will be adding numbers together by partitioning and also looking for numbers that total 10. Write the numbers 36 and 54 on the board. Together, partition them: 30 + 6 and 50 + 4. Ask them to add the tens using this thinking: *I know 3 + 5 = 8, so 30 + 50 must equal 80.* Then the units: *I know 6 + 4 = 10, finally recombine: 80 + 10 = 90.* Repeat this with similar numbers that have units that equal 10.
Paired work: Give each pair a copy of 'Add 'em up'. Explain that one child picks one of the numbers to add and the second picks the other, which must have a unit which when added to the other makes 10. Demonstrate the method for addition shown as being the same principle, just a different way of recording.

Differentiation

Less confident learners: This group works on the support version of the photocopiable page, working on additions of teens numbers that make 30.
More confident learners: This group works on the extension version of the photocopiable page working with numbers that will mainly produce answers of over 100.

Review

Invite pairs of children to share examples of their work, demonstrating on the board and explaining exactly what they did.

Write a two-digit number on the board and ask the children to give you another, which when added to the first, the units will make 10. For example, you write 43, they could say any number with a seven in the units place. Repeat with other two- and three-digit numbers.

Lesson 10 (Practise and evaluate)

Starter

Rehearse, refine and reason: Repeat the starter from lesson 7. This time when you draw the number lines, ask the children to tell you which numbers can be marked on easily and why: 50 because it's halfway between 0 and 100, 25 because it's halfway between 0 and 50 and 75 because it's halfway between 50 and 100.

Main teaching activities

Whole class: Explain to the children that in today's lesson they will be practising what they did last time. Write the numbers 43 and 17 on the board. Together, partition them in the way they did in 'Add 'em up' and find the total. Ask the children to explain their thinking: *I know 4 + 1 = 5, so 40 + 10 = 50; I know 3 + 7 = 10, so 30 + 70 = 100.* Repeat this with other two-digit, and this time, three-digit numbers with units that equal 10.

Paired work: Each pair needs a copy of the 'Make your own' activity sheet. Demonstrate what they need to do: choose two digits and make a number each. The second child needs to choose a unit that, when added to the first child's unit, makes ten. They then add the numbers in the same way as in Lesson 9.

Differentiation

Less confident learners: This group uses the support version of the photocopiable page to make teens numbers.

More confident learners: This group uses the extension version of the photocopiable page to make numbers that will produce answers of over 100.

Review

Invite pairs of children to share examples of their work, demonstrating on the board and explaining exactly what they did.

Transfer the skills they have been learning to money. Say: *I have 15p and need 20p, how much more do I need?* Encourage the children to explain how they know. Repeat with different amounts and totals to suit all ability ranges.

Name ____________________ Date ____________________

How many pennies?

Put out some pennies.

Estimate how many there are.
Write your estimate in the chart below.

Now count the pennies. Find the total.

Make groups of 10.

Write how many groups of 10 there are and how many are left over.

The first line in the chart is an example.

Estimate	Total	Groups of 10	Left over
30	**25**	**2**	**5**

Name ______________________ Date ______________________

Add and subtract

5	21	15	7
16	8	9	27
10	20	3	19
13	24	26	30

1. Choose two numbers from the grid, such as 10 and 7.
2. Make up two addition calculations, such as 10 + 7 = and 7 + 10 =.

______________________ ______________________

3. Do you think the answers will be the same? ____________
4. Work out the answers using a number line. Complete the two number sentences.
5. Make up two subtraction calculations with the same numbers, such as 10 – 7 = and 7 – 10 =.

______________________ ______________________

6. Do you think the answers will be the same? ____________
7. Work out the answers using a number line. Can you find both answers?

______________________ ______________________

8. What can you say about addition and subtraction?

____

____

____

9. Use the grid numbers to make up some more examples. Write them on the back of this sheet.

Unit 2 2 weeks

Counting, partitioning and calculating

Speaking and listening objective

- Speak with clarity and intonation when reading and reciting.

Introduction

This is a block of ten lessons. The first three focus on reading and writing numbers in words and figures, describing simple number sequences and identifying odd and even numbers. They also include reinforcement, rehearsal and consolidation of ordering, comparing and rounding numbers. It is always a good idea to take opportunities to do this as it really helps the children get a feel for number. The second three lessons focus on counting and place value with an element of estimating. This is an important skill to include; children should be encouraged to estimate answers to problems, measures and other amounts. The final lessons of the block focus on developing understanding of addition and subtraction through work on calculation strategies with a focus on using these to solve missing number problems. The using and applying objective threads throughout all the lessons as does the speaking and listening objective.

Using and applying mathematics

- Present solutions to puzzles and problems in an organised way; explain decisions, methods and results in pictorial, spoken or written form, using mathematical language and number sentences.

Lesson	Strands	Starter	Main teaching activities
1. Review and practise	Counting	Derive and recall multiplication facts for the 2, 5 and 10 times-tables and the related division facts; recognise multiples of 2, 5 and 10.	Read and write two-digit and three-digit numbers in figures and words; describe and extend number sequences and recognise odd and even numbers.
2. Practise	Counting	**Explain what each digit in a two-digit number represents, including numbers where 0 is a place holder.**	As for Lesson 1
3. Teach and practise	Counting	Describe and extend number sequences and recognise odd and even numbers.	As for Lesson 1
4. Teach and practise	Counting	Read and write two-digit and three-digit numbers in figures and words; describe and extend number sequences and recognise odd and even numbers.	**Count up to 100 objects by grouping them and counting in tens, fives or twos; explain what each digit in a two-digit number represents, including numbers where 0 is a place holder; partition two-digit numbers in different ways, including into multiples of 10 and 1.**
5. Teach and practise	Counting	As for Lesson 2	As for Lesson 4
6. Teach and practise	Counting	As for Lesson 1	As for Lesson 4
7. Teach and practise	Calculate	**Derive and recall all addition and subtraction facts for each number to at least 10.**	Add or subtract mentally a one-digit number or a multiple of 10 to or from any two-digit number; use practical and informal written methods to add and subtract two-digit numbers.
8. Teach and practise	Calculate	Read and write two-digit and three-digit numbers in figures and words; describe and extend number sequences and recognise odd and even numbers.	As for Lesson 7
9. Review, teach and practise	Calculate	Understand that halving is the inverse of doubling and derive and recall doubles of all numbers to 20, and the corresponding halves.	As for Lesson 7
10. Apply and evaluate	Calculate	Derive and recall multiplication facts for the 2, 5 and 10 times-tables and the related division facts; recognise multiples of 2, 5 and 10.	**Use the symbols +, -, ×, ÷ and = to record and interpret number sentences involving all four operations; calculate the value of an unknown in a number sentence (eg ❑ ÷ 2 = 6, 30 - ❑ = 24).**

Lessons 1-3

Preparation
Copy the 'Follow me cards' onto card and laminate, then cut out a set of cards. Copy 'Number words' onto A3 paper and cut out the words.

You will need
Photocopiable pages
'Which number goes where?' (page 29) for each child.
CD resources
'0-100 number cards', '0-100 number line' for each child, '0-50 number line' for each less confident child, 'Follow me cards', an A3 copy of 'Number words', an acetate and one copy per child of 'Number lines (0-20)', '(0-30)' and '(20-50)' (see General resources); 'Which number goes where?', support and extension versions.
Equipment
None.

Learning objectives

Starter
- Derive and recall multiplication facts for the 2, 5 and 10 times-tables.
- Explain what each digit in a two-digit number represents, including numbers where 0 is a place holder.
- Describe and extend number sequences and recognise odd and even numbers.

Main teaching activities
2006
- Read and write two-digit and three-digit numbers in figures and words; describe and extend number sequences and recognise odd and even numbers.

1999
- Read and write whole numbers to at least 100 in figures and words.
- Compare two given familiar numbers, say which is more or less, and give a number that lies between them.

Vocabulary
two hundred... one thousand, units, ones, tens, hundreds, digit, round, nearest, round to the nearest 10, more, larger, bigger, greater, fewer, smaller, less, most, least

Lesson 1 (Review and practise)

Starter
Read and refine: Use the 'Follow me cards' to practise multiplication and division facts for 2 and 10. The children work on their own or, if lacking confidence, with a partner. Give out all the cards (at least one for each individual or pair). Choose someone to read out a question. The child who has the answer calls it out and reads their question, and so on. Record the time it takes to go round the class. Shuffle the cards and repeat.

Main teaching activities
Whole class: This lesson is about writing, ordering and comparing numbers. Each child will need a set of single-digit number cards. Give the children instructions, such as: *Put a 7 on the table in front of you. Make it read 74. What did you do? Swap the digits round. What have you now? Is that bigger or smaller than 74? Is it odd or even? How do you know? Now add a card to make 147. What did you do? How much bigger is 147 than 47? Make the highest three-digit number you can using those cards. How did you do that? Why? Make it five more... 100 less... ten more...* This is a very good method for helping children grasp place value and number manipulation. Most children get this fairly easily after some practice. If any have difficulty, help them or allow them to work with a 'buddy'. Repeat the activity with the children writing and rubbing out digits on their whiteboards.

Hold up two two-digit number cards: *Which number is lower... higher?* Draw a number line and write these numbers at the ends. Invite some children to suggest a number that comes between the two, and to place these numbers on the line. Show the children the 'Number words' and ask them to find the correct words for some of these numbers. Repeat this several times, making some pairs of numbers from the same digits. For example:

34
43

34 37 40 42 43

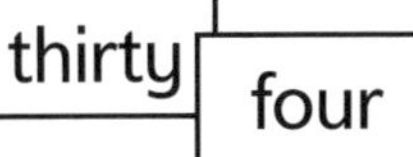

Differentiation

Less confident learners: Provide the support version of the 'Which number goes where?' sheet that involves making a teens number. Help this group to read and understand the instructions.
More confident learners: Provide the extension version that involves making 'in between' numbers from a limited choice of digits.

Group work: Distribute the 'Which number goes where?' photocopiable page and demonstrate the example shown.

Review

Draw a number line with ten divisions on the board. Write a two-digit number at each end. Ask a child to suggest an 'in between' number and mark it in place. Continue until there are ten numbers on the line. Repeat with another pair of numbers, but use a line without divisions. Ask the children to work out where to place the numbers. Encourage them to look for the halfway mark first.

Lesson 2 (Practise)

Starter

Revisit and reason: As in the main teaching activity from Lesson 1, ask the children to make and manipulate numbers on their whiteboards by following your instructions. For example, they might write the number 1; make it read 21; then 12, 312, the lowest/highest three-digit number possible with these digits, five more, ten less, ten more... Repeat with other single-digit starting numbers.

Main teaching activities

Whole class: Reinforce Lesson 1. Hold up two two-digit number cards. With the children's help, write these numbers at the ends of a number line without divisions, and place as accurately as possible some numbers that come between the two. Ask the children to find the correct number word cards for the numbers as you point to them. Repeat several times.
Group work: Let the children work in pairs with two-digit number cards. Each pair has a pile of number cards in front of them, face down on the table. They pick five cards and look at them. They then order them from smallest to largest on the 0–100 number line. For example, if they pick the cards 23, 17, 46, 89, 63:

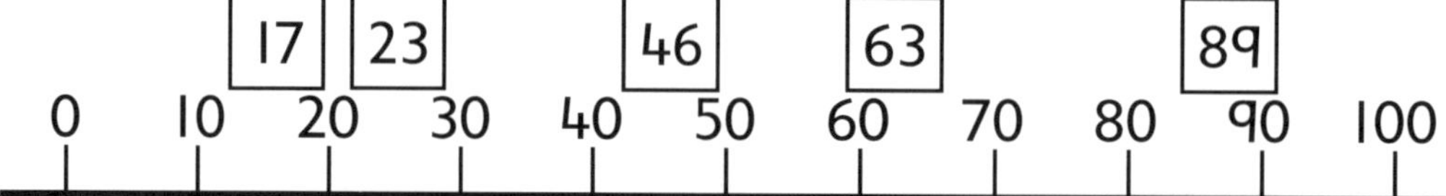

Differentiation

Less confident learners: Ask this group to order sets of numbers to 50 from least to greatest.
More confident learners: Ask this group to draw and complete blank number lines.

They then put the cards back, shuffle the pile and pick five more cards.

Review

Invite some more confident children to explain how they positioned their numbers on their lines. Ask some other children to place numbers picked from cards as accurately as they can on a line you have drawn on the board. Invite the rest of the class to comment on their accuracy.

Lesson 3 (Teach and practise)

Starter

Recall: Divide the class into two teams. As you swing a pendulum, call out a range of two-digit numbers from which the teams count alternately, on and back in ones, as the pendulum swings to the left and the right. Repeat for counting in tens from numbers such as 51 and 67.

Main teaching activities

Whole class: This lesson is about counting in steps. Put 'Number lines (0–30)' on the OHP or draw it on the board. Circle the zero and ask: *If we count in threes from zero, what is the first number we come to?* Draw a loop to the number 3. *What is the next number?* Each time, draw a loop from the previous number to the next multiple of 3. At 30, go back in jumps of three. Help the children to make the inverse connection by drawing arrow diagrams.

Ask questions such as: *How many jumps from 0 to 6? If I make three jumps from 0, will I land on an odd or an even number? How do you know? What about seven jumps? If we start on the number 1, will seven jumps of three still get me to 21? Why not?* Repeat, starting at different numbers. Focus on odd and even numbers. Ask: *What are they? What numbers do they end with?* Use cubes to demonstrate that even numbers can be divided equally into two but that odd numbers cannot.
Paired work: Demonstrate the number line activity described on 'Number lines (0–20)'. In addition to the given task, ask them to put a circle around two even numbers and a cross through two odd numbers. Let the children work with copies of the '0–30' number line.

Differentiation

Less confident learners: Provide the '0-20' number line.
More confident learners: Provide the 20-50' number line.

Review

Invite a few pairs to draw one of their number lines on the board and demonstrate what they did. Ask the children to look for patterns. Look for awareness that when we count in fours, the numbers are always even (if the starting number is even) or odd (if it is odd); but when we count in fives, the units digit alternates between two digits, one odd and one even.

Lessons 4-6

Preparation

Copy 'Vocabulary for estimating' onto A3 paper and cut out the words. Put different numbers of beads or centicubes (up to 50) into the string bags.

You will need

Photocopiable pages
'Straws' (page 30), 'How close can you get?' (page 31) for each child.
CD resources
'0-100 number cards', 'Spider charts for multiplying' and 'Spider charts for dividing', an OHT of the 'Dots 1', '2' and '3' sheets, 'Vocabulary for estimating cards' (see General Resources); copies of 'More straws'.
Equipment
At least 500 straws; elastic bands; an OHP; at least 16 small filled string bags; beads or centicubes; a bead string; Blu-Tack.

Learning objectives

Starter

- Read and write two-digit and three-digit numbers in figures and words; describe and extend number sequences and recognise odd and even numbers.
- Explain what each digit in a two-digit number represents, including numbers where 0 is a place holder.
- Derive and recall multiplication facts for the 2, 5 and 10 times-tables.

Main teaching activities

2006

- Count up to 100 objects by grouping them and counting in tens, fives or twos; explain what each digit in a two-digit number represents, including numbers where 0 is a place holder; partition two-digit numbers in different ways, including into multiples of ten and one.

1999

- Use and begin to read the vocabulary of estimation and approximation; give a sensible estimate of at least 50 objects.
- Understand that more than two numbers can be added.

Vocabulary

guess how many, estimate, nearly, roughly, close to, about the same as, just over, just under, exact, exactly, too many, too few, enough, not enough

Lesson 4 (Teach and practise)

Starter

Rehearse and recall: Count in twos from zero to 20 and back. Repeat with fives and tens. Divide the class in half, 'conduct' them by pointing to the groups alternately. As you do, one group should count in tens from 0 to 100 and back, and the other in fives from 0 to 50 and back. Repeat with different combinations of steps, for example, twos and five, twos and tens.

Main teaching activities

Whole class: This lesson is about counting and place value with an element of estimating. Show the children a large pile of straws and ask them to estimate how many there are. Begin to count, handing the straws one at a time to a child as you do, drop some, lose count and start again. Repeat this a few times. Ask: *Is there a better way to count these?* Discuss, remind them of previous work if necessary and establish that counting in twos, fives and tens would be more efficient. With the children's help, count out bundles of ten straws, counting the ten in ones, twos and fives to show the different possible methods. When you have a few bundles, ask the children how many straws you have. Add some singles and then ask them how many altogether. Record this, for example, 3 bundles and 4 straws: 30 + 4 = 34.

Group work: The children should work in mixed-ability groups of four. Give each group a tray of straws and some elastic bands. Ask them to group the straws into as many tens as possible and then record these and the left over straws in a number sentence as demonstrated. They should use the 'Straws' photocopiable page to record this, then ask them to make up other numbers of straws and partition these in the same way.

Review

Take feedback from the activity. Ask a child to hold five bundles of straws and ask everyone to close their eyes while you pick up a few bundles. Ask: *How many straws do you think I am holding? Am I holding more/less than 50? What can you use to help you?* Repeat a few times and then remind the children of the point of the lesson: there are more efficient ways to count than in ones.

Differentiation

If the less confident learners find the activity sheet difficult to understand, let the more confident children in the mixed-ability groups explain what they have to do.

Lesson 5 (Teach and practise)

Starter

Rehearse and reason: Repeat from Lesson 2, but use different instructions (such as: *Write the number 32, take away two, double it, add three*) to explore two-digit numbers.

Main teaching activities

Whole class: This lesson is about estimating and approximating amounts up to 50. Ask: *Who can say what 'estimating' is? Can anyone tell me some estimating words?* Display the appropriate word cards, and show and discuss any words the children leave out. Put up one of the 'Dots' OHTs and ask: *Who can estimate the number of dots?* Discuss using their fingers to make a sensible estimate: *Are there more dots than you have fingers? Yes – so you know there are more than ten. Put your hands next to a friend's. Are there more dots or more fingers now?* Build up groups of ten fingers until the number is close: *Do you think we have exactly the same amount, just over or just under?* Finally count, drawing loops around groups of ten. Repeat using the dots on another OHT.

Group work: The children work in mixed-ability groups of four. Give each group three string bags. For each bag, they take turns to feel the cubes and estimate how many are in the bag, recording on the 'How close can you get?' photocopiable sheet. Set a short time limit so they cannot count the cubes. Once everyone in the group has made a guess, they should count the cubes to find out who was closest. Finally, they can discuss and try to answer the problems at the bottom of the sheet.

Review

Discuss whether the children found it easy or hard to make a sensible estimate. Write 48 on the board and say: *Mrs Cook estimated there would be 48 children at the party, so she baked 48 cakes that morning. Her friends also baked cakes for the number of children they expected.* Write their estimates on the board: 53, 60, 24 and 49. Tell the children that there were 50 children at the party. Hold up these word cards from 'Vocabulary for estimating': just under, just over, too many, too few and nearest. Ask the children which word best describes each estimate. Stick the word they agree on beside each estimate.

Differentiation

Less confident learners: Check that these children are taking an active part in the discussions of the group.
More confident learners: Make sure that these children do not dominate the group discussions.

Lesson 6 (Teach and practise)

Starter

Recall and refine: Count in twos and tens together, using fingers so that, when you stop part of the way through, the children can tell you what the multiplication fact is. For example, if you stop on 12 (the sixth finger) the multiplication fact is 2 times 6. Move on to using spider charts to reinforce these times tables and the corresponding division facts.

Main teaching activities

Whole class: This lesson is about partitioning two-digit numbers in different ways. Use the straws from Lesson 4. Ask a child to make 67. Separate the bundles of ten from the singles. Write the number sentence on the board 60 + 7 = 67. Explain that there are different ways to make 67 and demonstrate by saying: *If we take a bundle of ten from this pile and give it to the single straws, what number sentence would that be?* Establish: 50 + 17 = 67. Ask them to write other similar sentences on their whiteboards: 40 + 27, 30 + 37, 20 + 47, 10 + 57. Repeat for another number.

Group work: Tell the children that they are going to practise this concept. Demonstrate, following the instructions on the 'More straws' CD page.

Differentiation

Ask the more confident learners to help the less confident children if they need assistance with following the instructions on the activity sheet.

Review

Take feedback from the activities, asking pairs to demonstrate what they did. Use this as an assessment opportunity. Say: *Show me on your whiteboards two ways that you might partition 58.*

Lessons 7-10

Preparation

Copy the 'Addition vocabulary cards' onto A3 paper and cut out the words. Copy the 'Lost in space gameboard' and 'Find the way! gameboard' onto card and laminate, and make an acetate copy of each. Fill in the template version of 'Making 10' for less confident and more confident children. Prepare spider charts for the five-times table to match those for the two- and ten-times tables.

You will need

CD resources

'Making 10' for each child, 'What am I?' for each child; '0-100 number cards', 'Spider charts for multiplying', 'Spider charts for dividing', 'Spider charts for ×5 and ÷5' and 'Addition and subtraction vocabulary cards', 'Lost in space gameboard' and 'Find the way! gameboard' - one for each group of three or four and an acetate of each (see General resources); a copy of the template version of 'Making 10' and support and extension versions of 'What am I?'.

Equipment

Blu-Tack; number lines; 100 squares; counting equipment.

Learning objectives

Starter

- Derive and recall all addition and subtraction facts for each number to at least 10.
- Read and write two-digit and three-digit numbers in figures and words; describe and extend number sequences; recognise odd and even numbers.
- Understand that halving is the inverse of doubling and derive and recall doubles of all numbers to 20, and the corresponding halves.
- Derive and recall multiplication facts for the 2, 5 and 10 times tables and the related division facts; recognise multiples of 2, 5 and 10.

Main teaching activities

2006

- Add or subtract mentally a one-digit number or a multiple of 10 to or from any two-digit number; use practical and informal written methods to add and subtract two-digit numbers.
- Use the symbols +, -, ×, ÷ and = to record and interpret number sentences involving all four operations; calculate the value of an unknown in a number sentence (eg □ ÷ 2 = 6, 30 - □ = 24).

1999

- Know that addition can be done in any order to do mental calculations: add three small numbers by putting the largest first and/or finding a pair totalling 10; partition additions into tens and units, then recombine; partition into '5 and a bit' when adding 6, 7, 8 or 9, then recombine.
- Understand that more than two numbers can be added.
- Choose and use appropriate operations and efficient calculation strategies (eg mental, mental with jottings) to solve problems.

Vocabulary

add, addition, more, plus, make, sum, total, altogether, score, tens boundary

Lesson 7 (Review, teach and practise)

Starter

Revisit: Write a number up to 10 on the board. Time the children for two or three minutes, depending on the number, to see how many addition and subtraction facts they come up with for that number, for example, for 3: 0 + 3 = 3; 3 + 0 = 3; 3 - 3 = 0; 1 + 2 = 3; 2 + 1 = 3; 3 - 1 = 2; 3 - 2 = 1. Share facts, then repeat for another number.

Main teaching activities

Whole class: Tell the class that they are going to practise some mental addition strategies and learn some new ones. Revise the vocabulary for addition, holding up word cards as the children suggest them. Attach the cards to the board with Blu-Tack. Remind the children that they already know how to add up more than two numbers by putting the largest number in their heads and counting on. Quickly revisit this strategy. Write 3, 6 and 9 on the board. Ask the children to put 9 in their heads and then count on 6 and then 3. Repeat with 7, 8 and 2, then with 60, 30 and 70.

Now introduce looking for numbers whose unit digits total 10. Write three numbers on the board, two of which total 10, such as 8, 4 and 2. Invite children to come to the board and circle the numbers that add up to 10. Now do the same with the numbers as sums: 4 + 8 + 6; 9 + 4 + 1; 3 + 7 + 9; 2 + 5 + 5. Point out that 10 is the highest number now, so they are also using the other strategy when they count on from the 10.

Gradually move on to adding two single-digit numbers and one two-digit number, such as 16 + 8 + 2. Encourage the children to hold the larger number in their heads and then count on, but now it is the 10 that will be counted: 16 + 10. Repeat several times.

Group work: The children can use the 'Making 10' CD page to practise what they have learned by generating their own additions from a given selection of numbers.

Differentiation

A template version of the activity sheet is provided for you to fill in with single-digit numbers for less confident children and half single-digit and half two-digit numbers for more confident children.

Review

Write on the board: 16 + 9 + 4. Ask: *How can we use both strategies to find the answer?* Aim towards adding the 6 and the 4 to make 10, which with the other 10 makes 20, then adding on the 9. Write a few more such problems on the board for the children to answer. Ask: *Could you have solved it in a different way?*

Lesson 8 (Teach and practise)

Starter

Recall and revisit: Give the children different two-digit starting numbers and ask them to count on and back in ones and tens. When they count in ones, ask them to clap when they say an even number and stamp when they say an odd one. Ask them what would happen if they did this when counting in tens.

Main teaching activities

Whole class: Develop the Review from Lesson 7. Ask: *Who can remember what we did?* If necessary, write on the board as a clue: 17 + 3 + 8. Invite someone to circle the two numbers that make 10, then ask the children to add that 10 to the remaining 10 and then add on the 8. Let the children use their whiteboards for any jottings necessary, and for their answers. Repeat with examples such as: 14 + 6 + 5; 7 + 1 + 19. Now try some with two two-digit numbers and a single-digit number, such as: 25 + 10 + 5; 15 + 23 + 7; 24 + 12 + 6.

Paired work: Demonstrate the 'Find the way!' game, which the children can play to practise these strategies. Use an OHT of the 'Find the way! gameboard' to explain that the aim is to get through the maze by adding lines of three digits together, two of which must total 10. The children

Differentiation
Children of all abilities can play this game. Provide number lines, 100 squares and counting apparatus where needed.

should try to use all the numbers. Ask them to record their additions and draw lines connecting the numbers that they use. Say, for example (see below): *I start on 5, and look for two numbers to add to it so the addition includes a 10. I can use 8 and 2, so I draw a line from 5 to 8 to 2, and record the sum 5 + 8 + 2 = 15. Now I am on 2, and I look for two more numbers so that the addition includes a 10. I can use the next 2 and 8 (= 12). Next I can use 9 and 1 to add to the last number, 2 (= 12). Where can I go next?*

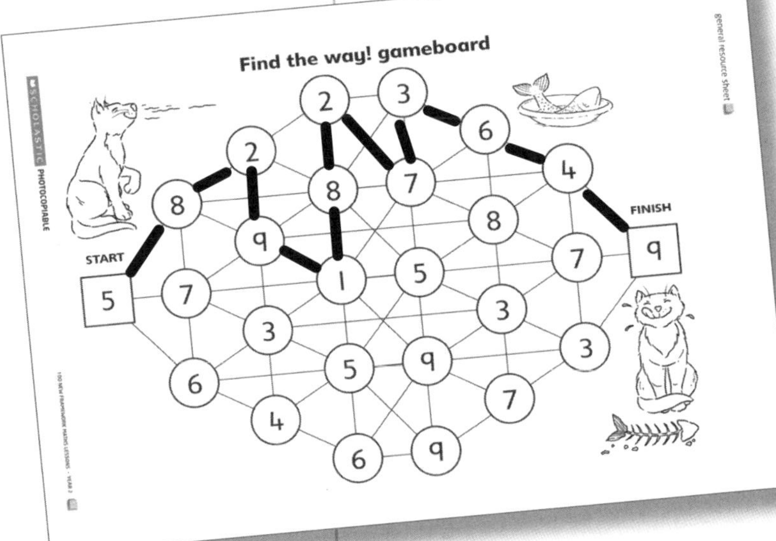

Review
Show the OHT of the 'Find the way! gameboard' and invite children to demonstrate how they got through the maze. Draw the route as they tell it to you. Write a '1' in front of some of the numbers to make teens numbers. Ask the children what difference this makes. Look for the answer that you can still find units digits to make 10 and then add on any extra tens. Suggest and demonstrate that jottings will help the children to keep track of their additions. Ask questions such as: *Is there another way you could have done this? Is your method the same as your neighbour's?*

Lesson 9 (Review, teach and practise)

Starter
Recall and read: Write the words 'double' and 'halve' on pieces of card or paper. Call out numbers to 10, and some to 20, and hold up a card. The children should double or halve the number depending on the word on the card and show you their answers with number cards 0–9.

Main teaching activities
Whole class: Recap the addition strategy of partitioning into tens and ones and recombining. Go through a few examples. Discuss what happens when the units digits total 10 or more, as in 34 + 27. This makes 30 + 20 + 4 + 7 = 50 + 11. Point out that 11 is 10 + 1, so you can add 50 and 10 and then add the 1 to make 61. Repeat this a few times with different starting numbers below 50.

Group work: Tell the children that they will practise this strategy by playing a game independently, but in groups of four, using the 'Lost in space gameboard'. Model the game, using an OHT. Some children may benefit from playing with a partner. Each group will need a set of 0–50 number cards and paper for recording. They take turns to pick two number cards to add by partitioning into tens and units, then move the number of spaces that the units digit of the answer shows. For example: *If I pick 27 and 38, I can partition them into 20 + 7 + 30 + 8 = 50 + 15 = 65. My unit number is 5, so I move on five spaces. The first space traveller to reach the home planet wins.*

Review
Divide the class into three teams and play the game on an OHT of the 'Lost in space gameboard'. Choose individuals to assess by asking them to demonstrate their additions on the board for their team. Ask questions such as: *How do you know you are right? Is there another way you could have done this? Is your method the same as your neighbour's?*

Differentiation
When playing the 'Lost in space' game, it may be helpful to pair less confident children with more confident children, or with an adult.

Unit 2 2 weeks

Lesson 10 (Apply and evaluate)

Starter

Rehearse and recall: Practise multiplication and division facts for two-, five- and ten-times tables, using the spider charts. Invite some children to come to the front to do the pointing. Time the children to see how quickly they can go round all the facts.

Main teaching activities

Whole class: Explain: *Today we are going to use the strategies we have been learning to help us solve missing number problems.* Recap on the strategies they have looked at, finding numbers to make 10 and partitioning and recombining. Write this on the board: 32 + ☐ = 40. Ask: *Which of the strategies will help us here?* Establish that it is the one for making 10. Write a list of similar calculations for the children to answer on their whiteboards. Begin with simple single and teens numbers and progress to more complicated ones, for example, 1 + ☐ = 10, 11 + ☐ = 20, 28 + ☐ = 40, ☐ + 37 = 70. This is a good way to differentiate - children who need extending will do most if not all, children needing support may just manage the first few.

Write a second type of calculation on the board: ☐ + 32 = 54. Discuss how this can be solved. Remind them of the counting on strategy they used last term for subtraction and encourage this. Repeat a few more examples. Move on to subtraction: 20 - ☐ = 13. Discuss how making 10 can help here. Go over a few more examples.

Individual work: The children should practise this work on the 'What am I?' CD page. It asks them to find missing numbers and explain how they found them. This activity concentrates on addition. Encourage the children to use appropriate resources to help them if necessary, for example, number lines, 100 squares.

Differentiation

Less confident learners: This group uses the support version of 'What am I?' to work with numbers to 20. Provide counters if you feel this would help.

More confident learners: This group uses the extension version of 'What am I?' to work with numbers to 100 and has two subtractions to tackle.

Review

Go through examples from each level of the activity, inviting children to share their thinking. Ask questions such as: *Is there another way you could have done this? Is your method the same as your neighbour's?*

Name ____________________ Date ____________

Which number goes where?

Choose two or more of these digits.

Make two two-digit numbers from them.

7	5	2	4

Write your numbers at the ends of a number line – for example, 75 and 54.
Now think of an 'in between' number and write that on the line – for example, 61.
Write your 'in between' number in words too – for example, sixty-one.

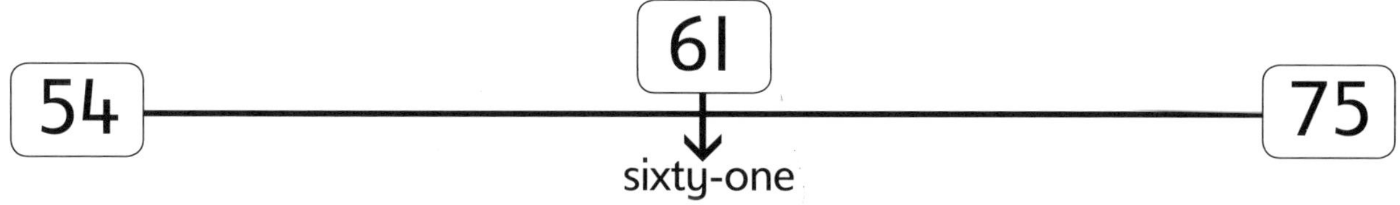

Try some more numbers, using the digits above.

1.

2.

3.

4.

5.

Make up some more of your own, using any digits.

BLOCK A

Counting, partitioning and calculating

Name ______________________ Date ______________

Straws

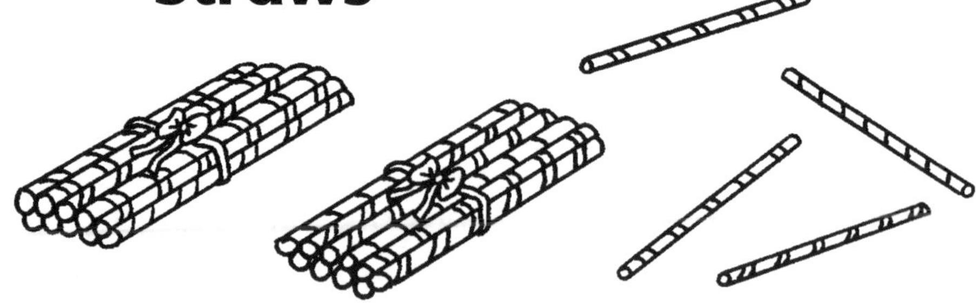

How many straws?

Bundles	Singles	Total ☐ + ☐ = ☐

How many more numbers can you make?

Bundles	Singles	Total ☐ + ☐ = ☐

Bundles	Singles	Total ☐ + ☐ = ☐

Bundles	Singles	Total ☐ + ☐ = ☐

Bundles	Singles	Total ☐ + ☐ = ☐

Bundles	Singles	Total ☐ + ☐ = ☐

Bundles	Singles	Total ☐ + ☐ = ☐

Name ______________________ Date ______________

How close can you get?

Estimate the number of things in the bag. Write your estimate in the table.
Count how many there are. Was your estimate close?
Do this for all the bags you have.

Name	Estimate	Count them	Were you close?

Name	Estimate	Count them	Were you close?

Name	Estimate	Count them	Were you close?

Sam had a bag of sweets. He estimated that there were 24 sweets in the bag. He counted them. There were 45.
Tick the best word to describe his estimate.

Tina had a bag of sweets. She estimated that there were 30 sweets in the bag. She counted them. There were 28.
Tick the best word to describe her estimate.

Sharma had a bag of sweets. He estimated that there were 28 sweets in the bag. He counted them. There were 28.
Tick the best word to describe his estimate.

Unit 3 2 weeks

Counting, partitioning and calculating

Speaking and listening objective

- Respond to presentations by describing characters, repeating some highlights and commenting constructively.

Introduction

This is a block of ten lessons. The first five focus on reading and writing numbers in words and figures. Within this objective are opportunities to describe simple number sequences; identify odd and even numbers; order, compare and round numbers. When comparing, the children are encouraged to use the symbols =, < and >. The children are also expected to partition numbers in different ways. The last five lessons focus specifically on understanding addition and subtraction. This involves rehearsing what the children should already know: vocabulary, inversions and calculating unknown values represented by symbols. There are also opportunities to rehearse and progress in a variety of mental calculation strategies.

This work is often conducted through the using and applying objective, with an emphasis on explaining and recording in an organised way.

The speaking and listening objective is fulfilled by way of the explanations and the encouragement of children's responses.

Lesson	Strands	Starter	Main teaching activities
1. Review and practise	Counting	Derive and recall multiplication facts for the 2, 5 and 10 times-tables and the related division facts; recognise multiples of 2, 5 and 10.	• Read and write two-digit and three-digit numbers in figures and words; describe and extend number sequences and recognise odd and even numbers. **• Count up to 100 objects by grouping them and counting in tens, fives or twos; explain what each digit in a two-digit number represents, including numbers where 0 is a place holder; partition two-digit numbers in different ways, including into multiples of 10 and 1.**
2. Teach and practise	Counting	As for Lesson 1	• Estimate a number of objects; round two-digit numbers to the nearest 10. • Read and write two-digit and three-digit numbers in figures and words; describe and extend number sequences and recognise odd and even numbers. • Order two-digit numbers and position them on a number line.
3. Review and practise	Counting	As for Lesson 1	As for Lesson 2
4. Apply	Counting	As for Lesson 1	• Read and write two-digit and three-digit numbers in figures and words; describe and extend number sequences and recognise odd and even numbers. • Order two-digit numbers and position them on a number line. • Estimate a number of objects: round two-digit numbers to the nearest 10.
5. Teach and practise	Counting	As for Lesson 1	• Read and write two-digit and three-digit numbers in figures and words; describe and extend number sequences and recognise odd and even numbers. • Order two-digit numbers and position them on a number line; use the greater than (>) and less than (<) signs.
6. Review and practise	Calculate	**Derive and recall all addition and subtraction facts for each number to at least 10, all pairs with totals to 20 and all pairs of multiples of 10 with totals up to 100.**	**• Add or subtract mentally a one-digit number or a multiple of 10 to or from any two-digit number; use practical and informal written methods to add and subtract two-digit numbers.** • Understand that subtraction is the inverse of addition and vice versa; use this to derive and record related addition and subtraction number sentences. **• Use the symbols +, –, ×, ÷ and = to record and interpret number sentences involving all four operations; calculate the value of an unknown in a number sentence (eg ❑ ÷ 2 = 6, 30 – ❑ = 24).**
7. Teach and practise	Calculate	As for Lesson 1	As for Lesson 6
8. Teach and practise	Calculate	As for Lesson 6	**Add or subtract mentally a one-digit number or a multiple of 10 to or from any two-digit number; use practical and informal written methods to add and subtract two-digit numbers.**
9. Teach and practise	Calculate	Read and write two-digit and three-digit numbers in figures and words; describe and extend number sequences and recognise odd and even numbers.	As for Lesson 8
10. Teach, apply and evaluate	Calculate	Derive and recall multiplication facts for the 2, 5 and 10 times-tables.	As for Lesson 8

SCHOLASTIC

Using and applying mathematics

- Present solutions to puzzles and problems in an organised way; explain decisions, methods and results in pictorial, spoken or written form, using mathematical language and number sentences.

Lessons 1-5

Preparation

Copy 'Round it!' onto acetate. Copy the 'Follow me cards' onto card and laminate, then cut out a set of cards.

You will need

Photocopiable pages
'Lunch money' (page 41).
CD resources
' 'Round it!' and 'Round it! gameboard 1', '2' and '3', '0-100 number cards', 'Arrow cards' for each less confident child, 'Up the mountain' gameboard, 'Spider charts for multiplying' and 'Spider charts for dividing', 'Spider charts for ×5 and ÷5', 'Follow me cards' (see General resources); 'Lunch money', 'In the balance' and 'Which number am I?', support and extension versions.
Equipment
Pennies; counters; class 100 square; individual whiteboards; balance scales; 1kg and two 500g weights; pendulum.

Learning objectives

Starter

- Derive and recall multiplication facts for the 2, 5 and 10 times-tables and the related division facts; recognise multiples of 2, 5 and 10.

Main teaching activities

2006

- Read and write two-digit and three-digit numbers in figures and words; describe and extend number sequences and recognise odd and even numbers.
- Count up to 100 objects by grouping them and counting in tens, fives or twos; explain what each digit in a two-digit number represents, including numbers where 0 is a place holder; partition two-digit numbers in different ways, including into multiples of 10 and 1.
- Estimate a number of objects; round two-digit numbers to the nearest 10.
- Order two-digit numbers and position them on a number line; use the greater than (>) and less than (<) signs.

1999

- Read and write whole numbers to at least 100 in figures and words.
- Compare two given two-digit numbers, say which is more or less, and give a number that lies between them.
- Describe and extend simple number sequences; recognise odd and even numbers to at least 30.
- Count reliably up to 100 objects by grouping them, eg in tens, then in fives or twos.
- Know what each digit in a two-digit number represents, including 0 as a place holder; partition two-digit numbers into a multiple of ten and ones (TU).
- Order whole numbers to at least 100, and position them on a number line and 100 square.
- Use symbols correctly, including less than (<), greater than (>), equals (=).
- Give a sensible estimate of at least 50 objects.
- Round numbers less than 100 to the nearest 10.

Vocabulary

two hundred... one thousand, units, ones, tens, hundreds, digit, round, nearest, round to the nearest 10, more, larger, bigger, greater, fewer, smaller, less, most, least, guess how many, estimate, nearly, roughly, close to, about the same as, just over, just under, exact, exactly, too many, too few, enough, not enough, round to the nearest ten

Lesson 1 (Review and practise)

Starter

Recall: Count in twos together, using fingers so that, when you stop part of the way through, the children can tell you what the multiplication fact is. For example, if you stop on 12 (the sixth finger), the multiplication fact is 2 times 6. Move on to using spider charts to reinforce these times tables and the corresponding division facts.

Repeat for the five- and ten-times tables.

Main teaching activities

Whole class: Explain that in this lesson the children will be recapping their knowledge of writing numbers, odd and even numbers, place value and counting by grouping objects. Call out five or six two- and three-digit numbers for the children to write on their whiteboards. For each ask: *Put your thumbs up if you think this is an odd number, thumbs down if you think it is even. How do you know? What do odd numbers end with? How about even? Why?* Discuss the place value of each number and ask them to count on from that number in ones and then tens, fives and twos. Discuss the patterns seen.

Refer to one of the two-digit numbers the children have written and ask: *If we had that number of pennies, how could we count them?* Demonstrate with around 57 pennies, changing lots of ten to 10p coins, five to a 5p coin and the remaining two to a 2p coin. Ask: *If I had 105 pennies, how many 10 pence coins would I need? What could I use instead of those (£1 coin)?* Repeat with similar examples.

Paired work: Tell the children that they will be working on some problems that involve finding amounts of money that fit certain criteria. Demonstrate using the two puzzles on the 'Which number am I?' activity sheet. Work through each clue, eliminating numbers as you do, completing the 'I can't be....' statements.

Differentiation

Less confident learners: Provide the support version of the activity sheet 'Which number am I?' for these children.
More confident learners: Give these children the extension version of the activity sheet to work through.

Review

Take feedback from the activity, asking the children to share their clues with the class and ask the class to work out which numbers they could be thinking of. Write some missing number sentences on the board and ask the children to complete them, explaining how they know. Be sure to focus on the skill of partitioning in different ways:

53 = 30 + □   67 = □ + 27   49 = 19 + □   98 = □ + 38

Lesson 2 (Teach and practise)

Starter

Rehearse and recall: As for Lesson 1.

Main teaching activities

Whole class: This lesson is about rounding numbers to the nearest 10. Ask: *Does anyone know what we mean by rounding?* Take suggestions and then explain. Use a bead string or draw a numbered number line 0–20 on the board. Highlight 0, 10 and 20. Mark 13 with an arrow. Explain that rounding a number to the nearest 10 means deciding which 10 number it is closest to. Ask: *Is 13 closer to 10 or 20?* Repeat with other numbers to 20.

Explain to the children that with numbers ending in 5, the rule is to round up to the higher value, so 5 is rounded to 10 and 15 to 20. Now draw a number line with 11 marks but no numbers, and write 26 on the seventh mark (where it would be if the whole line were numbered 20–30). Ask: *Which two tens numbers shall I put on this number line? Which one is 26 closest to?* Repeat with a variety of numbers up to 100.

Group work: Tell the children that they are going to practise rounding numbers to the nearest 10. Demonstrate the 'Round it!' game using an OHT of the instructions. Let the children play in pairs or small groups. Encourage them to play twice, the second time recording in the way shown in the instructions.

Differentiation

If the less confident learners find the instructions for the 'Round it!' game difficult to understand, let them work with more confident learners or adult support.

Review

Call out some random numbers for the children to round to the nearest 10. Ask them to write the answers on whiteboards and show you. Next, ask the children (working in 'buddy' pairs) to think of occasions when rounding might be helpful. Take feedback, and try to elicit the idea that rounding makes mental calculation easier. Give the example of adding/subtracting 9 or 11 by rounding to the nearest 10 and adjusting. Ask the children questions such as: 15 + 9, 13 + 11, 17 - 9, 14 + 19, 18 + 21. Explain that in the following lesson they will look at another situation where rounding is useful.

Lesson 3 (Review and practise)

Starter

Rehearse and reason: Use the spider charts for multiplication and division by 2, 5 and 10, as before. Do this twice. Play the multiplication and division 'Follow me cards'. Record how long it takes to go round the class.

Main teaching activities

Whole class: Explain to the children that this lesson is about ordering numbers to 100 and rounding them to the nearest 10. Provide them with a pile of two-digit number cards. Invite five children to pick a card each and show them to the class, who should order them from the smallest to the largest by telling the children where to stand. Repeat a few times. The last time, ask the children to find the numbers on a class 100 square. Mark these numbers. Say: *We are going to round these numbers to the nearest 10.* Remind the children of the work they did in Lesson 2 and particularly the Review: add/subtract 9 or 11 by adding/subtracting 10 and adjusting. Explain that it is useful to round to tens because these are easy numbers to work with.

Round the numbers on the class 100 square. Ask, for example: *Is 23 closer to 20 or 30?* On the 100 square, count how far 23 is from each number. Repeat with the other numbers. Pick more number cards and repeat several times. Hold up cards for the children to round on their whiteboards. Let the children refer to the class 100 square if they need to.

Hold up a card with 5 as the 'units' digit. Ask which multiple of 10 it is closest to. Establish that it is halfway between two multiples of 10. Explain that the rule is to round numbers ending in 5 up, not down.

Group work: Explain that the children will now practise this in pairs or small groups. Demonstrate the game 'Round it!' using the instruction sheet, then distribute 'Round it! gameboard 2'. When the children have played the game once, they should play again and record their work.

Differentiation

Less confident learners: Give these children 'Round it! gameboard 3', with 10 and 20 only. Ask the children to generate numbers from 10 to 19 using arrow cards.

More confident learners: The children could try the challenge described on 'Round it!'.

Review

Call out random numbers for the children to round on their whiteboards. Now ask them to talk to a partner about when they think rounding might be helpful. Take feedback; look for the idea of estimating the answer to a calculation (for example, when adding up prices in a shop).

Lesson 4 (Apply)

Starter

Rehearse and recall: Use the 'Up the mountain gameboard' for a whole-class game to practise halving multiples of 10 to 100. Follow the instructions for this lesson, given on the activity sheet.

Main teaching activities

Whole class: Ask the children what they learned in Lessons 2 and 3. Call out a few numbers for them to round on their whiteboards. Include numbers that end in 5. Ask why it can be useful to round. Recap on adding or subtracting 10 and adjusting as a strategy for adding or subtracting 9 or 11.

Move on to estimating the answers to problems through rounding: *Imagine I am in a shop and I have 30p. I would like to buy three chews. They cost 9p each. Do I have enough money? How can I decide quickly?* Ask the children to talk to each other and come up with suggestions. Discuss how useful this strategy is for shopping.

Give another example: *I am in the shop and I have 50p. I want to buy a bag of crisps for 32p and a can of cola for 29p. Have I enough money?* Ask the children what they think, then work through the problem on the board.

Repeat with more problems from 'Lunch money'.
Group work: Demonstrate how to complete the rest of 'Lunch money'. Emphasise that the children do not need to calculate the exact answers, only estimate the answers by rounding.

Differentiation
Less confident learners: Provide the support version of 'Lunch money' with smaller amounts. The children should work in pairs.
More confident learners: Provide the extension version where the full calculation is used to check.

Review
Invite some children to explain how they made their estimations. Make sure every problem completed is covered. Check each estimate by working out the answer. Recap the < and > symbols and ask them to make sentences to compare their estimates with the actual answers.

Lesson 5 (Teach and practise)

Starter
Refine and reason: Repeat the Starter from Lesson 4, but offer bonus points for telling you a quarter of the number as well as half. You may need to remind the children that a quarter is half of a half, and encourage them to find a quarter by halving and halving again.

Main teaching activities
Whole class: Say that this lesson is about the special jobs of zero, the equals sign and the symbols < and >. Write the number 25 on the board. Ask the children to partition 25 into tens and ones on their whiteboards in as many ways as they can. Write 20 + 5 = 25 and 10 + 15 = 25 on the board and ask them to check they have written those. Make 25 using arrow cards; invite two children to help you. Ask the child with the 5 to move away. Say: *What is left in the place of the 5? What would the number say if the zero wasn't there? The zero holds the place for the units or ones numbers. We call it a place holder.* Repeat this with 49, 18, 67 and 34. Then write 104 on the board. Ask which number the zero is the placeholder for. Repeat with 108 and 2045.

Ask the children what the = sign means. Invite a child to draw one on the board. Many children think the = sign means 'the answer'. It is very important for them to understand that it means 'what is on one side of the = sign is the same as what is on the other side'. Demonstrate this with balance scales. Put a 1kg weight in one side and ask whether the two sides are equal. Add a 500g weight to the other side and ask whether both sides are equal now. Add another 500g weight. Write a number sentence on the board to show this: 1kg = 500g + 500g.

Write on the board: 10 + 5 = 11 + □. Ask: *What can you put in the box to make this number sentence true? How do you know?* Encourage the children to work out the left-hand side and then decide how to make the other side the same (10 + 5 = 15, 11 + 4 = 15 so the missing number must be 4). Repeat with other numbers, with the box in different places, for example: 12 - □ = 10 - 1, 20 - 6 = □ + 4, □ + 10 = 10 x 2.
Paired work: Demonstrate the example from the 'In the balance' activity sheet. Let the children complete the sheet in pairs.

Differentiation
Less confident learners: Provide the support version of 'In the balance' with simpler calculations.
More confident learners: Provide the extension version with more complex calculations.

Review
Invite some children to go through some of the number sentences they made equal. Write an incorrect number sentence on the board, such as: 11 + 5 = 20 - 10. Ask: *Is that correct? How can I make the two sides equal? On your whiteboards, change one of the numbers so that the number sentence is correct. Show me.* Repeat with other incorrect number sentences. Next, ask what symbol they could have used in place of the = sign to make 11 + 5 = 20 - 10 correct, establish that it is >. Recap the use of the symbols < and > in this way, asking the children to help you make up some more sentences like this.

Lessons 6-10

Preparation

Copy 'Home we go! gameboard' onto acetate. Copy the 'Addition and subtraction vocabulary cards' onto card and laminate, then cut out a set of cards.

You will need

Photocopiable pages
'What's in the box?' (page 42) for each pair.
CD resources
OHT of 'Review questions', '0-100 number cards', 'Find the way! gameboard', 'Home we go!', 'Target boards 1', '2' and '3', 'Addition and subtraction vocabulary cards', Spider charts for multiplying' and 'Spider charts for dividing', 'Spider chart for ×5 and ÷5' (see General resources); 'Figure it out!', 'What's in the box?', 'Keeping it whole' and 'Number bonds' support, extension and template versions.
Equipment
Pendulum.

Learning objectives

Starter

- Derive and recall all addition and subtraction facts for each number to at least 10, all pairs with totals to 20 and all pairs of multiples of 10 with totals up to 100.
- Derive and recall all multiplication facts for the 2, 5 and 10 times-tables and the related division facts; recognise multiples of 2, 5 and 10.
- Read and write two-digit and three-digit numbers in figures and words; describe and extend number sequences and recognise odd and even numbers.

Main teaching activities

2006

- Add or subtract mentally a single-digit number or a multiple of 10 to or from any two-digit number; use practical and informal written methods to add and subtract two-digit numbers.
- Understand that subtraction is the inverse of addition and vice versa and use this to derive and record related addition and subtraction number sentences.
- Use the symbols +, –, ×, ÷ and = to record and interpret number sentences involving all four operations; calculate the value of an unknown in a number sentence (eg □ ÷ 2 = 6, 30 - □ = 24).

1999

- Extend understanding of the operations of addition and subtraction.
- Understand that subtraction is the inverse of addition (subtraction reverses addition).
- Use the +, - and = signs to record mental additions and subtractions in a number sentence, and recognise the use of a symbol such as □ or △ to stand for an unknown number.

Vocabulary

two hundred... one thousand, units, ones, tens, hundreds, digit, round, more, larger, bigger, fewer, smaller, less, most, nearest, round to the nearest 10, exact, exactly, multiply, divide

Lesson 6 (Review and practise)

Starter

Recall, refine and reason: Use a simple pendulum (as before) to practise number pairs to make 20 (for example, if you call out 13, the children call out 7) and pairs of multiples of 10 to make 100 (for example, 20 and 80); as a challenge progress to 200 (130 + 70). Discuss how their knowledge of pairs to 20 will help them.

Main teaching activities

Whole class: Say that for the next three lessons, the children will be focusing on addition and subtraction. Ask them to tell you all they can remember about these two areas, particularly: numbers can be placed in any order for addition and the answer will be the same; for subtraction the answer will usually be different; addition and subtraction are inverse operations. Write examples of these concepts on the boards to demonstrate.

Write these 'arrow diagrams' on the board:

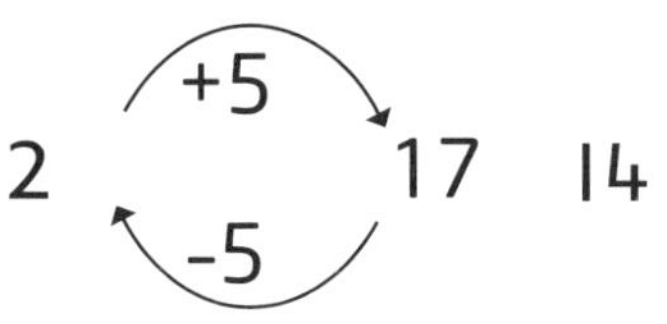

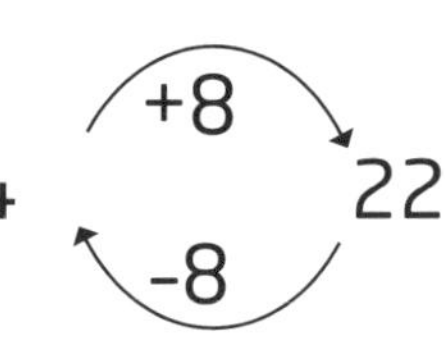

Ask the children what these show. Ask them to write down two number sentences for each diagram on their whiteboards. Use the arrow diagrams to make up questions, such as: □ + 5 = 17, □ - 5 = 12, 14 + □ = 22. Ask the children to find the answers, using arrow diagrams. Repeat with several similar examples, including higher two-digit numbers. Discuss strategies for finding the answers reinforcing the aspect of inversion.
Group work: Distribute the 'What's in the box?' activity sheet and model the example, then let the children complete the sheet.

Differentiation
Less confident learners: Present the support version of the activity sheet with lower totals.
More confident learners: Present the extension version with higher totals.

Review
Project the OHT of 'Review questions'. Work through these SATs-type problems. Ask the children such questions as: *What do you need to do here? What strategy can you use to help you?*

Lesson 7 (Teach and practise)

Starter
Refresh and read: Write some missing number sentences on the board and time the children to see how many they can answer in two minutes. Expect varying results. Repeat this two or three times. Using talk partners, ask them to think of as many words as they can for addition and subtraction.

Main teaching activity
Whole class: Remind the children of the problems they solved in Lesson 6. Explain that today they will use other symbols for the missing numbers. Pick two number cards to 50 (such as 45 and 23) and make a number sentence with the triangle symbol representing the first number and the cards as the second and answer numbers. Relate this to an arrow diagram.

Ask: *What do we know that can help us?* Write these number sentences on the board:
△ + 23 = 45   45 - 23 = △
Which sentence can help us see what the triangle stands for? (The subtraction sentence.) Work through five or six examples.
Paired work: Demonstrate the 'Figure it out!' activity sheet. Ask pairs of children to complete it.

Review
Ask some volunteers to share an example of their work and explain what they did.

Look at number sentences with symbols in the middle. Write on the board: 23 + △ = 45. Can the children tell you how to solve this? Ask what other sentences they can make from it. Say that because addition can be done in any order, △ + 23 = 45. Use an arrow diagram to show that △ = 22. Repeat with examples from the children's work.

Differentiation
Less confident learners: Provide the support version of 'Figure it out!' with lower numbers.
More confident learners: Provide the extension version with higher numbers.

Lesson 8 (Teach and practise)

Starter
Refresh: Write a number up to 10 on the board. Time the children for two or three minutes (depending on the number) to see how many addition and subtraction facts they can write down on their whiteboards for that number. For example, possible facts for 3 are: 0 + 3 = 3; 3 + 0 = 3; 3 - 0 = 3; 3 - 3 = 0; 1 + 2 = 3; 2 + 1 = 3; 3 - 1 = 2; 3 - 2 = 1. Share facts, then repeat for another number.

Main teaching activities
Whole class: Recap what the children did in the previous lesson. Continue to work on addition and subtraction. Begin by revising appropriate vocabulary: hold up the vocabulary cards as the children say them. Stick them on the board; add any the children have forgotten.

Say that today the children will try keeping the first number of a calculation whole and adding or subtracting the other number by partitioning. Demonstrate this using a class 100 square. Write 24 + 15 on the board. Explain that we can keep 24 whole in our minds, but partition the 15 to add 10 (making 34) and then 5 (making 39). Show these stages on the 100 square. Record on the board: 24 + 10 + 5 = 34 + 5 = 39. Check by subtraction.

Repeat with four or five additions, showing what you are doing on the 100 square. Move on to a subtraction, such as 53 - 24. Ask the children to keep 53 whole in their minds and take away 20 to leave 33, then 4 to leave 29. Record on the board: 53 - 20 - 4 = 33 - 4 = 29. Repeat with four or five subtractions. Check by addition.

Group work: Distribute and demonstrate the 'Keeping it whole' activity sheet, which asks the children to practise what they have learned by generating calculations and working them out.

Differentiation

Less confident learners: Fill in the template version of 'Keeping it whole' with numbers to 30 before copying it for the group. Allow the children to use 100 squares.
More confident learners: Fill in the template version with numbers to 100.

Review

Link this lesson's work to money problems. For example: *Sally had 67p. She spent 23p. How much did she have left?* Ask the children to work it out on their whiteboards: 67p - 20p - 3p = 44p. Try a few similar problems. For each problem, check using the inverse operation.

Lesson 9 (Teach and practise)

Starter

Read and reason: Ask the children to tell you what they know about odd and even numbers. If necessary, remind them that an odd number always has 1 left over when it is divided by 2, and an even number has nothing left over. Give them various two-digit starting numbers and ask them to count on and back in ones, clapping when they say an even number and stamping when they say an odd number. Repeat for counting in tens.

Main teaching activities

Whole class: Say that today, the children will use known number facts to help them add up other numbers. Go through the number bonds of 10, writing them on the board: 0 + 10 and 10 + 0; 1 + 9 and 9 + 1; 2 + 8 and 8 + 2; 3 + 7 and 7 + 3; 4 + 6 and 6 + 4; 5 + 5.

Write on the board some calculations that can be solved with these facts, and talk them through with the children. For example:

- 60 + 40: We know that 6 + 4 = 10, so what must 60 + 40 equal? How about 30 + 70?
- 12 + 8 + 6: We know that 2 + 8 = 10, so this must be 10 + 10 + 6, which is 26.
- 24 + 16: 4 + 6 = 10, so we could say 20 + 10 + 10, which equals 40.

Work through several examples, asking the children to spot the number bonds.

Group work: Distribute and demonstrate the 'Number bonds' activity sheet.

Differentiation

Less confident learners: Provide the support version of 'Number bonds' with totals to 30, or use the template version to simplify the work further.
More confident learners: Provide the extension version with totals to 100.

Review

Invite some children to share the calculation they found the most difficult and explain their method on the board. Play a class game of 'Find the way!' using the OHT. Split the class into three teams, who take turns making the next move. You could add a further challenge by leaving counters on the numbers used, so no-one can use them again. Play the game two or three times.

Lesson 10 (Teach, apply and evaluate)

Starter

Recall and refresh: Use the 'Spider charts for multiplying' and 'Spider charts for dividing' to practise the two-, five- and ten-times tables facts. Point to all the outside numbers on the multiplication charts in random order, and see how quickly the children can say the answers. Invite some children to do the pointing. Repeat with the division charts.

Main teaching activities

Whole class: Explain that today the children are going to think about bridging through 10. Check that they understand what that means: going through a tens boundary, as from 29 to 31. Write 26 + 8 on the board. Ask the children: *What is the next tens number? How many units are needed to get to it? How can you break the 8 into two numbers, one to make 30 and the other left to add on to 30?* Write what they say as a number sentence on the board, such as: 26 + 8 = 26 + 4 + 4 = 30 + 4 = 34. Repeat with other 'two-digit add single-digit' additions.

Now move on to 'two-digit add two-digit' calculations, such as 28 + 16. Remind the children about the strategy of keeping the first number whole and partitioning the second. Following that idea, demonstrate how to add the tens number first and then add the units by making a 10 and adding what is left: 28 + 16 = 28 + 10 + 6 = 38 + 6 = 38 + 2 + 4 = 40 + 4 = 44. Talk through the process. Do a few more examples.

Group work: Ask the children to apply this strategy using a game. Demonstrate how to use the 'Home we go!' gameboard with 'Target board 1'. Ask the children to add the numbers on the gameboard to those on 'Target board 1', using the strategy for bridging through 10. After they have played once, ask them to record their work as you demonstrated in the lesson.

Differentiation

Less confident learners: Provide 'Target board 2' with numbers to 10.

More confident learners: Provide 'Target board 3' with two-digit numbers only.

Review

Invite some children from each group to demonstrate which numbers they chose, and to explain clearly how they worked out the calculation. Write 19 + 26 on the board and ask the children to think of as many different ways of calculating it as possible (for example, 20 + 26 – 1; 10 + 20 + 10 + 5). Make sure they include today's strategy. Ask them which strategy they thought was the best.

Name ____________________ Date ____________________

Lunch money

Work in small groups of 3 or 4.
Imagine you are in a café.
Estimate whether you have enough money by rounding the prices to the nearest 10p.

For example:
I have 70p. I would like to buy a drink for 39p and a biscuit for 42p.
Have I got enough money?
In your head, round the amounts: 40p and 40p. Add them: 80p.
Answer: No.

I have 80p. I would like to buy chips for 51p and a drink for 43p. Have I got enough money? ______ Why?	I have £1. I would like to buy a sausage for 51p and a burger for 58p. Have I got enough money? ______ Why?
I have 90p. I would like to buy a slice of cake for 48p and a sandwich for 52p. Have I got enough money? ______ Why?	I have 80p. I would like to buy 3 fish fingers for 21p each. Have I got enough money? ______ Why?
I have £2. I would like to buy a bag of chips for 68p and a piece of fish for £1.29. Have I got enough money? ______	I have £1. I would like to buy a drink for 54p and crisps for 38p. Have I got enough money? ______

Name ______________________ Date ______________________

What's in the box?

Work out what number needs to go in the box.

Write down what you did to find the answer. Use the 'arrow diagram' to help you.

Here is an example:

12 + 6 = 18

I did 18 – 6 = 12 so

12 goes in the box.

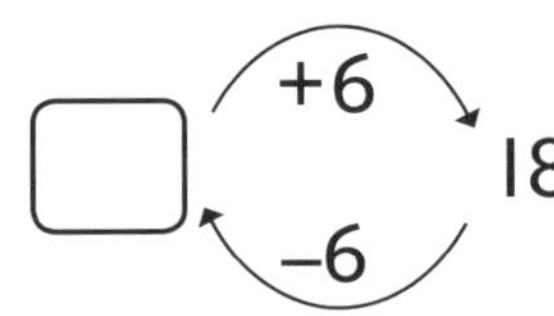

Now you try:

☐ + 9 = 15

I did:

+9 15 –9

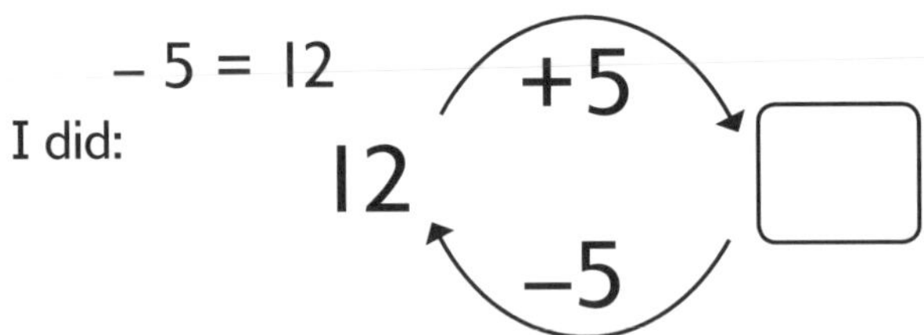

☐ – 5 = 12

I did:

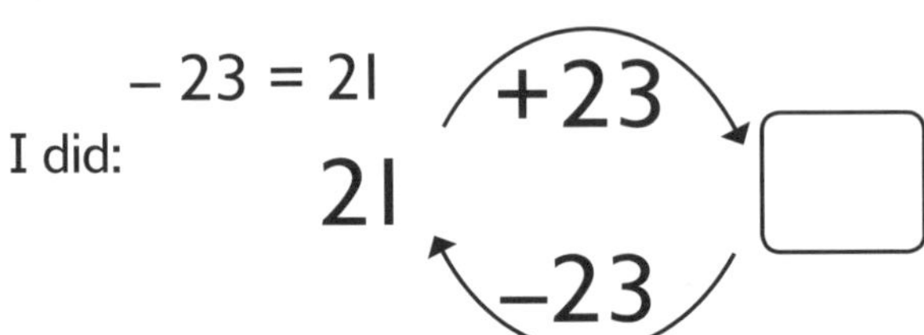

☐ – 23 = 21

I did:

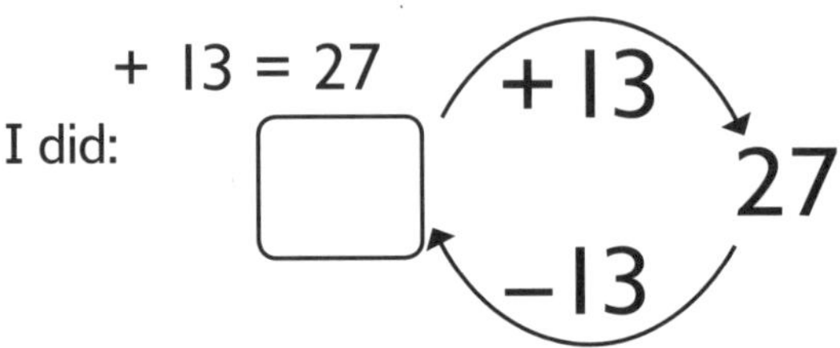

☐ + 13 = 27

I did:

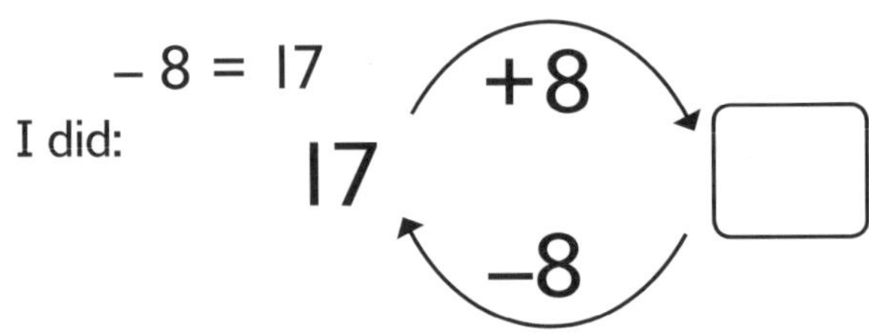

☐ – 8 = 17

I did:

☐ – 31 = 25

I did:

+31 25 –31

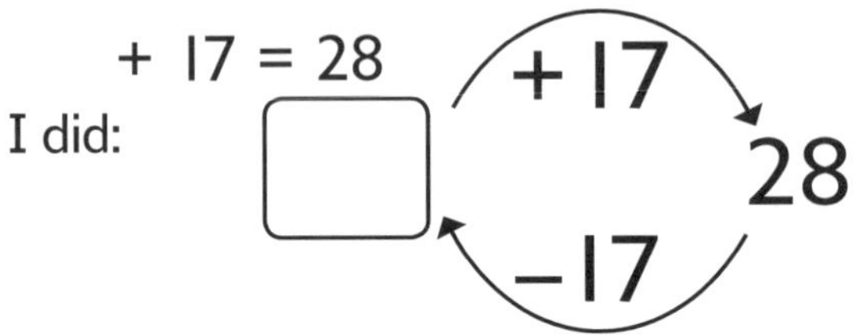

☐ + 17 = 28

I did:

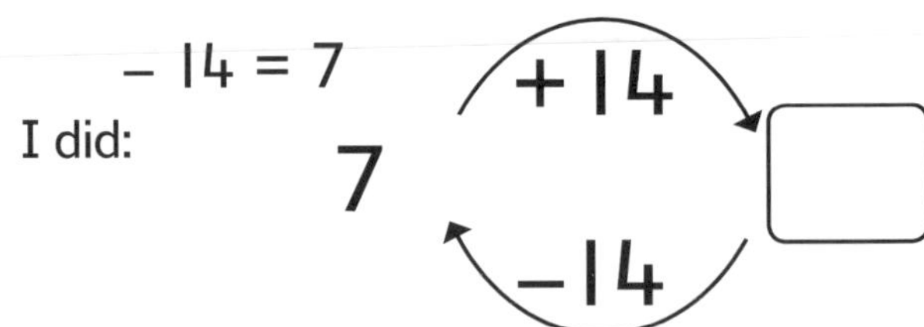

☐ – 14 = 7

I did:

15 + ☐ = 23

I did:

15 23

☐ + 15 = 31

I did:

+15 31 –15

☐ – 20 = 35

I did:

+20 35 –20

30 + ☐ = 42

I did:

30 42

Securing number facts, understanding shape

Key aspects of learning
- Problem solving
- Creative thinking
- Information processing
- Motivation

Expected prior learning

Check that children can already:
- describe simple patterns and relationships involving numbers or shapes
- solve problems involving counting, adding, subtracting, doubling or halving in the context of numbers, measures or money; recognise the value of coins
- recall addition and subtraction facts to 10 and doubles of all numbers to at least 10
- use informal written methods to add or subtract a one-digit number or multiple of 10 to or from a two-digit number, recording an addition or subtraction number sentence
- name common 2D shapes and 3D solids and describe their features
- use diagrams to sort objects into groups according to a given criterion.

Objectives overview

The text in this diagram identifies the focus of mathematics learning within the block.

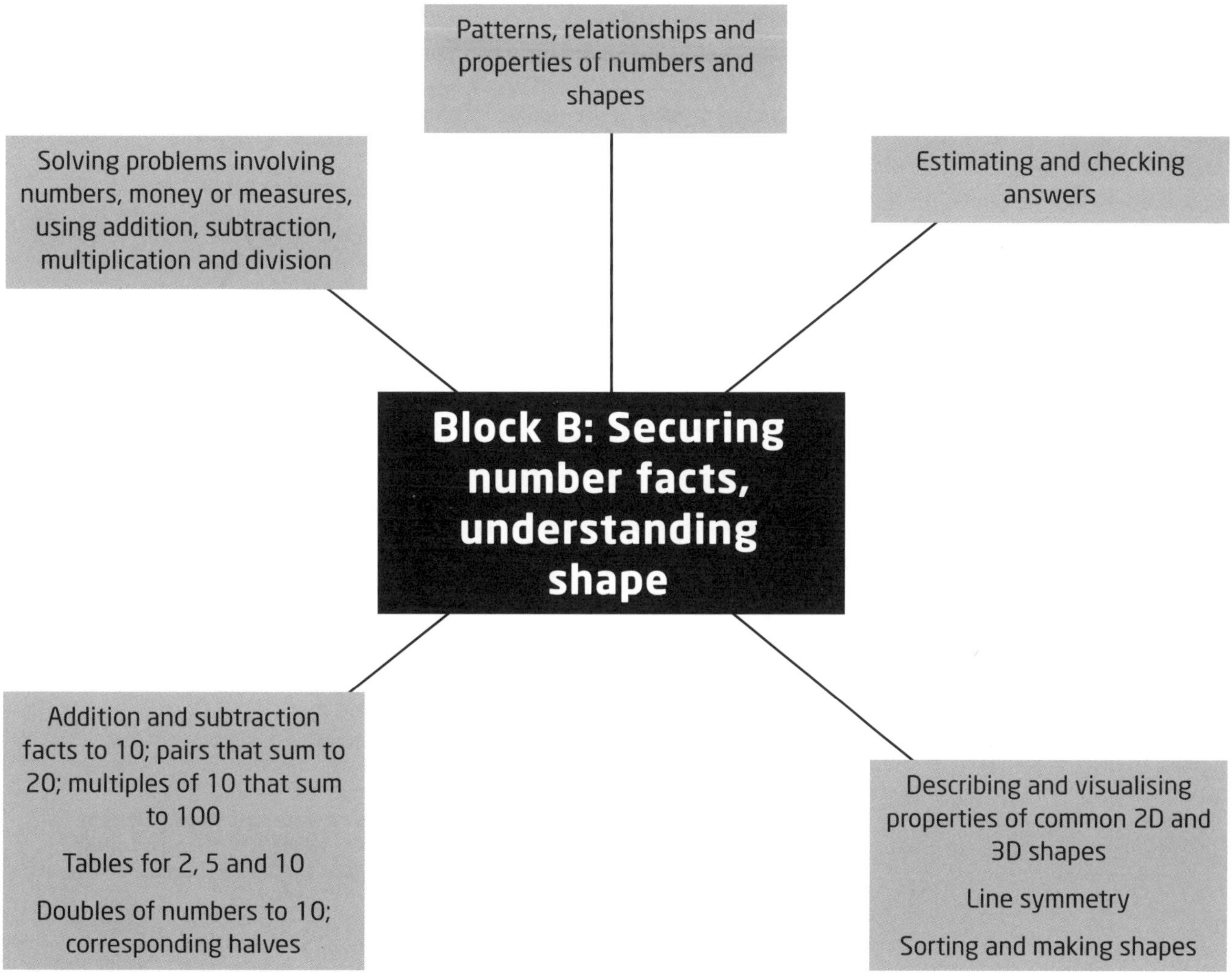

Patterns, relationships and properties of numbers and shapes

Solving problems involving numbers, money or measures, using addition, subtraction, multiplication and division

Estimating and checking answers

Block B: Securing number facts, understanding shape

Addition and subtraction facts to 10; pairs that sum to 20; multiples of 10 that sum to 100

Tables for 2, 5 and 10

Doubles of numbers to 10; corresponding halves

Describing and visualising properties of common 2D and 3D shapes

Line symmetry

Sorting and making shapes

Unit 1 3 weeks

Securing number facts, understanding shape

Lesson	Strands	Starter	Main teaching activities
1. Teach and practise	Use/apply	Understand that halving is the inverse of doubling and derive and recall doubles of all numbers to 20, and the corresponding halves.	Describe patterns and relationships involving numbers or shapes, make predictions and test these with examples.
2. Teach and apply	Use/apply	Identify near doubles, using doubles already known (eg 8 + 9, 40 + 41).	As for Lesson 1
3. Teach and apply	Use/apply	• Read and write two-digit and three-digit numbers in figures and words; describe and extend number sequences and recognise odd and even numbers. • Recognise multiples of 2, 5 and 10.	As for Lesson 1
4. Review and apply	Use/apply	Recognise multiples of 2, 5 and 10.	Solve problems involving addition, subtraction, multiplication or division in contexts of numbers, measures or pounds and pence.
5. Review, teach and apply	Use/apply	Derive and recall multiplication facts for the 2, 5 and 10 times-tables and the related division facts.	As for Lesson 4
6. Review and apply	Use/apply	**Derive and recall all addition and subtraction facts for each number to at least 10, all pairs with totals to 20 and all pairs of multiples of 10 with totals up to 100.**	As for Lesson 4
7. Review and apply	Use/apply	As for Lesson 6	As for Lesson 4
8. Review, teach, apply and evaluate	Use/apply	As for Lesson 6	As for Lesson 4
9. Evaluate and apply	Use/apply Knowledge	• Understand that halving is the inverse of doubling and derive and recall doubles of all numbers to 20, and the corresponding halves. • Identify near doubles, using doubles already known (eg 8 + 9, 40 + 41).	• Solve problems involving addition, subtraction, multiplication or division in contexts of numbers, measures or pounds and pence. • Understand that halving is the inverse of doubling and derive and recall doubles of all numbers to 20, and the corresponding halves.
10. Review, apply and evaluate	Use/apply Knowledge	As for Lesson 9	As for Lesson 9
11. Review and practise	Shapes	Read and write two-digit and three-digit numbers in figures and words; describe and extend number sequences and recognise odd and even numbers.	**Visualise common 2D shapes and 3D solids; identify shapes from pictures of them in different positions and orientations; sort, make and describe shapes, referring to their properties.**
12. Review, teach and apply	Shapes	Understand that halving is the inverse of doubling and derive and recall doubles of all numbers to 20, and the corresponding halves.	As for Lesson 11
13. Review, teach and practise	Shapes	As for Lesson 9	As for Lesson 11
14. Review and apply	Shapes	As for Lesson 12	**• Visualise common 2D shapes and 3D solids; identify shapes from pictures of them in different positions and orientations; sort, make and describe shapes, referring to their properties.** • Identify reflective symmetry in patterns and 2D shapes and draw lines of symmetry in shapes.
15. Teach and practise	Shapes	As for Lesson 6	As for Lesson 14

Speaking and listening objective
- Listen to others in class, ask relevant questions and follow instructions.

Introduction
This block of work contains 15 lessons. The first two specifically focus on patterns and relationships. The third begins a series of eight lessons on problem solving, starting with number-based problems and leading into 'real life' problems involving money. These include elements of recalling addition and subtraction facts and also halving and doubling. The last five lessons involve a variety of aspects of shape including a focus on symmetry in patterns and 2D shapes. The starters of each lesson focus on rehearsing the skills involved with doubling, halving, near doubles, number pairs to 10 and 20 and multiples of 2, 5 and 10. It is important that these are practised frequently to keep them fresh in the children's minds. At all times, the children should be encouraged to listen to others in class as they explain their answers or thinking, ask relevant questions and follow instructions.

Using and applying mathematics
- Describe patterns and relationships involving numbers or shapes; make predictions and test these with examples.
- Solve problems involving addition, subtraction, multiplication or division in contexts of numbers, measures or pounds and pence.

Lessons 1-2

Preparation
Photocopy all the gameboards onto card and laminate.

You will need
CD resources
A copy of 'Diamond number line for ones' and 'Diamond number line for twos' for each pair of children, a class set of '0-100 number cards', at least four A3 copies of the 'Diamond number line' (see General resources).
Equipment
Whiteboard pens; counters.

Learning objectives

Starter
- Understand that halving is the inverse of doubling and derive and recall doubles of all numbers to 20, and the corresponding halves.
- Identify near doubles, using doubles already known (eg 8 + 9, 40 + 41).

Main teaching activities
2006
- Describe patterns and relationships involving numbers or shapes; make predictions and test these with examples.

1999
- Describe and extend simple number sequences.
- Begin to recognise two-digit multiples of 2.
- Investigate a general statement about familiar numbers.

Vocabulary
zero, one hundred, two hundred... one thousand, count on, count back, count in ones/twos/tens, multiple of, sequence, continue, predict, pattern, rule

Lesson 1 (Teach and practise)

Starter
Recall: Ask the children to set their number cards 0-9 out in front of them. Call out random numbers from 1 to 10 and ask the children to show you their doubles, using number cards. Then call out even numbers to 20 and ask the children to show you their halves. Finally, mix the questions.

Main teaching activities
Whole class: Explain that today, the children will be learning about number sequences that go up and down in ones or tens. Pick a two-digit number card and ask the children to start counting forwards and then backwards from it. Repeat this a few times, counting alternately in ones and in tens.

Next, invite a child to pick a card and write the number on the board. Ask the children to discuss with a partner what they think the next eight numbers will be on either side, counting on and back in ones. Ask the children what they notice. Elicit the response that the units number is one more each time. Invite some children to write these numbers on the board.

Repeat for counting in tens; what do the children notice? (The units number remains the same.)

Paired work: Ask the children to play the game in pairs. Use an A3 copy of 'Diamond number line' to model the instructions on 'Diamond number line for ones'. For example: *I've picked 2 and 4, so I'm going to make 24 and write it in the first diamond. If my partner picks 8 and 2, what two numbers can we make? Can one of them be written in a diamond?* (Ask a child to write 28 in the correct place.) *If 7 and 5 are picked now, what numbers can we make? Will either of them fit on the line? No, so it's the other player's turn. What about 2 and 5? Great, 25 can be added to the line...* Children must start with a number below 90.

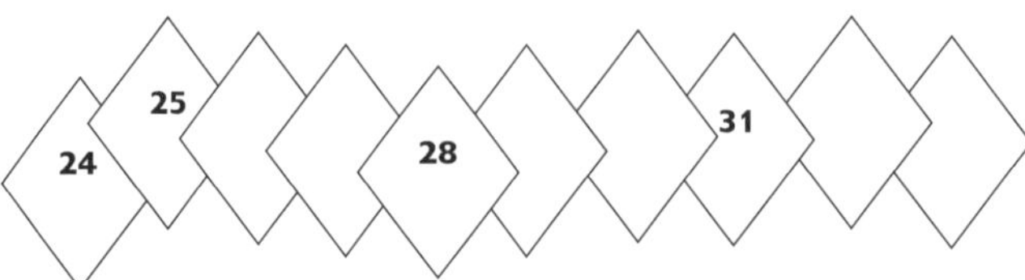

Differentiation

Less confident learners: Give these pairs a starting number below 20 and a pile of number cards with ten extra 1s and 2s.

More confident learners: Ask these pairs to write their starting number in the 'middle' diamond on the line, so that they need to count forwards and backwards.

Review

Play the game again as a class, using another A3 copy of 'Diamond number line' but counting in tens. Pick single-digit number cards to make a two-digit number and write it in the middle diamond. Invite the children to pick single-digit cards and replace the tens number each time to make a new number. Ask the class to tell you what the numbers are, and invite children to write them in the correct places. Each time, ask the children what has happened to the tens number and to the units number. Reiterate the fact that the units number stays the same: only the tens number is changing.

Lesson 2 (Teach and apply)

Starter

Refine and rehearse: Set up as in Lesson 1. Call out pairs of numbers to 10 that are near doubles. Ask the children to find the answer by doubling one number and adjusting, then show you the answer with their cards. Ask them to explain their method and suggest alternative methods. Which way do they think is best? Extend to numbers such as 10 + 11, 20 + 21, 30 + 32.

Main teaching activities

Whole class: Have a pack of number cards 0–50 face down in front of you. Invite a child to pick one card and write the number on the board. Write up the next five numbers counting in twos, and ask the children to tell you what the sequence is. Focus on the fact that the numbers go up in twos, and explain that today the children will be counting in twos and looking for patterns in the sequences. Invite another child to pick a card and ask others to make a sequence as you did.

Draw a number line with ten divisions. Ask another child to pick a card from the pack and write it in the middle of the line. Invite other children to complete the line. Talk about whether the numbers get bigger or smaller in each direction. Repeat this a few times. If the children mention that the numbers are all either odd or even, congratulate them for remembering and ask how they know, but don't make 'odd' and 'even' a teaching point for this lesson.

Paired work: Use an A3 copy of 'Diamond number line' to model the instructions on 'Diamond number line for twos'. Let the children play the game in pairs.

Differentiation

Less confident learners: Give these pairs a starting number below 10 and a set of single-digit number cards with ten extra 1s and 2s.

More confident learners: Ask these pairs to write their starting number in the 'middle' diamond on the line, so that they need to count forwards and backwards.

Review

Invite a few pairs to draw one of their completed number lines on the board and share what they noticed about this pattern. If any of the children have already mentioned odd and even numbers, ask them to repeat this. Write a few random numbers going down from left to right onto an A3 copy of the

'Diamond number line' sheet, and invite the children to say what the missing numbers are.

When the line is completed, write down the units number pattern (for example: 8, 6, 4, 2, 0, 8, 6...) and link it to even or odd numbers.

Lessons 3-4

Preparation

Photocopy 'Dicey digit problems' and cut into strips. Copy each set of 'Calculator cards' onto card, laminate and cut out. OHP calculators can vary, so practise first! Check that you can carry out the programming instructions on the calculator cards, and amend them if not.

You will need

Photocopiable pages
'Dicey digit problems' (page 56) and a copy of 'Number investigations' (page 57) for each group.

CD resources
Number cards 0-50, and number cards 0-9 for each group (from '0-100 number cards'), one of each set of 'Calculator cards' (see General resources); 'Dicey digit problems' and 'Number investigations' support and extension versions.

Equipment
An OHP calculator; dice; dominoes.

Learning objectives

Starter

- Read and write two-digit and three-digit numbers in figures and words; describe and extend number sequences; recognise odd and even numbers.
- Recognise multiples of 2, 5 and 10.

Main teaching activities

2006

- Solve problems involving addition, subtraction, multiplication or division in contexts of numbers, measures or pounds and pence.
- Describe patterns and relationships involving numbers or shapes, make predictions and test these with examples.

1999

- Solve mathematical problems or puzzles.
- Suggest extensions by asking 'What if...?' or 'What could I try next?'

Vocabulary

predict, sequence, multiple of, answer, solution, addition, add, total, subtract, take away, multiply, calculate, calculation, mental calculation, jotting

Lesson 3 (Teach and apply)

Starter

Read and reason: Use an OHP calculator to work through the three sets of calculator cards. The children need to identify the pattern each time and continue it orally until you say *Stop*. For example, key in: + 2 = = = (counts in steps of 2); 2 + 5 = = = (counts in steps of 5 from 7); or 110 - 10 = = = (counts back in steps of 10 from 100).

Main teaching activities

Whole class: Explain that you are going to give the class some problems and puzzles to solve, and will be asking them to make predictions. Do an example together: *We need to make 11 by adding three numbers. How many different ways can we do this? First predict the answer - that is, say what you think it will be.* Take some predictions and write them on the board. *Now we need to find the answer. Talk to your maths partner and write some ways of making 11 with three numbers on your whiteboards. You have two minutes.* Collect the ways. Use questioning, and ask the class to comment on each other's answers. For example: *What is the highest number that can be used? How do you know? Do you agree with that? What other thoughts do you have? Can you use three of the same number? Would it make a difference if you could only use each number once? What if you could use four numbers?*

Group work: After exploring this problem, ask the children to work in small groups to solve some of the problem strips from 'Dicey digit problems'.

Differentiation

Less confident learners: This group can use the support version of 'Dicey digit problems' with simplified problems.

More confident learners: This group can use the extension version with more complex problems.

Review

Take problems from each ability level and ask the children who solved them to explain what they did. Encourage them to talk about: how they made their predictions; whether they agreed on these; how they started their investigation; whether they had a 'system' or just made random guesses;

how they knew they had found all the possible solutions; and how close their predictions were.

Lesson 4 (Review and apply)

Starter

Revisit: In the Starter, hold up some number cards to 50. As you hold up each one, the children should perform an action if it is a multiple of 2, 5 or 10. For example, they could clap for multiples of 2, jump once for multiples of 5 and stick their tongues out for multiples of 10! If a number is a multiple of 2 and 5 (for example), they can carry out both actions.

Differentiation

Less confident learners: This group can use the support version of 'Number investigations' with simplified problems.
More confident learners: This group can use the extension version of 'Number investigations' with more complex problems.

Main teaching activities

Whole class: Recap on the work the children did in Lesson 3.
Group work: Develop the Group work from Lesson 3, asking the children to use the 'Number investigations' sheet. These problems are more extended than in Lesson 3, encouraging the children to think of more possibilities for solutions.

Review

Develop the Review from Lesson 3.

Lessons 5-10

Preparation

Copy the 'Coin cards and labels' onto card and colour; laminate the sheets and cut out the coins and labels. Make a copy of each coin card on acetate and cut out the coins. Prepare plastic (or real) pennies in groups of 200, 100, 50, 20, 10, 5, 2 and 1 for demonstration. Put the larger amounts into plastic bags. Copy a set of the relevant 'Shopping cards' for each child.

You will need

Photocopiable pages
'Shopping cards 1' for each child (page 58); 'Ivor Dog's dog and puppy food' (page 59).
CD resources
Number cards 0-9 for each child, acetates of 'Spider charts for multiplying' and 'Spider charts for dividing', 'Coin cards and labels', 'Shopping cards 2' and '3', 'Doubling and halving' (see General resources); 'Ivor Cat's cat food'; 'Ivor Dog's dog and puppy food' support and extension versions. Interactive resource 'Money'.
Equipment
400 × 1p coins; Blu-Tack; 2p, 5p and 10p coins; 0-100 number line; pendulum.

Learning objectives

Starter

- Derive and recall multiplication facts for the 2, 5 and 10 times-tables.
- Derive and recall all addition and subtraction facts for each number to at least 10, all pairs with totals to 20 and all pairs of multiples of 10 with totals up to 100.
- Understand that halving is the inverse of doubling and derive and recall doubles of all numbers to 20, and the corresponding halves.

Main teaching activities

2006

- Solve problems involving addition, subtraction, multiplication or division in contexts of numbers, measures or pounds and pence.
- Understand that halving is the inverse of doubling and derive and recall doubles of all numbers to 20, and the corresponding halves.

1999

- Recognise all coins and begin to use £.p notation for money.
- Find totals, give change, and work out which coins to pay.
- Choose and use appropriate operations and efficient calculation strategies (eg mental, mental with jottings) to solve problems.
- Derive quickly doubles of all whole numbers to at least 20 and the corresponding halves. (Year 3 objective)

Vocabulary

money, coin, penny, pence, pound, £, price, cost, buy, bought, sell, sold, spend, spent, pay, change, costs more, costs less, how much...?, total, groups of

Lesson 5 (Review, teach and apply)

Starter

Reason: Ask the children to count in twos and tens, using their fingers. Make the link to 'how many lots of'. Remind them that when they count in 'lots of' they are beginning to learn the two- and ten-times tables. Use 'Spider charts for multiplying' to practise random two- and ten-times table facts. Introduce the 'Spider charts for dividing' and ask questions such as: *How many twos make this number?* (Point to 12, they say six.) *How many tens make this number?* (Point to 80, they say eight.) Encourage them to use their fingers if they need to.

Main teaching activities

Whole class: Explain that the children will be looking at the coins in our money system. Show them some real coins and tell them that as these are very small for the whole class to see, you have prepared some larger copies. Blu-Tack each coin and its enlarged copy to the board. Hold up the coin labels and ask the children to match these to the coins. Ask: *Why do we need these different coins? What would happen if we only had pennies? What would it be like to pay for a comic that cost 50p if we only had pennies?* Using the plastic coins, show how many pennies each coin is worth. Ask the children to help you order the coins from the least to the greatest value.

Put 26 plastic pennies on the OHP, or use the interactive resource 'Money'. Remind the children that when you have a lot of things it is easier to count in groups than in ones. Invite someone to come out and count out ten pennies. Ask: *What could we have instead of these ten pennies?* (10p) Swap the ten pennies for the 10p coin.

Do the same for the next ten pennies. Now ask: *Can we make another group of ten? No, but we could change some of the remaining ones into another coin. Which one?* (5p) Replace the five pennies with the 5p coin. Ask: *How many pennies are left?* (1) Add them up: 10p + 10p + 5p + 1p. Reinforce by saying: *We started off with 26 pence. From that we could get two ten pences, a five pence and a penny.* Repeat several times with amounts to 50p.

Group work: Ask ability pairs or groups to try a matching activity. They will need a selection of coins and a set of coin labels. Say: *Pick a label, take that number of pennies and then try to swap them for other coins.* Encourage the children to make each amount in three different ways.

Differentiation

Less confident learners: This group can work with amounts to 15p.

More confident learners: This group can find the smallest number of coins and one other mixed-coin way of making the amount on each label.

Review

Ask the children to show you the different ways they found to make 50p, £1 and £2.

Lesson 6 (Review and apply)

Starter

Recall: Call out random numbers to 10 and ask the children to show you the other number that will make 10 with their number cards. Discuss how this can help them to make 100, and repeat the first activity for multiples of 10 to 100.

Main teaching activities

Whole class: Recap Lesson 5: why all the coins are useful and how much each is worth. Order the coins from the lowest value to the highest. Invite a child to find a 2p and a 1p coin. Ask the class how much this child has altogether. Repeat with a 5p and a 2p coin. Repeat for several combinations of two and three different coins.

Paired work: Tell the children that they will be investigating different ways of paying for something. Show the children the shopping cards for amounts to 20p. Tell them that one child in each pair is the 'shopkeeper' and the other child is the 'shopper' who is buying the toys. The 'shopper' picks a card and finds the right coins to give to the 'shopkeeper'. The 'shopkeeper' checks that there is the correct amount of money and keeps it, while the 'shopper' keeps the toy cards. After a couple of turns, they swap roles.

Give each pair a set of cards from the 'Shopping cards 1' sheet. After about 5 minutes, stop the class and add another element: they need to pick two cards (using 'Shopping cards 2') and work out the total, using any method they choose, then find the coins needed to pay that amount. Say that in the

Review, you will discuss the methods they used. Encourage recording in this form: Total = 37p = 20p + 10p + 5p + 2p.

Review

Hold up some shopping cards and ask for each one: *How can we make this amount using the most coins... the fewest coins?* Use the interactive resource 'Money' to show their suggestions. Hold up two cards and ask some children to explain the strategies they would use to find the total.

Differentiation

Less confident learners: This group can use the shopping cards for amounts to 20p, only using one card each time and using 1p, 2p, 5p and 10p coins to make the amount required, so they can concentrate on the money rather than the addition.
More confident learners: This group can pick two cards from the set with prices over £1 (see 'Shopping cards 3'). Ask them to use as few coins as possible.

Lesson 7 (Review and apply)

Starter

Refine and reason: Repeat the Starter from Lesson 6 and then progress to number pairs to 20. Discuss how this can help them find pairs of multiples of 10 to 200 and repeat the first activity for multiples of 10 to 200.

Main teaching activities

Whole class: Recap Lesson 6 by holding up some coin labels and asking for the totals and the least number of coins needed to make them. Say: *Today we will find some total prices, pay with a 20p, 50p, £1 or £2 coin, and work out the change by counting up in coins.*

Work through this process slowly, using partitioning to find the total and counting out coins for the change. For example: *I am going to spend 21p and 14p. I give the shopkeeper 50p. The first thing I need to do is add the amounts I spend. Watch how I do this.* (Write the calculations on the board.) *21p + 14p. I am going to partition these amounts. 21p becomes 20p and 1p. What does 14p become? (10p and 4p.) Now I'm going to add the tens numbers first: 20p + 10p = 30p. And then the ones numbers: 1p + 4p = 5p. Now I can recombine the tens and the ones to get 30p + 5p = 35p. My total is 35p.*

Repeat with a few examples before moving on to finding change. Go back to the first example: *To work out the change, I am going to count on from 35p to 50p using coins. What can I use to get me to 40p? (5p.) What can I use to get from 40p to 50p? (10p.) So how much have I counted from 35p to 50p? (10p and 5p, making 15p.)*

Demonstrate this a few times, using 20p, 50p and £1 as the coins to get change from.

Paired work: Repeat the activity from the previous lesson, but this time, when the children have found the total of two cards, they need to work out the change from 50p or £1.

Differentiation

Less confident learners: This group can use one card (from 'Shopping cards 1') to 20p and work out the change from 20p.
More confident learners: This group can use two cards over £1 (from 'Shopping cards 3') and work out the change from £3 or £4.

Review

Invite some of the children to demonstrate how they worked out their totals and the change. Ask: *What was the first thing you needed to do? Can you explain how you found the total? What was the next thing you did? Can you show us how you counted out the change? Which coins did you use?* Use the Interactive resource Money to show their suggestions.

Lesson 8 (Review, teach, apply and evaluate)

Starter

Recall: Practise number bonds to ten using the swinging pendulum. Call a number on one swing and, as it swings the other way, the children call out the number that goes with it to make 10. Repeat for 20 and multiples of 10 to 100.

Ask the children to write down on their whiteboards all pairs of numbers that make 15, 8, and so on.

Main teaching activities

Whole class: Repeat the whole-class and paired activities from Lesson 7, but instead of counting out coins, show the children how to use a number

line to find the change and then record. For example: To find the total of 15p and 14p, we can partition the numbers and add the tens first, just as we do when we add ordinary numbers: 10p + 10p + 5p + 4p = 20p + 9p = 29p. To work out the change from £1, we can use a number line and count from our total of 29p up to £1, just as we do when we find small differences in ordinary numbers. Remember that £1 is 100p. 29p plus 1p gets us to 30p. Now let's count in tens to £1: 40, 50, 60, 70, 80, 90, £1. That's 70p altogether.

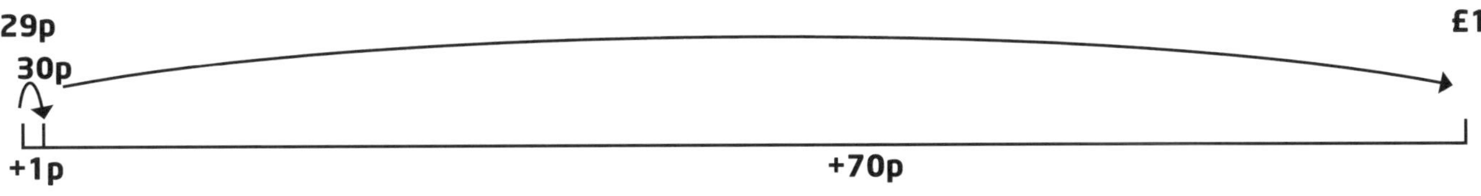

So our change is 1p and 70p, which makes 71p.
To find the total of 25p and 32p, let's partition the numbers and add the tens first: 20p + 30p + 5p + 2p = 50p + 7p = 57p. Now let's use a number line and count from our total of 57p up to £1: 57p plus 3p gets us to 60p.

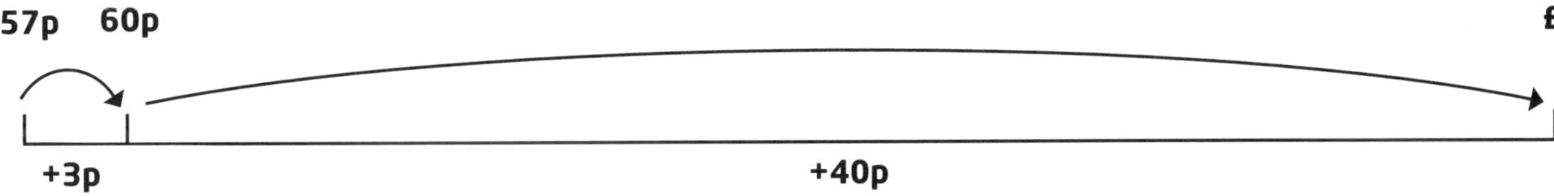

How many tens get us to £1? Let's count... 40p.
Our change is 3p and 40p, which makes 43p.

Review

Take feedback from the activity through questioning. Your questions could include: *Can you show us how you found the difference between your total and the money you gave to the shopkeeper?* Focus on checking the results of their totals. Remind them of work they have done about how addition can be done in any order. Ask some children to demonstrate how they could check their answers (by adding the amounts in a different order).

Differentiation
As for Lesson 7.

Lesson 9 (Evaluate and apply)

Starter

Recall and reason: Use the context of money in the following: *How would you work out double 4p?* The children will probably say '4 add 4'. Explain that the opposite of doubling is halving and that if you double 5 to get 10 you have to halve 10 to get back to 5. Call out even numbers to ten for the children to halve. Repeat for doubles of numbers to 10 and then 20 and their corresponding halves.

Main teaching activities

Whole class: A lot of ground was covered in the main teaching activities of Lessons 7 and 8, so spend some time continuing or revisiting them for consolidation purposes. As part of the lesson, use two lots of the same number up to 20p - for example, 12p and 12p. Discuss the word *double* and ask the children to think of a good way to describe it. They should think and then share with a partner. Discuss ways to double: partitioning and doubling each number; multiplying by two; recalling the fact.
Paired work: During this activity, the children are doing a similar activity to previous lessons but buying two of the same item, so will need to double the amount of money. They should use the cards from 'Shopping cards 2'. When the children have found the answer, they need to work out the change from 50p or £1.

Differentiation

Less confident learners: This group should concentrate on doubling numbers to 20p (from 'Shopping cards 1') and not worry about finding change. Let them use pennies if this would be helpful.
More confident learners: This group can double cards over £1 (from 'Shopping cards 3') and work out the change from £3 or £4.

Review

Take feedback from the activity and then focus on checking the totals of their doubling. Ask the children to tell you what they think they could do. Aim towards halving. Discuss halving as being the opposite of doubling. Draw arrow sentences as in Block A, Unit 1, Lessons 7 and 8 to show that doubling and halving are inverse operations. Tell the children that they will be working on this in their next lesson.

Lesson 10 (Review, apply and evaluate)

Starter

Rehearse and refresh: Ask a mixture of doubles, halves and near doubles questions of numbers to 20 as in Lessons 6 and 7, to reinforce concepts.

Main teaching activities

Whole class: Recap the work on doubling that the children did in the last lesson. Ask them to explain how they doubled higher numbers such as 24, 31 and 67. Show the 'Doubling and halving' pages on the CD and take them through this model. Ask the children to copy it as you explain step by step: partition the number, double the tens, double the ones and recombine. Go through each example. Write some amounts of money on the board and ask the children to double these on their whiteboard, using the method you have demonstrated. Repeat with the halving pages. Show the children the first of 'Ivor Cat's cat food' pages and explain that Ivor is putting up the price of his cat food. Ask: *By how much? How do you know? What word tells you? How can you work out the new prices?* Work through this page, asking different children to work out the new cost of different cat foods, using the method demonstrated. Take feedback and then repeat with the next page which works on halving.
Paired work: Give the children Ivor Dog's price list for dog food ('Ivor Dog's dog and puppy food'). They should work out the prices for double the original amount and then half the amount, recording as you have demonstrated.

Differentiation

Less confident learners: This group should work on the price list for prices to 50p ('Ivor Dog's dog and puppy food' support).
More confident learners: This group should work on the price list for prices £1 and over ('Ivor Dog's dog and puppy food' extension).

Review

Take feedback from their activity. Focus on the idea that Ivor Dog will halve the prices that the children have just doubled. Invite children to take the class through halving some of their prices. Ask: *What do you notice?* Hopefully, they will notice that they are back to their original prices. Re-emphasise that halving and doubling are inverse operations. Finish by asking questions such as: *I'm thinking of a number. I halved it and the answer is 13. What number was I thinking of? Explain how you know.*

Lessons 11-15

Preparation

Prepare a collection of 3D and 2D shapes as listed in the '2D shape vocabulary' and '3D shape vocabulary'. Provide two of each 2D shape, one regular and one irregular. If necessary, photocopy 'Templates for irregular shapes 1' and '2' and 'Templates for regular shapes' onto card and cut them out. Make A3 card copies of '2D shape vocabulary' and '3D shape vocabulary' and cut out the cards. Make an OHT copy of 'Mirror, mirror...'.

Learning objectives

Starter

- Read and write two-digit and three-digit numbers in figures and words; describe and extend number sequences; recognise odd and even numbers.
- Understand that halving is the inverse of doubling and derive and recall doubles of all numbers to 20, and the corresponding halves.
- Derive and recall all addition and subtraction facts for each number to at least 10, all pairs with totals to 20 and all pairs of multiples of 10 with totals up to 100.

Main teaching activities

2006

- Visualise common 2D shapes and 3D solids; identify shapes from pictures of them in different positions and orientations; sort, make and describe

You will need
Photocopiable pages
'3D shapes' and '2D shapes' (pages 60 and 61) for each child.
CD resources
Number cards 0-50 from '0-100 number cards', 'Templates for regular shapes', 'Templates for irregular shapes 1' and '2', 'Mirror, mirror...', '2D shape vocabulary' and '3D shape vocabulary' cards (see General resources); an acetate and one copy per child of 'Make me symmetrical' support and extension versions; copies of 'Sort us', one per group and copies of 'Sort us again'.
Equipment
3D and 2D shapes; a feely bag; a cardboard tube; a pentagonal prism; A4 paper; Plasticine; pendulum.

shapes, referring to their properties.
- Identify reflective symmetry in patterns and 2D shapes and draw lines of symmetry in shapes

1999
- Use the mathematical names for common 3D and 2D shapes.
- Sort shapes and describe some of their features.
- Make and describe shapes.

Vocabulary
shape, pattern, flat, curved, straight, round, solid, corner, point, face, side, edge, surface, cube, cuboid, pyramid, sphere, cone, cylinder, circle, circular, triangle, triangular, square, rectangle, rectangular, star, pentagon, hexagon, octagon

Lesson 11 (Review and practise)

Starter
Rehearse: Divide the children into two groups. Ask a child to pick a number card 0-50 as a starting number. With your right hand, point towards each group at random intervals for them to count on in ones. From time to time, change to your left hand for counting backwards. Repeat for counting in tens.

Main teaching activity
Whole class: This is a whole-class lesson. Show the children a cube, cuboid, pyramid, sphere, cone and cylinder. Discuss their properties: number of edges, corners and faces; the 2D shapes of the faces. Recap on these terms as they occur. Now show the 3D shape vocabulary cards, asking children to match the words with the shapes and properties.

Follow the instructions and discussion prompts on the '3D shapes' photocopiable sheet, and demonstrate as you go along, guiding the children through the instructions. It is important for continuity to follow the instructions in order: the discussion of each 3D shape, and the 2D shapes of its faces, should follow on naturally from the previous one.

Review
Put a 3D shape in the feely bag. Invite a child to feel the shape and describe it. Encourage the child to use all the properties that were discussed in the lesson, including the shapes of curved faces where appropriate. The class has to work out what the shape is. Repeat with different children and different shapes.

Lesson 12 (Review, teach and apply)

Starter
Refine and rehearse: Call out random numbers to 5 and ask the children to show you the double of each number with their number cards. Discuss the opposite of doubling as halving and that if you double 5 to get 10 you have to halve 10 to get back to 5. Call out even numbers to 10 for the children to halve. Repeat for doubles of numbers to 10 and then 20, and their corresponding halves. Extend to numbers to 50.

Main teaching activities
Whole class: Ask the children to tell you what they did during the last lesson. Recap: show the children a cube, cuboid, pyramid, sphere, cone and cylinder. Discuss their properties: number of edges, corners and faces; the 2D shapes of the faces. This time, include the properties of the faces of the shapes with reference to number of sides and corners and line of symmetry. You may need to remind the children of the property of symmetry as one half being the same as the other. Show the 3D shape vocabulary cards, asking children to match the words with the shapes and properties.
Group work: The children should work in groups of about four. Each group

needs a cube, cuboid, pyramid, sphere, cone and cylinder. Their task is to think of ways of sorting the different shapes using two criteria, for example, square faces and not square faces. This is a basic Carroll Diagram, a good way to sort even though it isn't strictly in the Year 2 objectives. Go through an example with them. They should think of three different ways and record on 'Sort us'.

Differentiation

Less confident learners: Suggest that they think of ways of sorting related to the number of faces.
More confident learners: Suggest that they think of ways of sorting related to the shapes of the faces of their 3D shapes.

Review

Take feedback from each group. Focus on symmetry and together find a way of sorting the shapes that involves the lines of symmetry on the faces of the shapes.

Lesson 13 (Review, teach and practise)

Starter

Read and refresh: Revisit doubling and halving as in Lesson 9 but stress the aspect of inversion. Draw arrow diagrams to demonstrate the inversion concept:

7 —Double→ 14, 14 —Halve→ 7   8 —Double→ 16, 16 —Halve→ 8

Use the pendulum and, as it swings one way, call out a number to 20. As it swings the other way, the children call back its double. Repeat for corresponding halves.

Main teaching activities

Whole class: This is a whole-class lesson. Explain that today the children will be looking at 2D shapes. In order to make the link with 3D shapes, show the children the 3D shapes from Lesson 12 and discuss the 2D shapes of their faces. Show the pictures of the 2D shapes on 'Templates for regular shapes' and 'Templates for irregular shapes 1' and '2'.

Talk about the shapes. You don't need to use the terms 'regular' and 'irregular', but it is important for the children to understand that only certain shapes have the properties of equal side length and symmetry (remind the children of symmetry work in Year 1: folding shapes in half to give identical parts). Call out the names of some 2D shapes and ask the children to draw them on their whiteboards. Then hand out the '2D shapes' sheet for the children to complete. Demonstrate and explain what they are doing as they work.

Review

Attach to the board the 2D shape name cards from the '2D shape vocabulary' sheet. Ask the children to bring their shape and their drawing to the carpet. Call out some shape names and properties, and ask the children to stand up if their shape has the name or property that you say. Ask the children to Blu-Tack their shape on the board beside the correct name. If any children are unable to do this, ask them why. Stick their shapes on a different part of the board and ask them to try to find out their shape's name at home this evening.

Lesson 14 (Review and apply)

Starter

Rehearse and refine: Repeat the starter from Lesson 12 (but without the money context), asking for more challenging doubling and halving in addition to those stated, for example, double 35, halve 48, discussing methods from those that can answer.

Main teaching activities

Whole class: Ask the children to tell you what they did during the last lesson. Show the pictures of the 2D shapes on 'Templates for regular shapes' and 'Templates for irregular shapes 1' and '2'. Discuss their properties: number of sides, corners and lines of symmetry. Show the 2D shape vocabulary cards, asking children to match the words with the shapes and properties.

Group work: The children should work in groups of about four. Each group needs a copy of the 2D shapes discussed in the main part of the lesson. Their task is to think of ways of sorting the different shapes using two criteria, for example, four corners and not four corners. Again, this is the basic Carroll Diagram. Go through an example with them. They should think of three different ways and record on 'Sort us again'.

Differentiation

Less confident learners: Suggest that they think of two ways of sorting.

More confident learners: Suggest that they think of ways of sorting related to symmetry.

Review

Take feedback from each group. Focus on symmetry and together find a way of sorting the shapes that involves the lines of symmetry on the faces of the shapes.

Lesson 15 (Teach and practise)

Starter

Recall: Practise number bonds using the swinging pendulum. Call a number on one swing and, as it swings the other way, the children call out the number that goes with it to make any number to 20 or multiples of 10 to 100.

Main teaching activities

Whole class: Today the children will focus on 2D shapes and their property of symmetry. Ask them to name and describe as many 2D shapes as they can. Give eight children a '2D shape vocabulary' card. Give 14 others a shape each from 'Templates for irregular shapes 1' and '2', and 'Templates for regular shapes'. Discuss irregular and regular shapes; compare their properties. Ask each child in turn to take their shape to the correct label. Discuss the properties of each shape: sides, angles and so on.

Now ask: *What can you tell me about symmetry?* Hold up pairs of regular and irregular shapes. *Which have the most lines of symmetry, regular or irregular shapes?* Show OHTs of a regular and an irregular hexagon. Draw one line of symmetry on the regular hexagon. *Can anyone draw another line of symmetry on this hexagon? Regular shapes have more than one line of symmetry. Can anyone draw a line of symmetry on the irregular hexagon?* Ask the vocabulary card holders to Blu-Tack their cards and shape examples to the board.

Use the 'Mirror, mirror...' OHT to demonstrate how to find lines of symmetry using a mirror. (You won't be able to see the reflection while doing this.) Ask the children to help you fill in the mirror image of the squared pattern at the bottom of the sheet.

Paired work: Ask the children to complete the 'Make me symmetrical' CD page, working in pairs.

Differentiation

Less confident learners: Provide the support version of the photocopiable sheet with simpler patterns to reverse.

More confident learners: Provide the extension version with more complex patterns.

Review

Using an OHT of the 'Mirror, mirror...' sheet, work through the first two patterns. Ask: *Where on the other side of our mirror line should we colour this square? Why? When we have finished colouring this side, what should we see?* (The original pattern in reverse.) *Can anyone see another line of symmetry?*

Name ______________________ Date ______________

Dicey digit problems

Photocopy and cut out these problem strips.

How many different ways could you score 8 by throwing three dice?
Make a prediction first, then work it out.
How many more ways could you score 8
if you had four dice?

How many different ways can you add three odd numbers to make 11?
Make a prediction first, then work it out.
What if you could only add two odd numbers
to make 11?

What numbers can you make with the digit cards 4, 5 and 6?
You can use either two or three cards.
You can add, subtract or put the digits side by side.
Do you think you will be able to make more than 10 new numbers?
Have a go.

Take ten dominoes and sort them into two groups: dominoes with an odd total of spots and dominoes with an even total.
Which group has the higher total of spots? Make a prediction first, then work it out.

Using the digit cards 2, 3 and 4, and the signs + or – and =, what different answers can you make? Use either two or three of the cards.

Find an answer you could make if you used the + and the – sign in the same calculation, such as 4 + 3 – 2 = 5.

Name ______________________ Date ______________

Number investigations

Photocopy and cut out these problem boxes.

0	1
2	3

Sam throws three darts at this board.
Each dart lands in a square.
They could all land in the same square.

What is the highest score he could get? ☐

Find all the different scores he can get. ______________________

5	6
7	8

Pick a pair of numbers from the box.
Add them together.
Write the numbers and the answer. ______________

Pick a different pair of numbers and do the same thing.

____

Keep doing this. How many different answers can you get? ☐

5	1	4
2	3	6

You will need a dice and some counters.
Throw the dice and put a counter on the number thrown. Do this four times.

Add up the numbers where the four counters are.

What is your total? ☐

Can you find other ways to make that total using the numbers 1 to 6?
Write down all the possible ways. ______________________

____

Name ______________________ Date ______________

Shopping cards 1

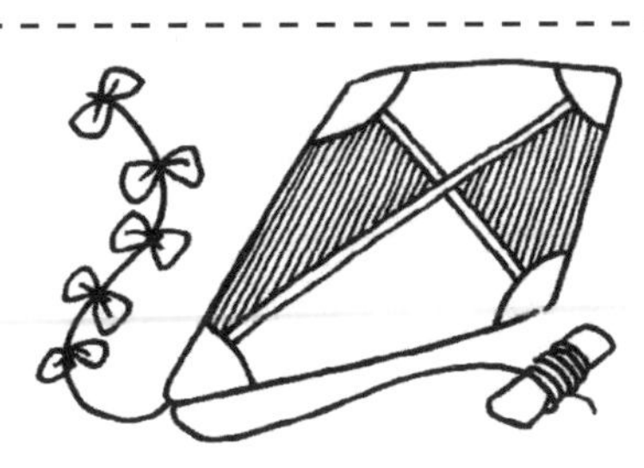		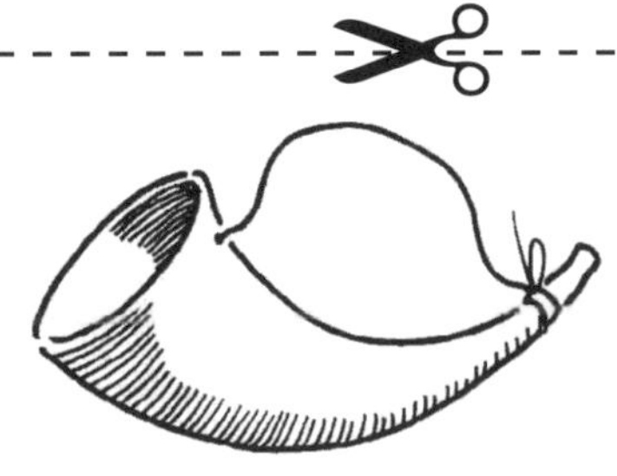
4p	3p	6p

7p	8p	6p

4p	2p	3p
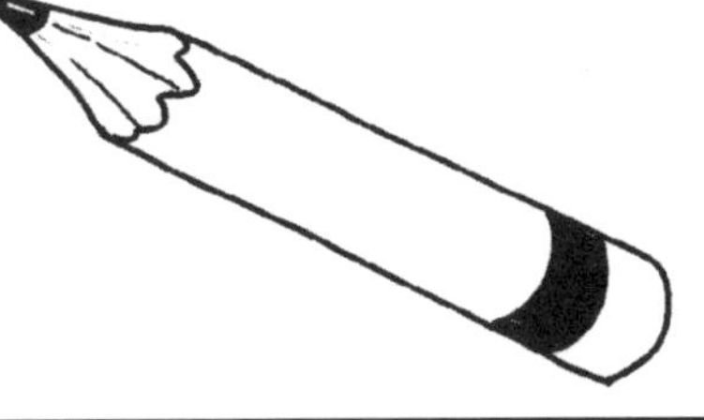	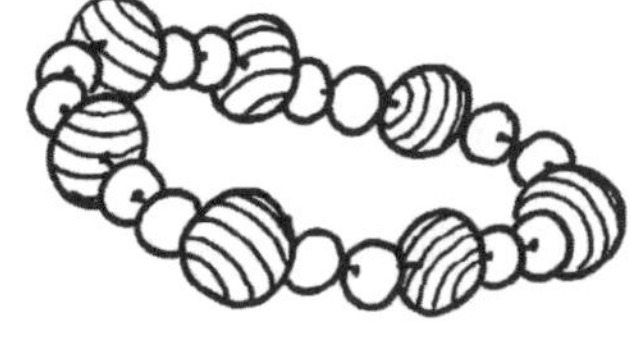	
14p	12p	13p
	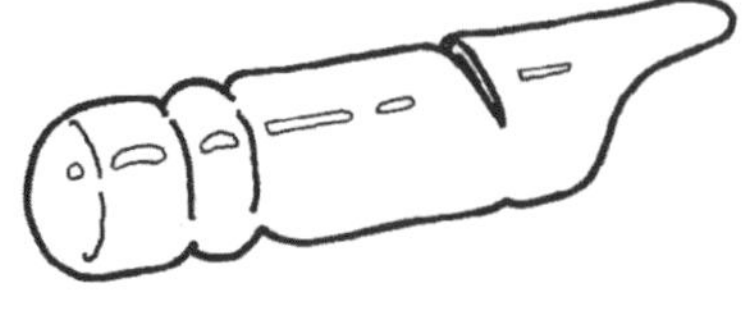	
14p	12p	13p

Name ____________________ Date ____________________

Ivor Dog's dog and puppy food

	Lamb 46p		Beef 39p
	Chicken and rice 49p		Beef 42p
	Mixed meat 48p		Chicken 27p
	Chicken and vegetable 36p		Tripe 38p
 	Chicken and liver 32p		Beef and turkey 35p

Ivor Dog has doubled his prices! What are they now?

Name ______________________________ Date ____________________

3D shapes

You will need:
a small lump of Plasticine
a sheet of paper and a pencil.

- Make the Plasticine into a sphere. Say the word 'sphere'.

- What are you doing to make your Plasticine into a sphere? What things in 'real life' are spheres?
- What are the properties of your sphere? What is special about it? Does it roll? Is it smooth? Is it round?

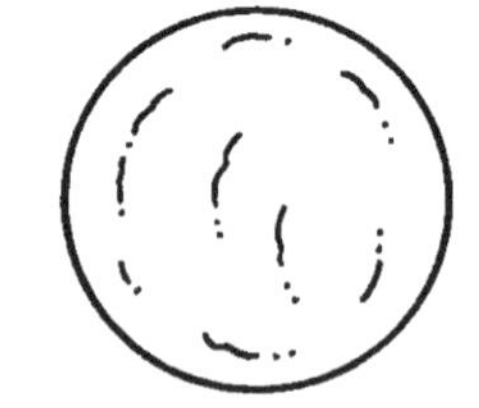

- Hold your sphere at arm's length. Look at it and draw the shape that you can see.
- Now turn your sphere into a cube. What are you doing to change the sphere? Will you squash in the sides? Will you take the 'roundness' away?

- What do we see in everyday life that is shaped like a cube?
- How many edges/corners/faces does your cube have? What is the shape of each face?

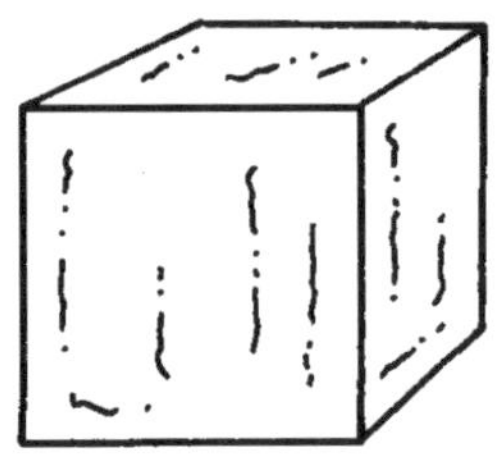

- Look at a cube from a distance and draw the 2D shape you can see.

Name ______________________ Date ______________

2D shapes

You will need:
a sheet of coloured A4 paper
a sheet of white paper
a pencil.

- Fold the coloured paper once to make it into an irregular shape.
- Describe your shape.
- Describe the properties of your shape to your neighbour.
- Repeat this, making a second fold and then a third and fourth.
- Draw around your shape on a sheet of white paper. Write down how many sides it has, how many corners and how many lines of symmetry (if any).
- Label your shape and keep it for the Review.

Securing number facts, understanding shape

Lesson	Strands	Starter	Main teaching activities
1. Review, teach, apply and evaluate	Use/ apply Shape	**Use units of time (seconds, minutes, hours, days) and know the relationships between them; read the time to the quarter hour; identify time intervals, including those that cross the hour.**	• Describe patterns and relationships involving numbers or shapes, make predictions and test these with examples. • Identify reflective symmetry in patterns and 2D shapes and draw lines of symmetry in shapes.
2. Teach and apply	Use/apply	As for Lesson 1	Describe patterns and relationships involving numbers or shapes, make predictions and test these with examples.
3. Review and apply	Use/apply	As for Lesson 1	Solve problems involving addition, subtraction, multiplication or division in contexts of numbers, measures or pounds and pence.
4. Apply and evaluate	Use/apply	Derive and recall multiplication facts for the 2, 5 and 10 times-tables.	As for Lesson 3
5. Apply and evaluate	Use/apply	Add/subtract 9 or 11; add/subtract 10 and adjust by 1.	As for Lesson 3
6. Apply and evaluate	Use/apply	Understand that halving is the inverse of doubling and derive and recall doubles of all numbers to 20, and the corresponding halves.	As for Lesson 3
7. Teach, apply and evaluate	Use/apply	Derive and recall multiplication facts for the 2, 5 and 10 times-tables and the related division facts; recognise multiples of 2, 5 and 10.	As for Lesson 3
8. Review and apply	Knowledge Counting	As for Lesson 7	• **Derive and recall all addition and subtraction facts for each number to at least 10, all pairs with totals to 20 and all pairs of multiples of 10 with totals up to 100.** • Read and write two-digit and three-digit numbers in figures and words; describe and extend number sequences and recognise odd and even numbers.
9. Teach and apply	Knowledge Counting	As for Lesson 7	As for Lesson 8
10. Apply and evaluate	Knowledge Counting	Recognise multiples of 2, 5 and 10.	As for Lesson 8
11. Review and practise	Shapes	**Derive and recall all addition and subtraction facts for each number to at least 10, all pairs with totals to 20 and all pairs of multiples of 10 with totals up to 100.**	• **Visualise common 2D shapes and 3D solids; identify shapes from pictures of them in different positions and orientations; sort, make and describe shapes, referring to their properties.** • Identify reflective symmetry in patterns and 2D shapes and draw lines of symmetry in shapes.
12. Review and practise	Shapes	Read and write two-digit and three-digit numbers in figures and words; describe and extend number sequences and recognise odd and even numbers.	As for Lesson 11
13. Review and practise	Shapes	As for Lesson 7	As for Lesson 11
14. Teach and practise	Shapes	As for Lesson 12	As for Lesson 11
15. Apply and evaluate	Shapes	**Visualise common 2D shapes and 3D solids; identify shapes from pictures of them in different positions and orientations; sort, make and describe shapes, referring to their properties.**	As for Lesson 11

Speaking and listening objective

- Tell real or imagined stories (using conventions of familiar story language).

Introduction

This block of work contains 15 lessons. The first two specifically focus on patterns and relationships in number and shape with an element of symmetry in the first. The third begins a series on problem solving with 'real life' problems involving money and measures. These aim to reinforce the calculation strategies that the children focused on in Block A Unit 2: putting the largest number first, partitioning, finding numbers that total 10. The lessons carefully go through the stages of problem solving. The children will work on visualising, drawing and acting out problems. There are three lessons linked to these which rehearse and reinforce all addition and subtraction facts for each number to at least 10, all pairs with totals to 20 and all pairs of multiples of 10 with totals up to 100, and the following lessons then put these facts into problem solving contexts. All lessons 1-10 expect the children to read and write numbers, so there is no one lesson specifically designed for this as in Block A. Rather, the expectation is reinforced for a purpose. The last five lessons involve a variety of aspects of shape including recognising 2D shapes from 3D solids; there is a focus on symmetry in patterns and 2D shapes. The starters of each lesson focus on rehearsing the skills involved with time, mental calculation, tables, number pairs and counting. These are practised frequently to keep them fresh in the children's minds. During the lessons on shape in particular, there are opportunities to fulfil the speaking and listening objective.

Using and applying mathematics

- Describe patterns and relationships involving numbers or shapes, make predictions and test these with examples.
- Solve problems involving addition, subtraction, multiplication or division in contexts of numbers, measures or pounds and pence.

Lessons 1-2

Preparation

If necessary, make an A3 copy of the 'Up the mountain' gameboard. Copy the shapes from 'Templates for irregular shapes' and 'Templates for regular shapes' onto acetate and also onto card. Each pair of children will need six shapes: three regular and three irregular. Copy one of the strips on 'Symmetry investigation' onto acetate and cut out the shapes. Make a collection of symmetrical 2D shapes and pictures. Copy 'Puzzle practice 1' and '2' onto acetate.

You will need

Photocopiable pages

An acetate of 'Puzzle practice 1' and '2' (pages 74 and 75) for each pair.

CD resources

'Up the mountain' gameboard (A3), 'Templates for irregular shapes 1' and '2', 'Templates for regular shapes' on card and acetate, 'Months of the year cards', 'Symmetry investigation' cut up for each two pairs of children, plus acetate (see General resources).

Learning objectives

Starter

- Use units of time (seconds, minutes, hours, days) and know the relationships between them; read the time to the quarter hour; identify time intervals, including those that cross the hour.

Main teaching activities

2006

- Describe patterns and relationships involving numbers or shapes, make predictions and test these with examples.
- Identify reflective symmetry in patterns and 2D shapes and draw lines of symmetry in shapes.

1999

- Solve mathematical problems or puzzles, recognise simple patterns and relationships, generalise and predict.
- Suggest extensions by asking 'What if...?' or 'What could I try next?'

Vocabulary

jotting, answer, right, correct, wrong, what could we try next?, how did you work it out?, number sentence, sign, operation, symbol

Equipment
Symmetrical 2D shapes and pictures; card clocks; two counters; an OHP and OHP pen; plain paper; squared paper; scissors.

Lesson 1 (Review, teach, apply and evaluate)

Starter

Rehearse: Say the months of the year together. Give 12 children a month card each at random, and ask the rest of the class to put them in the right order.

Main teaching activities

Whole class: Explain that, in the next two lessons, the children will be solving problems and puzzles to do with shapes. Ask them what the word 'symmetrical' means. Expect them to say that one half is the same as the other. Show your examples of symmetrical items.

Figure 1

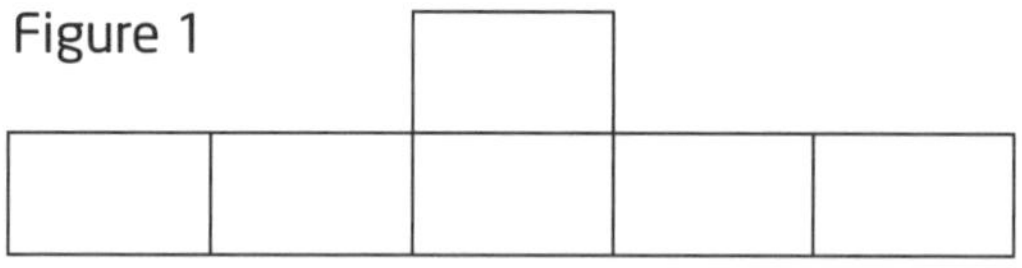

Put a regular card shape (from 'Templates for regular shapes') on the OHP. Draw round it. Demonstrate how you can flip it over so that one of its sides is still joined to the original shape to make a new shape that is symmetrical: the two halves are the same. Explain that the middle line is called the line of symmetry, because it shows where the two halves are. Repeat this a few times using different shapes, both regular and irregular. Invite individuals to help you.

Group work: Give the children sets of shape templates ('Templates for irregular shapes 1' and '2' and 'Templates for regular shapes'), pens and plain paper. Ask them to work in pairs to create patterns by drawing around some of their shapes. Allow about ten minutes for this, then bring the class back together and look at some of the shapes they made. Put an acetate strip from 'Symmetry investigation' on the OHP and say: *Take the shapes you have that look like these, and use them to make a symmetrical shape.* (See Figure 1.) *You must use the large piece in all your shapes, but then you can add as many of the small pieces as you want. Then you can investigate other symmetrical shapes that you can make. Try to find as many different ones as you can. Draw them on squared paper, then draw the line of symmetry on each one.*

Differentiation
Organise the children in mixed-ability pairs. Children who appear less confident in work with numbers may be more successful in work of this kind.

Review

Put the acetate shapes on the OHP and invite children, particularly those whom you wish to assess, to show the class some of the shapes they made. Ask them to indicate the line of symmetry (or mirror line). Encourage their thinking by asking questions such as: *How did you start? What did you try next? How do you know your shape is symmetrical?*

Lesson 2 (Teach and apply)

Starter

Reason: Give each child a card clock. Play an 'Up the mountain' game with two teams: call out times for the children to show. The first child to hold up a clock with the correct time wins a point. As well as asking for times such as 4 o'clock, half past seven and quarter to six, also try: *Find half past three, now find one hour after that time, half an hour earlier...*

Main teaching activities

Whole class: Show the children the OHT of the puzzle on 'Puzzle practice 1'. Explain that each shape stands for a number. Focus on the shape names and properties. Now ask: *Which are the columns? Which are the rows? Can anyone think of a good starting point? Can we work out any numbers from this row? What about this column? Could we use jottings to help us? What can we try now? Can you tell me a number sentence that shows us what you have said?*

Paired work: Organise children into mixed-ability pairs. They can then work on 'Puzzle practice 2'. Any children finishing these quickly could make up puzzles of their own.

Differentiation

Let the children work together in mixed-ability groups, supporting each other.

Review

Display the OHTs of the puzzles that the children have solved. Discuss the solutions, asking questions similar to those above. Assess whether the children can find the starting point and work systematically through the puzzle to reach a conclusion.

Lessons 3-7

Preparation

Copy 'How to solve a problem' onto A3 paper. Copy 'Small spider charts' onto A4 card and laminate (as a whole sheet) for each pair. Make acetates of 'Problems' and 'Making up problems'. Copy 'Money problem cards' onto card and cut into strips.

You will need

Photocopiable pages
'Problems at the zoo' (page 76) for each child.
CD resources
'Spider charts for multiplying', 'Spider charts for dividing', 'Spider charts for ×5 and ÷5' per child, an A3 copy of 'How to solve a problem', 'Small spider charts' per pair, acetates of 'Making up problems', a copy of 'Visualising problems 1' per child, 'Money problem cards' on card (see General resources); acetates of 'Problems'; 'Problems at the zoo' support and extension versions.
Equipment
Card clocks; pendulum; class 100 square; individual 100 squares; large sheets of paper; colouring pens; coins.

Learning objectives

Starter

- Use units of time (seconds, minutes, hours, days) and know the relationships between them; read the time to the quarter hour; identify time intervals, including those that cross the hour.
- Derive and recall multiplication facts for the 2, 5 and 10 times-tables and the related division facts; recognise multiples of 2, 5 and 10.
- Add/subtract 9 or 11: add/subtract 10 and adjust by 1.
- Understand that halving is the inverse of doubling and derive and recall doubles of all numbers to 20, and the corresponding halves.

Main teaching activities

2006

- Solve problems involving addition, subtraction, multiplication or division in contexts of numbers, measures or pounds and pence.

1999

- Use mental addition and subtraction, simple multiplication and division to solve simple word problems involving numbers in 'real life', money or measures, using one or two steps.
- Explain how the problem was solved.
- Recognise all coins and begin to use £.p notation for money.
- Find totals, give change and work out which coins to pay.
- Choose and use appropriate operations and efficient calculation strategies (eg mental, mental with jottings) to solve problems.

Vocabulary

money, coin, penny, pence, pound, £, price, cost, buy, bought, spend, spent, pay, change, dear, costs more, cheap, costs less, cheaper, how much...?, how many...?, total

Lesson 3 (Review and apply)

Starter

Read and refine: Give each child a card clock. Ask the children to show you various o'clock, half past, quarter to and quarter past times. Move on to questions such as: *My clock says 3 o'clock, but it is one hour slow. Show me what time it really is. My clock says 7 o'clock, but it is two hours fast... My clock says 1 o'clock, but it is half an hour slow... My clock says half past 8, but it is 15 minutes fast...*

Main teaching activities

Whole class: Explain that the children will use the mental strategies from the previous unit to solve 'real life' problems. Project the 'Problems' OHT and display the 'How to solve a problem' poster. Use the poster to talk through the steps needed to solve the first problem. When you reach Step 4, ask the children to think of a strategy to work out the answer. Remind them of the strategies they used in Block A: largest number first, looking for pairs that make 10, partitioning into different tens and ones; ask them to decide which one is the best. Allow them to discuss with a partner and then feed back to the class. Repeat the process with the other two problems on the OHT.

Differentiation
Less confident learners: Provide the support version of 'Problems at the zoo' with easier numbers. Let this group use counting apparatus such as counters, beads or toy animals if necessary.
More confident learners: Provide the extension version with more challenging numbers. Encourage the children to think of two strategies for each problem, decide which is better and explain.

Group work: Ask the children to work in ability pairs to solve the problems on the 'Problems at the zoo' photocopiable sheet and explain the strategies they used. Talk through the first problem.

Review
Write up some basic information, such as: *3kg, 50p, potatoes, how much?* Ask the children to talk to a partner and make up a problem involving this information. Use this example: *I bought 3kg of potatoes. Each kilogram cost 50p. How much did I spend?* Discuss how knowledge of tables facts might help: 3 × 5p = 15p, so 3 × 50p = 150 or £1.50. Invite some pairs to share their problems for the class to solve. Write the answers on the board. You could try writing a pounds and pence answer like this: £350. Ask the children whether this is correct and talk about why.

Lesson 4 (Apply and evaluate)

Starter
Revisit: Count in twos and tens together, using fingers so that, when you stop part of the way through, the children can tell you what the multiplication fact is. For example, if you stop on 12 (the sixth finger) the multiplication fact is 2 times 6. Move on to using spider charts to reinforce these times tables and division facts. Repeat, counting in fives.

Main teaching activities
Whole class: Explain that the children will work with a partner to make up their own problems, as in the Review of Lesson 3. Encourage them to think clearly about the information provided and the operations needed, and to check their answers. Use the 'Making up problems' OHT to talk through possible one-step and two-step problems. For example: '2m, 1m, sunflower' could be used to ask *I had three sunflowers: one was 1m tall, one was 2m tall and the third was as tall as both of the others together. How tall was the third sunflower?* As you model these problems, encourage the children to think visually and record with drawings instead of words.
Paired work: Pose problems for the children that involve one and two steps. Encourage them to make jottings or draw their problems as far as possible, so they don't waste time writing too many words. For example: *You have 14 monkeys and 26 bananas. What might your problem be? You have 5 ice creams, 50p and £5. What might your problem be?*

Differentiation
Less confident learners: Use simpler numbers and times. You or another adult could scribe for this group.
More confident learners: Provide more demanding numbers and times. Ask this group to solve each other's problems and explain how they did them.

Review
Invite some pairs to share their problems for the class to solve. Each time, ask: *How did you solve the problem? How many steps did you need to take?*

Lesson 5 (Apply and evaluate)

Starter
Refine and rehearse: Recap on adding or subtracting 9 and 11 by adding or subtracting 10 and adjusting. Demonstrate on the class 100 square, then provide individual 100 squares. Ask the children to put their finger on 4. Give a series of instructions, such as: *Add on 9, add on another 9, take away 11. What number are you?* Repeat several times.

Now ask them to turn their 100 squares over and close their eyes. Can they see the square in their heads? *Put your finger on the 3 on the 100 square in your head. Go down to the next row – what number are you on now? Move your finger back one – where are you now? Go down two rows and along two – where are you?* Repeat with a few numbers, including two-digit ones.

Main teaching activities
Whole class: Say that during the next two lessons the children will be seeing problems in their heads, drawing them and acting them out. Ask

them to close their eyes and visualise what you say. *You are sitting in your bedroom with a money box. It is shaped like a pig; it is blue and has yellow flowers on it. You take out the stopper underneath its tummy and tip the money onto your bed. You pick up one 10 pence piece, another 10 pence piece, then another and another. How many 10 pence pieces are you holding? How much is that altogether?* Act this out, asking children to collect the correct coins. Repeat in the same way with different scenarios. You can find more examples on the 'Visualising problems 1' sheet.
Group work: The children should work in mixed-ability groups to act out Maths problems, so that the rest of the class can identify each problem and work out the answer. They will need a selection of coins and may use pens and paper to draw pictures, but they must try not to use words (written or spoken). Use a problem from 'Money problem cards' to demonstrate, then give each group a strip from that sheet. Allow time for the groups to plan their 'scenario'. They should use the correct coins, finding the totals and the change (where appropriate).

Differentiation
The children should work together in mixed-ability groups, supporting each other.

Review
Model a second example from the 'Money problem cards' sheet.

Lesson 6 (Apply and evaluate)

Starter
Recall and refine: Call out numbers to 10 and then 20 and ask the children to double them and write their answer down on their whiteboards. Encourage them to partition any two-digit numbers if they cannot remember by memory. Repeat with numbers to 40, but ask the children to halve them. Mix them up, say that you will say a number and then clap if you want them to double it or stamp if you want them to halve it.

Main teaching activities
Whole class: Continue the mixed-ability activity in Lesson 5, but have a few 'mini reviews' during the session when you look at a group's little playlet. After they have acted it out, ask the rest of the children: *Can you tell us this problem in words? What are the important ideas here? What information have you been given? Can you work out what the answer might be?* Once they have finished and shown their problem play, give the group another card or ask them to make up their own.

For each scenario seen, make sure that the children can answer the questions above and assess whether they can identify the important pieces of information that will enable the problem to be solved and also whether they can work out the answer.

Differentiation
Less confident learners: Check that the children are taking an active part in the activity.
More confident learners: Check that these children do not dominate the 'problem play' scenarios.

Review
Ask the children to tell you what they have been doing over the last few sessions and to self-assess as to whether the activities have helped them to problem solve and in what way. Ask: *What do you need to do to be able to solve a problem?*

Lesson 7 (Teach, apply and evaluate)

Starter
Read, refine and revisit: Give each child the spider charts for multiplying and dividing by 2, 5 and 10. Count together in multiples, using fingers. Stop at various points, such as the seventh finger, and ask: *How many lots of 2 make 14? So we can say* $2 \times 7 = 14$. Give the children some timed challenges to complete in pairs, using the 'Small spider charts' sheet. They take turns to point at the numbers around whichever chart you say and then give the answers. Time them for two minutes. How many times can they go round the chart?

Main teaching activities

Whole class: Explain that the type of problem called an 'investigation' can sometimes have more than one correct answer. Talk through this example: *I want to buy a bar of chocolate. It will cost me 50p. I have some coins in my pocket.* (Show five 10p pieces, two 20p pieces and four 5p pieces.) *How could I use them to pay for the chocolate?* Ask the children to work with a partner to think of as many different ways of paying as they can. They should jot down their ideas on their whiteboards to share later. After about five minutes, take feedback and find as many answers as possible: 10p × 5; 10p × 3 + 20p; 5p × 4 + 20p + 10p, and so on. Ask the children which coins they used first and why.

Group work: Write the following on the board: *Jamie has three 10p coins, three 5p coins and three 2p coins in his pocket. He uses three coins to buy some bubble gum. How much might the gum have cost? Find all the possible amounts.* The children should work in pairs on this investigation. Tell them: *There are lots of answers. How many can you find?* Children record their answers on their whiteboards.

10p × 3
5p × 3
2p × 3
10p × 2 + 2p
5p × 2 + 2p
10p × 2 + 5p
5p + 2p × 2
10p + 5p × 2
10p + 5p + 2p
10p + 2p × 2

Review

Invite some pairs of children to talk through their work and their results. Ask the others whether they can add anything to these results. Aim for a complete list of answers, listed in a systematic way. Write them on the board as the children say them, in three columns – one for 10p starting coins, another for 5p and a third for 2p. Find the total number of answers, and explain that it is easier to keep a record if we work systematically.

Differentiation

Less confident learners: If possible, ask a teaching assistant to work with this group. Give the children the actual coins to work with. Ask them to start by combining 10p and 2p coins in threes and telling you what they 'make'. Expect answers such as: 30p, 6p, 22p, 14p. Then repeat, including 5p coins.
More confident learners: Encourage this group to be systematic, using all the 10p combinations first, then the 5p and finally the 2p combinations. Ask them to repeat the problem using four coins.

Lessons 8-10

Preparation

Collect a set of number cards to 20 for each group of four children, make six operation cards for each group, three with + and three with –.

You will need

CD resources
'What could it be?' and 'What could it be this time?' support and extension versions.
Equipment
Counting stick, coins.

Learning objectives

Starter

- Derive and recall multiplication facts for the 2, 5 and 10 times-tables and the related division facts; recognise multiples of 2, 5 and 10.

Main teaching activities

2006

- Derive and recall all addition and subtraction facts for each number to at least 10, all pairs with totals to 20 and all pairs of multiples of 10 with totals up to 100.
- Read and write two-digit and three-digit numbers in figures and words; describe and extend number sequences and recognise odd and even numbers.

1999

- Know by heart all addition facts for each number to at least 10.
- Know by heart all pairs of numbers with a total of 20.
- Know by heart all pairs of multiples of 10 with a total of 100.

Vocabulary

add, subtract, addition, subtraction, pairs, multiples

Lesson 8 (Review and apply)

Starter

Recall and reason: Use the counting stick to rehearse multiples and tables facts for the two-, five- and ten-times tables. Point to each division and ask the children to count in multiples of each number in turn to the tenth and back again. Say: *The beginning of my stick is zero and the end is 50, what will this number be?* (Point to the third division: 15.) Repeat this questioning for 0 to 20 and 0 to 100. Rephrase your questioning: *This is 25, what am I counting in? How many lots of 5 is that?* As you do this, make the link with multiplication, so reinforcing the concept of inversions.

Main teaching activities

Whole class: Tell the children that over the next three lessons they will be thinking about the usefulness of addition and subtraction facts and multiplication and division facts. Focus on all addition and subtraction facts to 10 and multiples of 10 to 100 for this lesson. Give them this problem: *I bought a candy stick and a toffee, they cost 10p. How much was each of them?* Discuss how they should go about this and then ask them to write down the possibilities on their whiteboards. Take feedback, systematically writing their responses on the board. Ensure that you have all the number bonds to 10. Repeat for other amounts of money to 10p. Say: *I have 10 counters, some are blue and some are red. How many are blue and how many are red?* Repeat for 100 counters, for example, say: *I have 100 counters, some are red and some are blue. How many are red and how many are blue?* Ask how they can use the 10 counters to help. Aim towards the fact that if they know that 7 + 3 = 100, then they know that 70 + 30 = 100, if they know that 2 + 8 = 10, they know that 20 + 80 = 100, and so on. Explain why this is, linking 1 to 10 with 10 to 100.

Individual work: The children should complete the task on 'What could it be?'

Differentiation

Less confident learners: This group should use the support version of 'What could it be?' and concentrate on all addition and subtraction facts for each number to at least 10. Let them use pennies as a practical resource to help them.

More confident learners: This group should use the extension version and work with facts to 10 and then 100 in multiples of 5.

Review

Go through a few examples from the children's work and then write on the board: □ + ○ = 100 and ask: *What two numbers could go in the square and circle? Are there any other possibilities?*

Lesson 9 (Teach and apply)

Starter

Recall and reason: Repeat the starter from Lesson 8.

Main teaching activities

Whole class: Recap on the last lesson by writing questions similar to the Review session on the board, eg □ + ○ = 10, □ + ○ = 8, □ + ○ = 100. Ask: *What two numbers could go in the square and circle? Are there any other possibilities?* For this lesson, focus on amounts to 20. Ask: *My friend and I have 20p between us. How much could we each have? How many possibilities are there? If we have 20p and I have 8p, how much does my friend have? How can you write that as a number sentence?*

Discuss £1 and the fact that it is 100 pennies. Say: *My friend and I have £1, how much could we each have?* Encourage the children to use number facts to 10 to help as in the previous lesson.

Individual work: The children should complete the task on 'What could it be this time?' This task encourages them to find different ways to make numbers and also looks at corresponding subtractions.

Differentiation

Less confident learners: This group should use the support version of 'What could it be this time?' to concentrate on all addition and subtraction facts for each number to at least 10. Let them use pennies as a practical resource to help them.

More confident learners: This group should use the extension version which is the same version as for the whole-class work, but work with multiples of 5 as appropriate.

Review

Take feedback from the children's task, inviting volunteers to write some of their examples on the board. Ask: *How can these skills help us?* Aim towards the answer that they can help in our calculations when we solve problems.

Lesson 10 (Apply and evaluate)

Starter

Rehearse and reason: Count from 1 to 20 and ask the children to jump if you say a multiple of 2, and clap for a multiple of 5. Ask them on which numbers they will need to do both. Discuss what a multiple of 2 ends with, linking to even numbers and write those digits on the board. Repeat for 5. Next, call out random numbers to 30, then 40 and ask them to jump and clap as before.

Main teaching activities

Whole class: Start off by recapping all the children have worked on in the last two lessons with examples. Today they will be reinforcing and in some cases extending this through an activity that involves making up 'real life' problems. Demonstrate with the whole class. Each group will need a set of number cards to 20 and six operation cards. Each pair should take it in turns to pick a number and an operation card, and then make up a sentence and problem to go with it. For example, pick 14 and +, sentence: 14 + 3 = 17, problem: *I had 14 books, my mum gave me 3 more so I now have 17.*

Group work: The children should undertake this task in pairs in mixed-ability groups of four, supporting each other. Encourage self-differentiation through the number sentences they make up, for example, instead of 14 + 3 = 17, some children could write 14 + 16 = 30.

Differentiation

Let the children work together in mixed-ability groups. Encourage the more confident learners to help the less confident members of the group.

Review

Take feedback from the activity by asking pairs to share their problems with the class and ask the class to find the answers.

Lessons 11-15

Preparation

An acetate and one copy per child of 'Creating patterns'.

You will need

Photocopiable pages

'Creating patterns' (page 77).

CD resources

'0-100 number cards', acetates and enlarged copies of 'Templates for irregular shapes 1' and '2', 'Templates for regular shapes', enlarged '3D shape vocabulary' cards, 'Shape patterns' (see General resources); 'Creating patterns' support and extension versions; copy of 'Shapes 2' for each child; '3D shapes 2'.

Equipment

Enough of the following shapes for small groups to handle: cube, cuboid, pyramid, sphere, cone, cylinder; pendulum; mirrors; scissors; Blu-Tack; 3D and 2D shapes (as listed in 'Vocabulary'); scissors; glue; A3 paper; Plasticine; feely bag; squared paper; two sets of shape labels.

Learning objectives

Starter

- Derive and recall all addition and subtraction facts for each number to at least 10, all pairs with totals to 20 and all pairs of multiples of 10 (and 5) with totals up to 100.
- Read and write two-digit and three-digit numbers in figures and words; describe and extend number sequences; recognise odd and even numbers.
- Visualise common 2D shapes and 3D solids; identify shapes from pictures of them in different positions and orientations; sort, make and describe shapes, referring to their properties.

Main teaching activities

2006

- Visualise common 2D shapes and 3D solids; identify shapes from pictures of them in different positions and orientations; sort, make and describe shapes, referring to their properties.
- Identify reflective symmetry in patterns and 2D shapes and draw lines of symmetry in shapes.

1999

- Use the mathematical names for common 3D and 2D shapes, including pyramid, cylinder, pentagon, hexagon, octagon.
- Relate solid shapes to pictures of them.
- Sort shapes and describe some of their features, such as the number of sides and corners, symmetry.
- Make and describe shapes, pictures and patterns.
- Begin to recognise line symmetry.

Vocabulary

shape, pattern, flat, curved, straight, round, solid, corner, point, face, side, edge, surface, cube, cuboid, pyramid, sphere, cone, cylinder, circle, circular, triangle, triangular, square, rectangle, star, pentagon, hexagon, octagon, plus: right angle, line symmetry, mirror line

Lesson 11 (Review and practise)

Starter

Recall and refine: Using the pendulum, practise the number facts concentrated on in the last few lessons. Write a number from 10 to 20 on the board. As it swings one way call out a number, and as it swings the other way the children call out its partner to total the number you have written. Repeat this idea for 100, calling out multiples of 5 as well as 10.

Main teaching activities

Whole class: Ask the children to think about all they can remember to do with shape. Invite them to share their thoughts with a partner and then with the rest of the class. Bring out these points, showing/drawing/discussing examples as you do: 3D, 2D, regular, irregular, all the shape names they should know, the different properties of face, corner, edge, side and symmetry. Remind them of the work they covered in Unit 1 and say that today they are going to rehearse and reinforce 3D shape. Show each of the following shapes: cube, cuboid, pyramid, sphere, cone and cylinder in turn. For each discuss: edges, corners, and number and shape of faces.

Group work: The children should work in mixed-ability groups of about four. They need at least one of each shape on the table in front of them plus a set of shape labels. As a group they should match the shapes to their labels. Using the second set of cards, they take it in turns to describe all the shapes one at a time, using properties but not names. The others need to guess which shape they are describing. Once the first child has done this, the second has a go. They should find that the third and fourth children will describe much more quickly because they have listened to the descriptions of the other two. Once they have all had a go, they should come up with a good, written description for all the shapes.

Differentiation

Let the children work together in mixed-ability groups. Check that the less confident learners are taking an active part in the discussions and make sure the more confident learners do not dominate proceedings.

Review

Take feedback, by listening to the groups' descriptions of shapes. Pick one description for each from different groups and repeat the group activity with the class: describe and expect the children to tell you quickly which shape you are describing.

Lesson 12 (Review and practise)

Starter

Rehearse and revisit: Divide the children into two groups. Ask a child to pick a number card 0–50 as a starting number. With your right hand, point towards each group at random intervals for them to count on in ones. From time to time, change to your left hand for counting backwards. Repeat for counting in tens.

Main teaching activities

Whole class: This is a whole-class lesson. Recap what the class did in the previous lesson. Discuss the properties of the 3D shapes they looked at (number of edges, corners and faces) as well as the 2D shapes of the faces. Recap on these terms as they occur. Now show the '3D shape vocabulary' cards, asking children to match the words with the shapes and properties.

Remind the children of the work they did in Unit 1 with Plasticine and say that they are going to have another go at this, but this time they will make more shapes.

Quickly follow the instructions and discussion prompts on '3D shapes 2', and demonstrate as you go along, guiding the children through the instructions. It is important for continuity to follow the instructions in order:

the discussion of each 3D shape, and the 2D shapes of its faces, should follow on naturally from the previous one.

Review

Put a 3D shape in the feely bag. Invite a child to feel the shape and describe it. Encourage the child to use all the properties that were discussed in the lesson, including the shapes of curved faces where appropriate. The class has to work out what the shape is.

Differentiation
Encourage all the children to take an active part in examining the 3D shapes during the Review.

Lesson 13 (Review and practise)

Starter

Recall: Call out multiplication and division facts for the children to answer using their whiteboards. Target the questioning so that all can access. Expect the more confident to answer all your questions and those that need support to concentrate on one or two. Let them use their fingers as a resource to help if necessary.

Main teaching activities

Whole class: Recap the work from Lesson 12. Show each 3D shape and ask them to look at it carefully and draw what they see on their whiteboards. They should see a 2D shape. Use this to lead into a discussion of 2D shapes and their properties.

Show the shapes from 'Templates for irregular shapes 1' and '2' and 'Templates for regular shapes', one type at a time. For each, discuss the properties including regularity and symmetry.

Paired work: Give mixed-ability pairs a copy of 'Shapes 2' each and one piece of A3 paper, folded or with a line drawn down the middle. Demonstrate their task which is to label each shape, then cut it out and together make a symmetrical pattern as follows: one child should put a shape on one side of the fold/line, the other take their matching shape and put it in the same position on the other side of the fold/line. They stick these down and then continue with another shape, finishing when all the shapes are stuck down.

Differentiation
Let the children work together in mixed-ability pairs. Ask more confident learners to help their partner if they are experiencing difficulty with cutting out and labelling their 2D shapes.

Review

Look at each pair's pattern and together assess their accuracy. Ask the class to think of some good clear definitions of symmetry.

Lesson 14 (Teach and practise)

Starter

Refine, revisit and reason: Practise two-, five- and ten-times tables using the spider charts. Next, call out an answer and ask the children to write the 'fact' that goes with it. For example, call out 18 and they write down 2 × 9. Put these into problem contexts, for example: *I had 5 buttons, my friend had 3 times as many, how many did he have? My friend and I had 25 sweets, she had 5 times as many as me, how many did I have?*

Main teaching activities

Whole class: Today the children will continue to think about 2D shapes and symmetry. Discuss what they did in the previous lesson and recap their work on symmetry. Hold up pairs of regular and irregular shapes cut from the templates and discuss how many lines of symmetry each has and then which have the most: the regular or irregular shapes? Ensure at least one of the shapes you hold up has no lines of symmetry. Ask the children to draw a shape on their whiteboards that has one line of symmetry, then two, and ask them to identify the name of their shape by counting the number of sides they have drawn. Next ask them to draw a shape that has no lines of symmetry and ask them to justify this to a partner.

Paired work: Give each pair of children a piece of squared paper and ask them to draw some square shapes. Once they have drawn about eight with different numbers of lines of symmetry, they should cut them out. Next, they draw a table in the form of a Carroll diagram, headed 'symmetry' in one column and 'no symmetry' in the other. They should then stick their shapes in the appropriate place. They should ensure that they have several to go in each section.

Differentiation

Less confident learners: Provide these children with a 'ready made' Carroll diagram with appropriate headings.

More confident learners: These children should make up a table with six columns, one headed 'no lines', the second '1 line', the third '2 lines', and so on, finishing with a final column of 'more than 4 lines'. They should ensure they have at least two shapes to stick into each column.

Review

Take feedback from the children about the activity. On the board, draw a large table similar to the one the more confident children were working with. Invite pairs of children to draw one of their shapes in the correct column. Ask the class to identify the lines of symmetry and ask them to tell you where they should go in the table.

Finish by showing the children a shape that you have folded. Ask them to imagine opening it up and then to draw the shape they think will be made. Repeat this a few times.

Lesson 15 (Apply and evaluate)

Starter

Rehearse and read: Give each child a shape and a different shape vocabulary card, using a mixture of 3D and 2D regular and irregular shapes. Call out some names and properties. Ask the children to stand up if their shape or vocabulary card has that property or name.

Main teaching activities

Whole class: Tell the children that in this lesson they will be investigating shape patterns. Display the 'Shape patterns' OHT, and ask the children to describe the first pattern. Use the questions on the OHT to discuss the first two patterns. Repeat with the other two patterns, asking similar questions.

Paired/individual work: The children may work on their own or with a partner. Use an OHT of the 'Creating patterns' photocopiable sheet to demonstrate this shape and pattern investigation, then ask the children to work through it.

Differentiation

Less confident learners: Provide the support version of 'Creating patterns' with simpler shape templates.

More confident learners: Provide the extension version of the activity.

Review

Look at the shapes the children have made; ask some children to sketch their work on the board. Discuss the properties of these shapes: the number of sides, angles and lines of symmetry.

Name ______________________ Date ______________________

Puzzle practice 1

Work out the value of each shape and the total of each row and column.

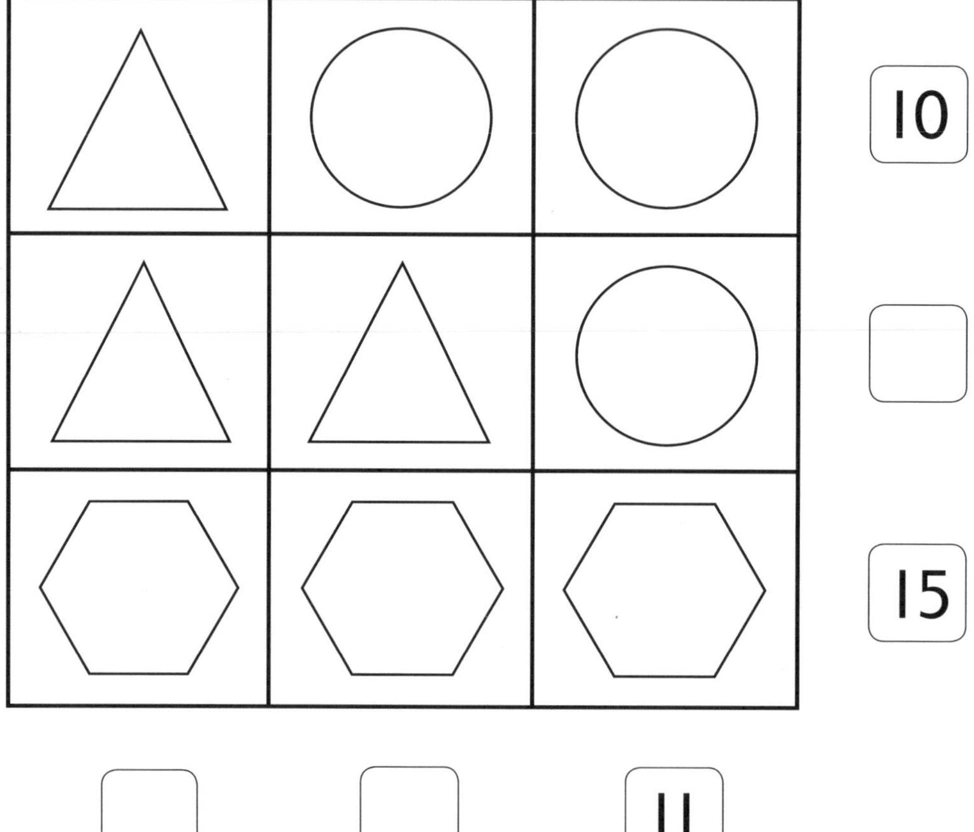

Value

Value

Value

Name ______________________ Date ______________

Puzzle practice 2

Work out the value of each shape and the total of each row and column.

Value

Value

Value

Name ______________________ Date ________________

Problems at the zoo

Work out the answers to these problems.

Show your working out in the boxes.

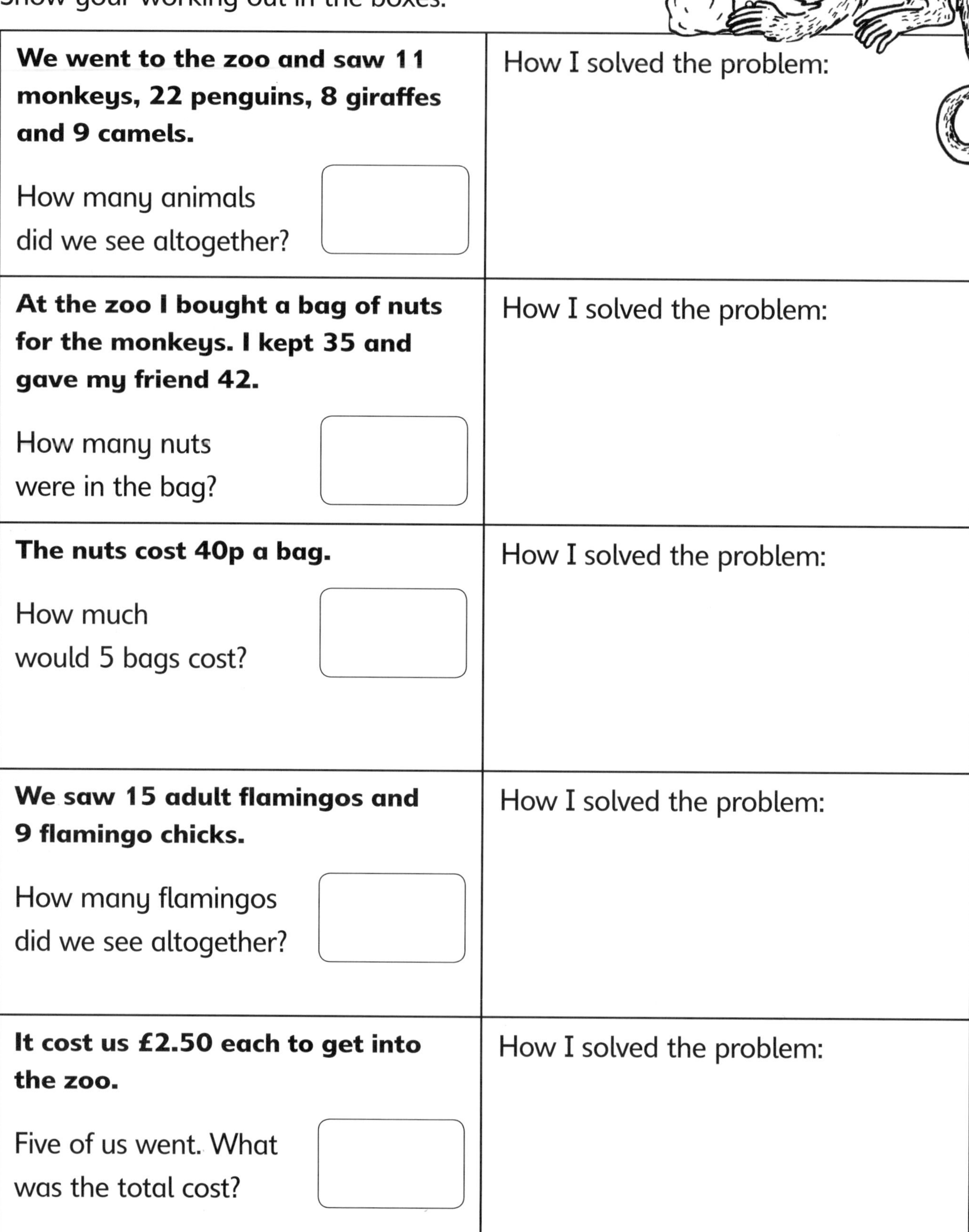

We went to the zoo and saw 11 monkeys, 22 penguins, 8 giraffes and 9 camels. How many animals did we see altogether?	How I solved the problem:
At the zoo I bought a bag of nuts for the monkeys. I kept 35 and gave my friend 42. How many nuts were in the bag?	How I solved the problem:
The nuts cost 40p a bag. How much would 5 bags cost?	How I solved the problem:
We saw 15 adult flamingos and 9 flamingo chicks. How many flamingos did we see altogether?	How I solved the problem:
It cost us £2.50 each to get into the zoo. Five of us went. What was the total cost?	How I solved the problem:

Name ______________________ Date ______________________

Creating patterns

Cut out the square, triangle and pentagon templates at the bottom of this sheet.
Use them to make new shapes like this:

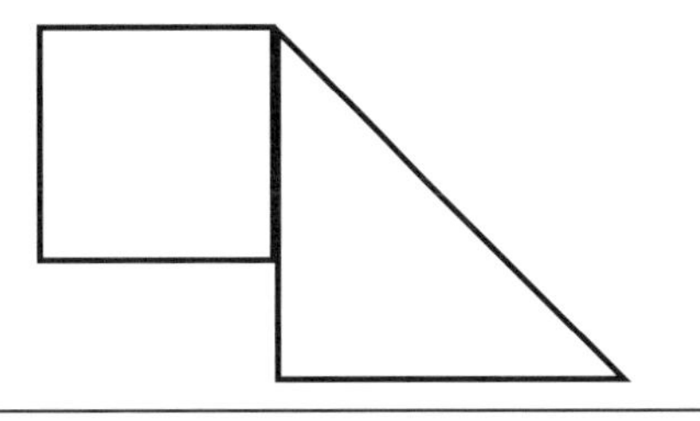

Now you try. Draw and name your new shapes in these boxes:

My new shape is a hexagon.

1. Use the square and the triangle.	**2.** Use the pentagon and the square.
My new shape is a	**My new shape is a**

3. Use the pentagon and the triangle.	**4.** Use all three templates.
My new shape is a	**My new shape is a**

Use two of your new shapes to make a pattern on another sheet of paper.

Here is an example:

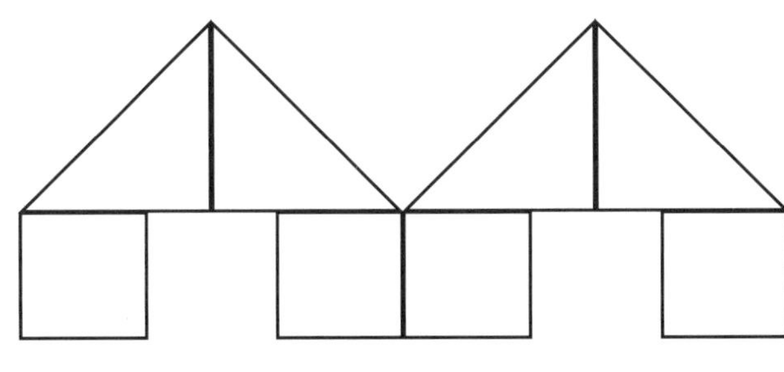

These are the shapes to cut out and use:

Unit 3 3 weeks

Securing number facts, understanding shape

Lesson	Strands	Starter	Main teaching activities
1. Teach and apply	Use/apply	**Use units of time (seconds, minutes, hours, days) and know the relationships between them; read the time to the quarter hour; identify time intervals, including those that cross the hour.**	• Solve problems involving addition, subtraction, multiplication or division in contexts of numbers, measures or pounds and pence. • Describe patterns and relationships involving numbers or shapes, make predictions and test these with examples.
2. Apply	Use/apply	As for Lesson 1	As for Lesson 1
3. Apply	Use/apply	**State the subtraction corresponding to a given addition, and vice versa.**	As for Lesson 1
4. Teach and apply	Use/apply	As for Lesson 3	As for Lesson 1
5. Teach, apply and evaluate	Use/apply	Derive and recall multiplication facts for the 2, 5 and 10 times-tables and the related division facts; recognise multiples of 2, 5 and 10.	As for Lesson 1
6. Review, teach and practise	Use/apply Knowledge	**Derive and recall all addition and subtraction facts for each number to at least 10, all pairs with totals to 20 and all pairs of multiples of 10 with totals up to 100.**	• Solve problems involving addition, subtraction, multiplication or division in contexts of numbers, measures or pounds and pence. **• Derive and recall all addition and subtraction facts for each number to at least 10, all pairs with totals to 20 and all pairs of multiples of 10 with totals up to 100.**
7. Apply	Use/apply Knowledge	As for Lesson 6	As for Lesson 6
8. Teach and apply	Use/apply Knowledge	**Visualise common 2D shapes and 3D solids; identify shapes from pictures of them in different positions and orientations; sort, make and describe shapes, referring to their properties.**	As for Lesson 6
9. Teach and practise	Knowledge	• Derive and recall multiplication facts for the 5 times-table and the related division facts. • Describe and extend number sequences.	• Understand that halving is the inverse of doubling and derive and recall doubles of all numbers to 20, and the corresponding halves. • Derive and recall multiplication facts for the 2, 5 and 10 times-tables and the related division facts; recognise multiples of 2, 5 and 10. • Use knowledge of number facts and operations to estimate and check answers to calculations.
10. Teach and practise	Knowledge	Understand that halving is the inverse of doubling and derive and recall doubles of all numbers to 20, and the corresponding halves.	As for Lesson 9
11. Teach and practise	Knowledge	As for Lesson 10	• Understand that halving is the inverse of doubling and derive and recall doubles of all numbers to 20, and the corresponding halves. • Use knowledge of number facts and operations to estimate and check answers to calculations.
12. Review and practise	Shapes Use/apply	Derive and recall multiplication facts for the 2, 5 and 10 times-tables and the related division facts; recognise multiples of 2, 5 and 10.	**• Visualise common 2D shapes and 3D solids; identify shapes from pictures of them in different positions and orientations; sort, make and describe shapes, referring to their properties.** • Describe patterns and relationships involving numbers or shapes, make predictions and test these with examples.
13. Teach and practise	Shapes Use/apply	As for Lesson 12	As for Lesson 12
14. Apply	Shapes Use/apply	• Describe and extend number sequences. **• Sort shapes, referring to their properties.**	As for Lesson 12
15. Apply and evaluate	Shapes Use/apply	As for Lesson 14	As for Lesson 12

Speaking and listening objective

- Tell real or imagined stories (using conventions of familiar story language).

Introduction

This block of work contains 15 lessons. The first eight are related to problem solving with 'real life' problems involving money and measures. These aim to reinforce and consolidate the calculation strategies on which the children have previously focused. The children will work on visualising, drawing and answering two-step problems. The final three lessons of this sequence rehearse and reinforce all addition and subtraction facts for each number to at least 10, all pairs with totals to 20 and all pairs of multiples of 10 with totals up to 100, and then put these into problem-solving contexts. Following these are three lessons involving doubling and halving. The final four lessons involve a variety of aspects of shape, including recognising 2D shapes from 3D solids. Threaded throughout are the using and applying objectives where the children are using the taught skills and applying them to a variety of contexts. Also threaded throughout is the encouragement to use their knowledge of number facts and operations to estimate and check answers to calculations.

During the problem-solving Lessons 1 to 5 in particular, there are opportunities to fulfil the speaking and listening objective when the children make up and tell imagined problem scenarios. The lessons on shape also fulfil this objective as they use visual skills along with verbal reasoning and explanations.

The starters of each lesson focus on rehearsing the skills involved with time, mental calculation, tables, number pairs and counting. These are practised frequently to keep them fresh in the children's minds.

Using and applying mathematics

- Describe patterns and relationships involving numbers or shapes, make predictions and test these with examples.
- Solve problems involving addition, subtraction, multiplication or division in contexts of numbers, measures or pounds and pence.

Lessons 1-5

Preparation

Copy 'How to solve a problem' onto A3 paper. Copy 'Small spider charts' onto A4 card and laminate, but keep as a whole sheet. Copy 'Making up problems' onto an OHT. Copy 'Addition and subtraction cards' and 'Months of the year cards' onto A3 card and cut out the cards. Copy 'Money problem cards' onto card and cut out the cards. Copy 'Two steps' onto acetate.

You will need

CD resources

'How to solve a problem', 'Small spider charts', 'Making up problems', 'Addition and subtraction cards', 'Months of the year cards', 'Money problems cards', 'Visualising problems 2', 'Two steps' (see General resources); 'Down by the sea' and 'Beach maths' support, extension and template versions; 'Here kitty, kitty...'.

Learning objectives

Starter

- Use units of time (seconds, minutes, hours, days) and know the relationships between them; read the time to the quarter hour; identify time intervals, including those that cross the hour.
- State the subtraction corresponding to a given addition, and vice versa.
- Derive and recall multiplication facts for the 2, 5 and 10 times-tables and the related division facts; recognise multiples of 2, 5 and 10.

Main teaching activities

2006

- Describe patterns and relationships involving numbers or shapes, make predictions and test these with examples.
- Solve problems involving addition, subtraction, multiplication or division in contexts of numbers, measures or pounds and pence.

1999

- Use mental addition and subtraction, simple multiplication and division to solve simple word problems, using one or two steps.
- Recognise all coins and begin to use £.p notation for money.
- Find totals, give change, and work out which coins to pay.

Vocabulary

money, coin, penny, pence, pound, £, price, cost, buy, bought, spend, pay, change, costs more/less, how much... ?, total, difference between, altogether

If access is possible, you may like to use *The Toy Shop* from the NNS ICT CD as part of your modelling.

Lesson 1 (Teach and apply)

Starter

Refresh and read: Give each child a card clock. Ask the children to show you various o'clock, half past, quarter to and quarter past times. Move on to questions such as: *My clock says 8 o'clock. It is one hour slow. Show me what time it really is. My clock says 9:30. It is two hours fast... My clock says 1 o'clock. It is half an hour slow... My clock says half past 3. It is 15 minutes fast...*

Main teaching activities

Whole class: Say that this week, the children will use the mental strategies they learned in Unit 2 to solve 'real-life' problems that involve money and measures. Display the 'How to solve a problem' poster, and talk through the steps needed to solve the first problem on the OHT of 'Making up problems'. Can anyone remember what we need to do when we have a word problem to solve? Direct their attention to the poster. When you reach Step 4, ask the children to think of a strategy to work out the answer. Remind them of the strategies they have been learning about: partitioning one of the numbers; looking for pairs that total 10; near doubling; counting on; bridging through 10. Ask them to decide which one is 'best' to help them solve this problem. Allow them to discuss with a partner and then feed back to the class. Solve the other three problems on the OHT in the same way.

Paired work: Organise the children into ability pairs. Give each pair a copy of 'Down by the sea'. Encourage the children to write down how they worked out these problems, using numbers rather than words.

Differentiation

Less confident learners: Provide the support version of 'Down by the sea' with simpler numbers. Give support with reading and recording, and provide counting apparatus, if needed.

More confident learners: Provide the extension version with more complex numbers. You could offer a challenge by asking the children to find two different methods of solving each problem.

Review

Write some information on the board, such as *1m, 80cm, string, how much?* or *£5, £1.50, how much altogether?* Ask the children to talk to a partner and make up a problem from this information. For example: *I had 1m of string. I cut off 80cm to tie up a parcel. How much did I have left?* or *I had saved £5. My grandma gave me £1.50. How much have I now?* Invite some pairs to share their problems and the rest of the class to solve them. Record the answers on the board. If there is a pounds and pence answer such as £6.50, write it as £650. Ask the children whether this is correct. Remind them to put the decimal point after the number of pounds in order to separate pounds from pence. Write up some pence amounts (such as 150p) and ask the children to write them using pounds and pence notation (£1.50). Repeat this a few times.

Lesson 2 (Apply)

Starter

Refresh and read: Ask the children to say the months of the year in order together. Give 12 children a month card each and ask the others to order them by telling them where to stand. For each month, ask the children what the weather is like, what they may be doing and whether there are any significant dates (such as birthdays, Christmas, Divali or Hannukah).

Main teaching activities

Whole class: Remind the children of the Review in Lesson 1. Say that today they will be working with a partner to make up their own problems. They may remember doing this before (see Unit 2). Using an OHT of 'Making up problems', talk through some possible one-step and two-step problems. For example, the information 5 kilograms, 3 and a half kilograms, flour could be used to generate: *The baker has 3 and a half kilograms of flour. He needs 5 kilograms to bake his bread. How much more flour does he need?* or *The baker had two bags of flour. One had 5 kilograms in and the other had 3 and a half kilograms. How much flour did he have altogether?* As you make up the problems, encourage the children to think visually and to use drawings in

their recording when possible, rather than words. Model this idea simply.
Paired work: The children should work in ability pairs. Give each pair a copy of the 'Beach maths' activity sheet, which gives them information to make into problems. Encourage them to jot their ideas down simply, or draw them when possible, so they don't waste time writing too many words.

Differentiation

Less confident learners: Provide the support version of 'Beach maths' with simpler information.
More confident learners: Provide the extension version with more complex information and a final challenge.

Review

Invite the children to share their problems with the class. Ask the class to solve the problems. Each time, ask: *How did you solve the problem? Was there any information you didn't need? How many steps did you need to take?*

Write some information on the board that could involve multiplication and division, and ask the children to make up a problem from it.

Lesson 3 (Apply)

Starter

Recall: Hold up the 'Addition and subtraction cards' that have at least one single-digit number. For each one, ask the children to write on their whiteboards the corresponding addition or subtraction to show you. Ask someone to demonstrate, using a number line, why their answer matches the original calculation. For example: you hold up 12 + 7 = 19, they write down 19 - 7 = 12 and demonstrate:

12 + 7 = 19

19 – 7 = 12

Main teaching activities

Whole class: Tell the children that today they will act out some problems to do with money. Ask whether they can remember what 'visualising' means. Ask them to shut their eyes and visualise what you say. *Imagine a tree. It is short and round with green leaves. Does your tree have lots of leaves or just a few? On the tree there are ten apples. They look very tasty. Pick half of them. How many have you picked? How many are left on the tree?* Repeat with a few scenarios that require the children to visualise amounts of money, using the 'Visualising problems 2' resource sheet.
Group work: Organise the children into mixed-ability groups. The children will be revisiting the idea of making up problems, but these are purely money and are at a level of difficulty appropriate to this part of the year. Give each group a card from 'Money problem cards'. They will need to be able to act out the problem in class, so that everyone knows what it is about and can work out the answer. They may use pens and paper to draw pictures, but they must try very hard not to use any words (written or spoken). Model an example from the sheet. Allow about 20 minutes for this preparation, telling the children at five-minute intervals how long they have left

Differentiation

Let the children work together in mixed-ability groups. As they create their 'problem' scenarios, check that the less confident learners are taking an active part in the discussions and make sure the more confident learners do not dominate proceedings.

Review

Extend this Review session. Give each group of children time to act out their problem, and the rest of the class time to solve it. Assess whether the performers understand the problem. Then assess the other children's responses: *Did they work out what was being asked? How did they solve the problem? Did they handle the information correctly? What strategies did they use?*

Lesson 4 (Teach and apply)

Starter

Refine: Repeat the Starter from Lesson 3, but hold up the 'Addition and subtraction cards' with two-digit numbers only.

Main teaching activities

Whole class: Make sure the children understand that 'two-step' problems have two parts - that is, two things to work out in order to find the answer. Display the 'How to solve a problem' poster and talk through the steps necessary to solve a problem. Demonstrate this with a problem from the 'Two steps' activity sheet.
Paired/individual work: Give 'Two steps' to pairs or individuals. Ask them to solve the problems as you have just demonstrated.

Differentiation

Provide adult support for less confident learners if necessary. Encourage more confident learners to discuss how they worked out their answers.

Review

Work through each problem from the activity sheet. Display the problems on the OHP so that everyone can participate. Ask the class questions such as: *What question is being asked? What information do we need? How can we solve the problem? How can we add/subtract these numbers? Is there another way?*

Lesson 5 (Teach, apply and evaluate)

Starter

Rehearse and recall: Give each pair of children the 'Small spider charts' sheet. Count together in multiples of 2, using fingers. Stop at various points - for example, when they get to 10, ask: *How many fingers is that? How many lots of 2 make 10? We can say that 2 five times is 10.* Write on the board: 2 × 5 = 10. Repeat with multiples of 10. Now ask the children to look at their spider charts. Ask them to work with the ten-times table chart first. One child should point at the numbers around the chart and the other should answer. Time them for two minutes. How many times can they go round the chart? Ask them to swap over and repeat for the two-times table chart.

Main teaching activities

Whole class: Tell the children that in this lesson they will look at another type of problem called an investigation. This doesn't always have just one correct answer. Go through an example with the children: *I bought a cola pop. It cost 6p. I paid for it with the exact money. Which coins did I use? I could have done it in five different ways. Write down on your whiteboard as many of the ways as you can. You can talk to a friend about the answers.* Ask questions such as: *What do you need to find out? How are you going to start? What coins can you use? Would a 10p be any good? Why not? What coins did you use?*
Paired work: Organise the children into mixed-ability pairs to work on the investigation on the 'Here kitty, kitty...' activity sheet. Give them 5p, 10p and 20p coins to help them if necessary.

Differentiation

If the less confident learners find the activity sheet difficult to read and understand, suggest that a confident reader reads the sheet to the whole group. Then encourage the children to explain to each other what they have to do.

Review

Invite some pairs of children to talk through their work and the answers they found. Assess how well they coped with the investigation. Recap on the types of problem solving the children have been doing this week: one-step and two-step word problems and investigations.

Lessons 6-8

Preparation

Copy '+ and - 19 and 21 cards', 'Coin cards and labels', 'Price labels (pence)' and 'Price labels (£.p)' onto card and cut out one of each set of cards for each pair. Copy the 'Which strategy?' game onto A3 paper and cut out. Make an OHT of 'Problems'.

You will need

Photocopiable pages
'Solve me!' (page 90) for each child or pair; 'What's my answer?' (page 91) for each child or pair.
CD resources
'0-100 number cards, 'Coin cards and labels', 'Price labels (pence)', 'Price labels (£.p)', 'How to solve a problem' poster, 'Addition and subtraction vocabulary', 'Problems', '+ and - 19 and 21 cards', 'What did you do?', 'Which strategy?'; 'Shape vocabulary cards' (both 3D and 2D) (see General resources); 'What's my answer?' and 'Solve me!' support and extension versions; '3D shapes'; 2D shapes'.
Equipment
Blu-Tack; a class 100 square; individual 100 squares; plastic coins, real coins and large card coins; a pendulum; counters; counting apparatus.

Learning objectives

Starter

- Derive and recall all addition and subtraction facts for each number to at least 10, all pairs with totals to 20 and all pairs of multiples of 10 with totals up to 100.
- Visualise common 2D shapes and 3D solids; identify shapes from pictures of them; sort, make and describe shapes, referring to their properties.

Main teaching activities

2006

- Solve problems involving addition, subtraction, multiplication or division in contexts of numbers, measures or pounds and pence.
- Derive and recall all addition and subtraction facts for each number to at least 10, all pairs with totals to 20 and all pairs of multiples of 10 with totals up to 100.

1999

- Extend understanding of the operations of addition and subtraction.
- Add/subtract 19 or 21.
- Choose and use appropriate operations and efficient calculation strategies.
- Use mental addition and subtraction, simple multiplication and division to solve simple word problems, using one or two steps.
- Explain how the problem was solved.

Vocabulary

money, coin, penny, pence, pound, £, spend, pay, change, total, addition, subtraction, difference, equal, count on, how much more?, bridging, nearest 10, next 10

Lesson 6 (Review, teach and practise)

Starter

Reason: Write on the board: ○ + △ = 10. Ask the children to write on their whiteboards number sentences that will fit this. Discuss what they have written. Find all the possible sentences. Use fingers to check, as well as jumps along a 0-10 number line. Repeat for a total below 10.

Main teaching activities

Whole class: The next two lessons are about adding and subtracting money and measures. Ask the children to tell you some words about addition and subtraction. As they do this, show the appropriate word cards and Blu-Tack them to the board. Discuss the strategies the children have learned for mental addition and subtraction.

Use the 'Which strategy?' general resource sheet: hold up a calculation and ask the children which box you should put it in. Repeat. Now write 36 + 19 on the board and ask them how they would work this out. (Add 20, then adjust.) Practise some similar examples, using a class 100 square to demonstrate. Ask the children to close their eyes and visualise a 100 square, find 13 and then add 19 (by adding 20 and taking away 1). Repeat for + 21 and - 21. Let any children who need support use a small 100 square.

Ask the children which coins we use. As they say the coin names, hold up the coin label cards and real coins, plus large card coins for everyone to see. Attach these to a board. Give the children a money problem based on shopping, such as: *I went to the baker's and bought a roll for 35p and a doughnut for 19p. How much did I spend?* Ask them to estimate the answer roughly, then work it out together (using the same strategy as above). Repeat with a few similar problems.

Paired work: Give each pair a copy of 'What did you do?', a pile of pence price labels and a pile of '+ and - 19 and 21' cards. Model this activity. *Pick a card from each pile and follow their instructions. Try to visualise a 100 square when you are calculating. When you have an answer, record your work on the 'What did you do?' sheet. Now make up a money problem for your calculation. Do this five times.*

Differentiation

Less confident learners: Give these children an individual 100 square. If they really struggle, ask them to add and subtract 9 and 11.
More confident learners: Ask these children to add and subtract 18 and 22 as well as 19 and 21.

Review

Invite a few children to tell the class one of their made-up money problems. Ask the class to solve these and explain what they did. Ask questions such as: *Did you add or subtract 1 when you added 19? Why? What about subtracting 19? Why? Can you show me using a number line?*

Lesson 7 (Apply)

Starter

Rehearse and recall: Call out some numbers from zero to 20 and ask the children to write on their whiteboards the number that goes with each to make 20. After a few examples, use a pendulum to practise quick recall: as it swings one way, you call out a number; as it swings the other way, the children call out the number that goes with it to make 20.

Main teaching activities

Whole class: This lesson is about using the strategies from Lesson 6 to solve two-step problems that involve measures and money. Discuss the strategies for adding and subtracting that the children have learned. Ask them what they must do to solve a problem; show the problem-solving poster and the OHT of 'Problems'. Talk through each problem: pick out the information that is needed; decide on the best strategy; estimate and then calculate the answer; check that the answer makes sense in context.
Individual work: Ask the children to solve some problems individually, choosing the best strategies to answer them. Model an example from the 'Solve me!' photocopiable sheet.

Differentiation

Less confident learners: Provide the support version of 'Solve me!' with simpler measures and prices.
More confident learners: Provide the extension version with more complex measures and prices.

Review

Invite some children to explain how they solved their problems. Use this for assessment. Question them carefully about the process and about why they chose the strategy they used. Ask how they could check their answers; encourage them to use inverses. Demonstrate this with an arrow diagram.

Lesson 8 (Teach and apply)

Starter

Read and reason: Give each child a 3D and a 2D shape card. Hold up a shape vocabulary card and ask children holding any shape that links to it to stand up. Ask a few children to explain why they are standing. Repeat for as many vocabulary cards as possible.

Main teaching activities

Whole class: This lesson encourages using addition and subtraction facts to 10 and 20 and multiples of ten to 100 to solve problems that involve money. Begin with a brief rehearsal of these, by calling out a number to 20 and asking the children to write its pair to make 20 on their whiteboards. Repeat with multiples of 10 to 100, reminding them that they can make use of their knowledge of number pairs to 10 and adjust, for example, 2 + 8 = 10 so 20 + 80 = 100. Write a three two-digit number addition on the board, for example, 12 + 23 + 18. Ask the children how they can add using this strategy. Some might add the 10s first and then look for numbers totalling 10, some may choose to keep the 12 and add 8 to make 20 and then add 23 and 10. Encourage the second for those that are able to use it. Repeat with similar examples.

Individual work: Ask the children to solve some problems individually using the 'What's my answer?' activity sheet, focusing on the strategies discussed to answer them. Model an example from the photocopiable sheet. Some of the activities are more open-ended having different possible answers.

Differentiation

Less confident learners: Provide the support version of 'What's my answer?' with simpler prices. Give this group coins as a support resource.

More confident learners: Provide the extension version with more complex prices involving pounds and pence.

Review

Discuss the questions that ask what someone could have bought and ask the children to tell you their different answers and how they worked them out. Ask similar questions using the price lists on 'What's my answer?' in order to recap the strategy used today.

Lessons 9-11

Preparation

Make cards from 'Multiplication and division vocabulary' and 'Doubles and halves cards'. Make cards for each group of three children from 'What we know 1' and 'What we know 2'. Photocopy 'Dartboard doubles' onto card, laminate and cut up for each group. Make 'spider charts' for the three- and four-times tables.

You will need

CD resources

'0-100 number cards', 'Multiplication and division vocabulary' cards, 'Dartboard doubles' game, spinner and gameboard for each group, 'Doubles and halves cards', an A3 copy of 'Spider charts for ×5 and ÷5' (see General resources); 'What we know 1' cards and 'What we know 2' cards for each group.

Equipment

Blu-Tack; individual whiteboards and pens; counting apparatus; counters.

Learning objectives

Starter

- Derive and recall multiplication facts for the 5 times-table and the related division facts.
- Describe and extend number sequences.
- Understand that halving is the inverse of doubling and derive and recall doubles of all numbers to 20, and the corresponding halves.

Main teaching activities

2006

- Understand that halving is the inverse of doubling and derive and recall doubles of all numbers to 20, and the corresponding halves.
- Derive and recall multiplication facts for the 2, 5 and 10 times-tables and the related division facts; recognise multiples of 2, 5 and 10.
- Use knowledge of number facts and operations to estimate and check answers to calculations.

1999

- Know and use halving as the inverse of doubling.
- Use known number facts and place value to carry out mentally simple multiplications and divisions.

Vocabulary

lots of, groups of, times, multiplied by, multiple of, repeated addition, array, row, column, equal, repeated subtraction, divided by, plus, left, left over, times, group in

Lesson 9 (Teach and practise)

Starter

Rehearse: Show the A3 spider chart for ×5 and ask the children to count in fives slowly as you point to the numbers 1–10 in order. Repeat, but stop at certain places and ask how many lots of five make the number they have just said. Repeat with the children using their fingers, as in previous lessons. Point to random numbers and ask the children for the answer when 5 is multiplied by that number. Repeat this using the three- and four-times table charts you have made.

Main teaching activities

Whole class: The next three lessons are about multiplication and division. Ask: *What do we mean by 'multiply' and 'divide'? What vocabulary do we use for these operations?* Show the 'Multiplication and division vocabulary' cards as the children say the words, and stick them to the board; add any words that the children don't say. Group the cards into multiplying and dividing words, and any that could be for both.

Say that today's lesson is about doubling and halving. *What do we mean by 'doubling'? What can we do to double 4?* (Add 4 + 4 or multiply 4 × 2.)

Write 4 + 4 and 4 × 2 on the board. Ask: *What do we mean by 'halving'?* Use an arrow diagram to demonstrate to the class that halving is the inverse of doubling.

Write some more numbers on the board and ask for volunteers to draw the arrow diagrams. Say: *Doubling is the inverse of halving, as multiplication is the inverse of division. So if we know that double 12 is 24, we know that half of 24 is 12.* Say a few examples for the children to answer on their whiteboards, such as: *Double 18 is 36, write down half of 36; double 11 is 22, write down half of 22; half of 28 is 14, write down double 14.*

Ask the children to write 6 on their whiteboards, then draw an arrow diagram to double it and halve the double. They could do this in either of the ways shown above, perhaps using 'D' and 'H' to stand for 'double' and 'half'. Now ask them to write 10, then draw an arrow diagram to halve it and double the half.

Repeat with a variety of numbers until most (if not all) of the class are confident.

Group work: Ask the children to play 'Dartboard doubles' in pairs or groups of three. Use the instructions to demonstrate.

Differentiation

Less confident learners: These children should use only numbers to 20, with counting apparatus.
More confident learners: Write extra numbers on the blank cards provided, such as 34, 45, 16 and 150.

Review

Play the 'Doubles and halves' game as a class. Give a few cards to each group or pair. This is more effective than giving each child a card, for two reasons: it gives support to any children who are liable to become anxious; and it keeps the children involved throughout the game.

Lesson 10 (Teach and practise)

Starter

Recall: The children will need single-digit number cards. Call out numbers to 15 (except 11, which can't be answered using one set of single-digit number cards) and ask the children to double them, then show you the answers. Call out their doubles for the children to halve. Ask the children what double 11 is. Repeat for multiples of 5 to 50 and 10 to 100, giving instructions such as: *Double 7, double 40, halve 80, double 35, halve 16, halve 30, double 30, double 45.* Ask the children what double 50 is.

Main teaching activities

Whole class: Explain that today's lesson is about using what we know to multiply and divide mentally. The children know the two-, five- and ten-times tables, know that a number ×1 is the same number, are learning the five-times table and can count in threes and fours. Write these number sentences on the board: 1 × ☐ = 7; ☐ × 10 = 60; 2 × ☐ = 20; 15 = 3 × ☐; ☐ × 2 = 50; ☐ ÷ 2 = 20; 5 ÷ ☐ = 5; 80 ÷ ☐ = 8; ☐ ÷ 3 = 10. Ask the children to write on their whiteboards what they think should go in each box. Discuss what information they knew that helped them to find the answers.

Group work: Put the children in mixed-ability groups of three or four. Demonstrate the 'What we know 1' cards, then ask the children in each group to work together to solve the calculations on the sheet.

Differentiation

Check that all the children in each group are taking an active part in working out the calculations on the activity sheet.

Review

Go through the cards used. Ask the children to tell you the answers and explain what information they knew that helped them to find the answers. For example, ask: *What multiplied by 9 gives 9? How do we know that? What is the rule that helps us? Can that help us to work out what number divided by 9 gives 1?*

Lesson 11 (Teach and practise)

Starter

Refine and rehearse: Repeat the Starter from Lesson 10, but ask the children to write the answers on their whiteboards. During the activity, ask questions such as: *Write down double 5, now double that, double it again, halve it, halve it again, what have you got? Can you explain why?*

Main teaching activities

Whole class: Write some calculations on the board as in Lesson 10; ask the children to solve them and to explain what information they knew that helped them to find the answers. Explain that today the children will look at partitioning numbers as a way of multiplying and dividing. Write 23 × 2 on the board. *How can we use partitioning and doubling to help us solve this?* (We can partition 23 into 20 and 3, double these and add the answers.) Write up 36 ÷ 2 and ask the children to answer it, using partitioning and halving. Repeat for various similar calculations.

Group work: Repeat the activity from Lesson 10, using the 'What we know 2' cards.

Review

Go through the cards used. Ask the children to give you the answers and explain how partitioning helped them to use what they knew. For example, look at 22 × 2 and ask: *What do you get if you partition 22? What are you doing when you multiply by 2? How can you double 20?*

Differentiation

As for Lesson 10.

Lessons 12-15

Preparation

Laminate a copy of 'Function machine game' for each child; make laminated card shapes from 'Templates for irregular shapes 1' and '2'; make vocabulary cards from '3D shape vocabulary' for each group. Make copies of 'Treasure shapes' and 'Treasure shapes recording sheets'.

You will need

Photocopiable pages

A3 copy of 'Treasure shapes' and 'Treasure shapes recording sheet' (pages 92 and 93), one for each child; 'From 3D to 2D' for each child (page 94).

CD resources

'Function machine game' for each child, 'Templates for irregular shapes 1' and '2', and 'Templates for regular shapes', '2D and 3D shape vocabulary' cards for each group (see General resources); '3D shapes' and '2D shapes'.

Equipment

Plasticine; dry-wipe pens and cloths; coloured pencils; 3D shapes; 2D shapes.

Learning objectives

Starter

- Derive and recall multiplication facts for the 2, 5 and 10 times-tables and the related division facts; recognise multiples of 2, 5 and 10.
- Describe and extend number sequences.
- Sort shapes, referring to their properties.

Main teaching activities

2006

- Visualise common 2D shapes and 3D solids; identify shapes from pictures of them in different positions and orientations; sort, make and describe shapes, referring to their properties.
- Describe patterns and relationships involving numbers or shapes, make predictions and test these with examples.

1999

- Relate solid shapes to pictures of them.
- Investigate a general statement about familiar numbers or shapes by finding examples that satisfy it.

Vocabulary

shape, flat, curved, straight, solid, corner, point, face, side, edge, surface, cube, cuboid, pyramid, sphere, cone, cylinder, circle, triangle, square, rectangle, star, pentagon, hexagon, octagon

Lesson 12 (Review and practise)

Starter

Revisit and refine: Rehearse the two-, five- and ten-times tables by chanting multiples together, counting on fingers. Ask the children at various points what finger they are on and what that means (for example, sixth finger when counting in twos means 6 lots of 2, which is 12). Reverse the activity for division facts: chant multiples and when you reach 12 (for example) ask what you get if you divide 12 by 2; the children look at their fingers. Give the children 'Function machine game'; ask them to write some numbers from 1-10; then, when you say *Go*, to multiply them by 2, 5 or 10. Now ask them to write multiples of 2, 5 and 10, then divide when you say *Go*.

Main teaching activities

Whole class: Say that for the next few lessons the children will be focusing on 3D and 2D shapes. Ask them to turn to a partner and think of all the names of shapes that they can think of. Take feedback, asking them to describe the shapes in terms of their properties. Give each child a 3D or a 2D shape card. Hold up a shape vocabulary card and ask children holding a shape that links to it to stand up. Ask a few children to explain why they are standing. Repeat for as many vocabulary cards as possible.

Ask the children to stand up if their shape has any right angles. Use this as an opportunity to revise right angles, and look for examples around the classroom. Ask them to make a right angle using their thumbs and forefingers. Repeat this for lines of symmetry. Encourage children holding 3D words to think about the symmetry of the faces of these shapes.

Group work: The children will need a selection of 3D and 2D shapes. They should sort them according to their own criteria and record in their own way.

Differentiation

Less confident learners: Encourage these children to focus on simple sorting such as 2D/3D, straight/curved edges. Provide a 'frame' for their recording.

More confident learners: Encourage these children to think about more complex sorting, for example, 'has at least one triangular face', 'has at least one right angle' or 'has at least one curved edge' and to make a Carroll diagram to show their work.

Review

Take feedback from the group activities and ask the children to evaluate the way their peers have sorted their shapes. Look at two shapes and ask: *What is the same about them? What is different?* Reveal a shape from behind a 'wall' and ask: *What could it be? How do you know? What could it not be? Why?*

Lesson 13 (Teach and practise)

Starter

Refresh and refine: As for Lesson 12.

Main teaching activities

Whole class: Recap the work from the last lesson and then say: *This lesson is about recognising 3D shapes from 2D pictures.* Go over the vocabulary of 3D shapes, using the cards. Hold up a sphere and ask the children to describe it. Show the 'Treasure shapes' picture and ask whether they can see any spheres in it. Discuss how they recognised the spheres: round, no edges and so on. Repeat with cubes, cuboids, cylinders, cones and pyramids.

Group work: The children should work in mixed-ability pairs or small groups, with an A3 copy of the picture and some Plasticine. Between them, they should make each of the 3D shapes they have seen in the main teaching activity, and use these to identify the shapes in the picture. They should colour each type of shape with a different-coloured pencil, then record (on the 'Treasure shapes recording sheet') how many of each shape they found.

Differentiation

Let the children work together in mixed-ability groups. Check that the less confident learners are taking an active part in the discussions and make sure the more confident learners do not dominate proceedings.

Review

Discuss how many of each shape the children found and how they recognised them. Write this statement on the board: *All 3D shapes have faces.* Ask the children to say whether this is true and explain how they know, using 'Treasure shapes' and real shapes. Expect such responses as: *a face is a surface and all 3D shapes have surfaces; we can see three faces on this picture of a cube, so we know it must have six really.*

Lesson 14 (Apply)

Starter

Recall and reason: Hold up a triangle and ask how many sides it has. Ask a child to write the number on the board. Show two triangles and ask: *How many sides altogether?* Ask a child to come to the board and write that number. Repeat for up to ten triangles. Ask the children what they notice. (They are counting in threes.) Repeat for quadrilaterals. Can the children predict what will happen with pentagons? Try it and see.

Main teaching activities

Whole class: Recap what they did in the last lesson and then say: *Today you are going to make your own patterns or pictures using 3D shapes.* Give each child a piece of Plasticine and ask them to make a sphere, discuss its properties and then ask them to draw it. Ask what shape they will draw in their picture or pattern (a circle). Repeat for the other 3D shapes.

Individual work: The children should make each shape and then draw it, completing the recording sheet 'From 3D to 2D'. Once they have done this, they use their drawings for reference and make up a pattern or a picture using these shapes; they may draw their own backgrounds as in 'Treasure shapes' from Lesson 13.

Differentiation

Less confident learners: Give these children actual manufactured 3D shapes.

More confident learners: Ask these children to try to draw a representation of the whole, for example, rather than simply the square face.

Review

Show some examples of the children's work. Ask the others to identify each shape and to tell everyone something about it. Repeat the questioning from the Review of Lesson 12: *What is the same about these two shapes? What is different?* Show part of one of the children's shapes and ask: *What could it be? How do you know? What could it not be? Why?*

Lesson 15 (Apply and evaluate)

Starter

Recall and reason: As for Lesson 14.

Main teaching activities

Whole class: Recap what they did in the last lesson. Go over the 2D and 3D shapes and their properties. Give each child 4 or 5 interlocking cubes and ask them to make any shape. Ask them to describe their shape to a partner in terms of number of faces and edges. Ask them to make another, invite a volunteer to come forward and describe their shape without anyone seeing and ask the others to try to make it with their cubes. Compare.

Paired work: Their task is to complete a similar activity to the one they did during the whole-class activity: they take it in turns to make a shape and describe it to their partner, who has to try to make the same shape from this explanation. Once they have finished, they should compare and then try to draw a 2D representation from different angles: what it looks like when looking at it from above, from one side, from another side.

Review

Invite pairs of children to demonstrate what they did, including drawing from different views. Ask one of them to draw one of their views on the board and ask the rest of the class to make a 3D shape with their cubes that has the same view. Compare shapes; there will be a variety. Move briefly on to 2D shape patterns and draw the following on the board:

Ask the children: *How many rectangles can you count in this diagram?*

If you have time, draw another diagram (see right) and ask: *What about this diagram?*

Differentiation

Less confident learners: These children should use a maximum of three cubes.

More confident learners: Encourage these children to use up to eight cubes.

Name ______________________ Date ______________

Solve me!

Here are some problems to solve. Remember to:

1. look for the question
2. look for the information
3. decide what to do
4. estimate the answer
5. work out the answer
6. check!

1. Lucy's gran needs 2m of material to make Lucy a dress.

Each metre costs £1.50.
How much does she spend? [ ]
She gives the shopkeeper £5.
How much change is she given? [ ]

How I worked out my answer: ______________________

2. Kiefa needs to buy 3m of string for school.

The string costs 21p a metre.
How much money will he need? [ ]
He has 50p.
How much more does he need? [ ]

How I worked out my answer: ______________________

3. Sanjay needs 5m of rope.

Each metre costs £2.
How much money does he need? [ ]
He has four £1 coins.
How much more does he need? [ ]

How I worked out my answer: ______________________

4. Kanar needs to buy 2m of ribbon.

The ribbon costs 35p a metre.
How much does she need to pay? [ ]
She pays the shopkeeper £1.
How much change does she receive? [ ]

How I worked out my answer: ______________________

Name ______________________ Date ______________

What's my answer?

Here are some problems to solve. Remember to:

1. look for the question **2.** look for the information **3.** decide what to do
4. estimate the answer **5.** work out the answer **6.** check!

36p each	44p each	£1.25p each	25p each	75p bunch

Answer these problems.

Show how you worked out your answer...

Sally bought an apple and a banana. How much did she spend? ☐	How I worked out my answer:
Becka bought a pineapple and a bunch of grapes. How much did she spend? ☐	How I worked out my answer:
Andy bought two apples and two bananas. How much did he spend? ☐	How I worked out my answer:
Sanjay bought one of everything. How much did he spend? ☐	How I worked out my answer:
Carrie bought two bunches of grapes and two pears. How much did she spend? ☐	How I worked out my answer:

BLOCK B
Securing number facts, understanding shape

Name ______________________ Date ______________________

Treasure shapes

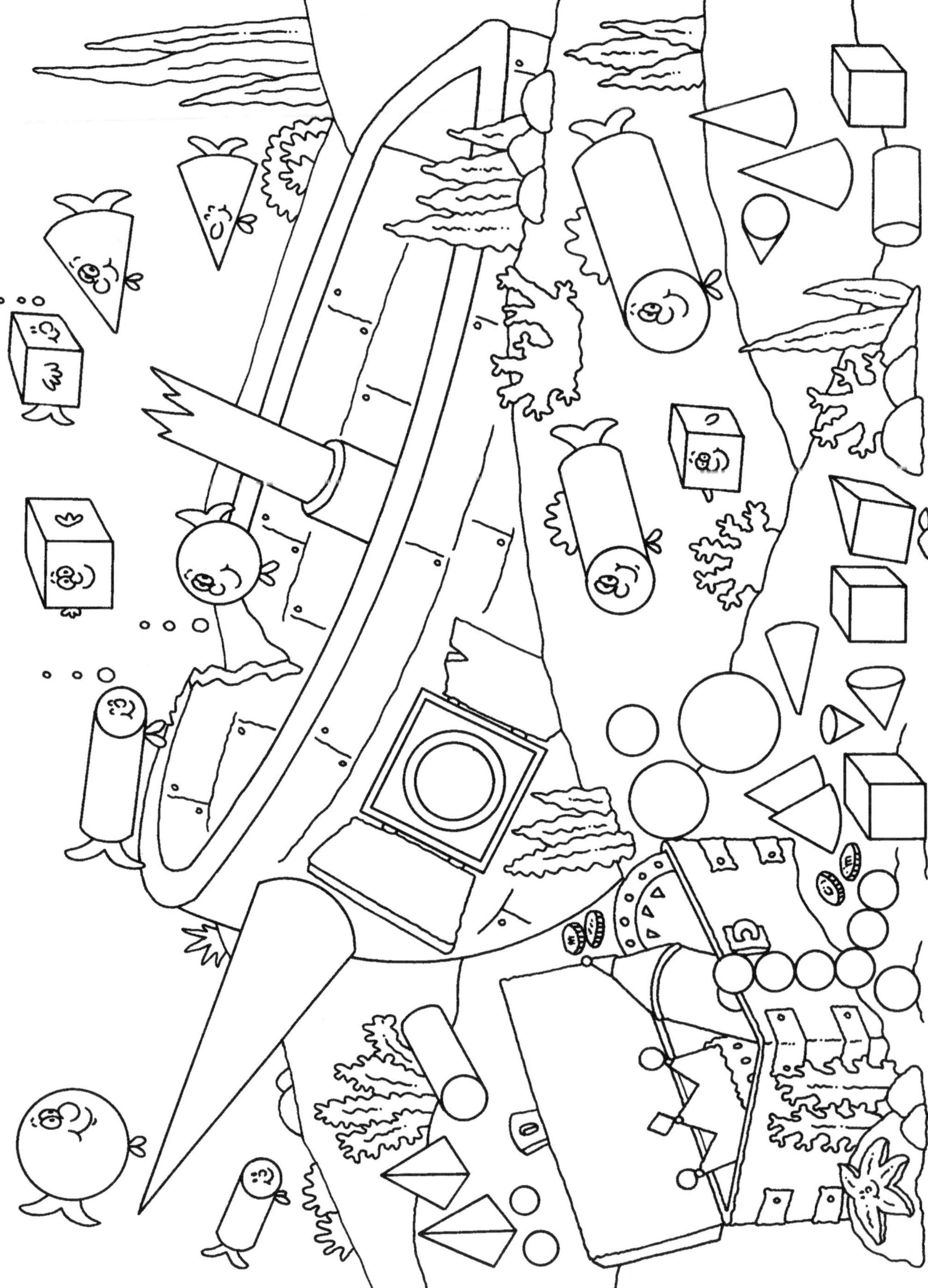

Name ______________________ Date ______________

Treasure shapes recording sheet

Fill in this chart to show what you found and what helped you to find it.

How many spheres?		What shape or shapes did you look for to help you?	
How many cubes?		What shape or shapes did you look for to help you?	
How many cuboids?		What shape or shapes did you look for to help you?	
How many cylinders?		What shape or shapes did you look for to help you?	
How many cones?		What shape or shapes did you look for to help you?	
How many pyramids?		What shape or shapes did you look for to help you?	

Name ______________________ Date ______________________

From 3D to 2D

Make the 3D shapes below from Plasticine or look at the real ones.

Draw the 2D shape that you can see.

3D shape	2D shape
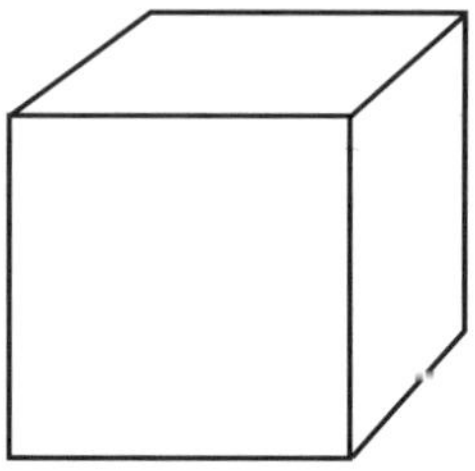	
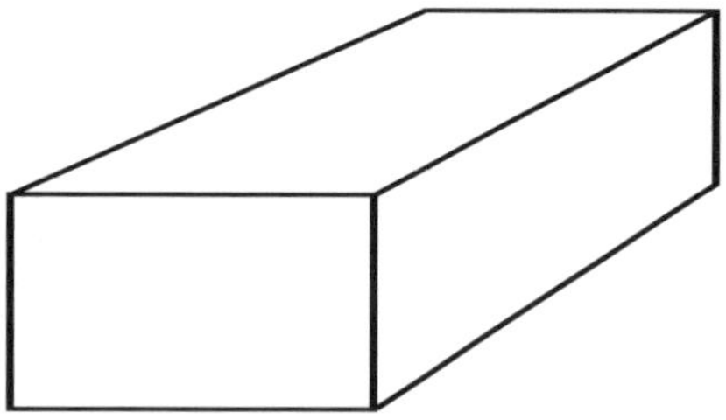	
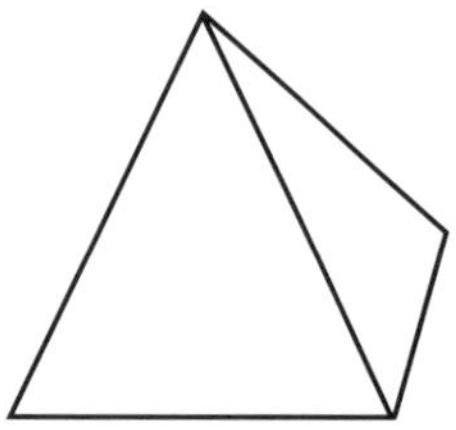	
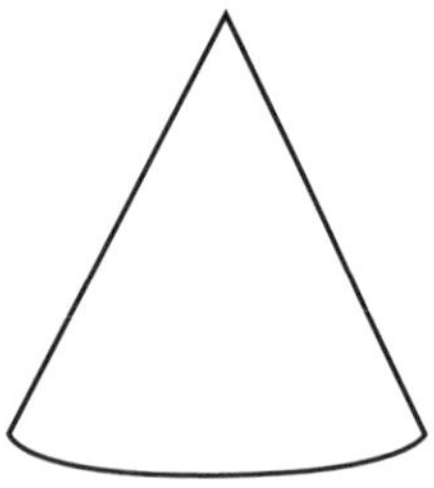	
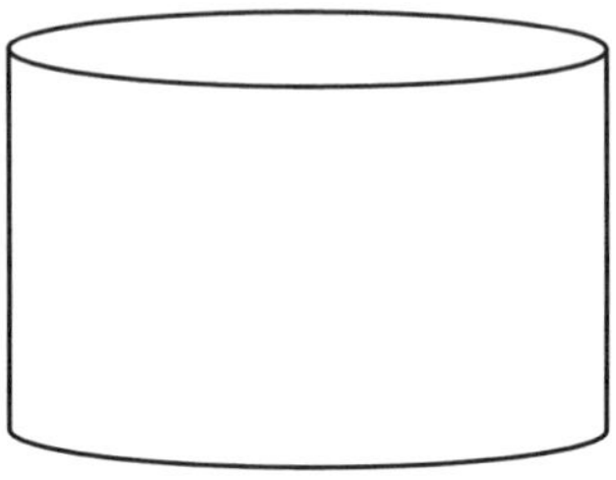	

Handling data and measures

Key aspects of learning
- Enquiry
- Information processing
- Social skills
- Reasoning

Expected prior learning

Check that children can already:
- answer a question by collecting and recording information in a list or table
- present outcomes using practical resources, pictures, block graphs or pictograms
- use diagrams to sort objects into groups according to a given criterion; suggest a different criterion for grouping the same objects
- estimate, measure, weigh and compare objects using suitable uniform non-standard units and measuring instruments, for example a lever balance, metre stick or measuring jug
- name common 2D shapes and 3D solids and describe their features.

Objectives overview

The text in this diagram identifies the focus of mathematics learning within the block.

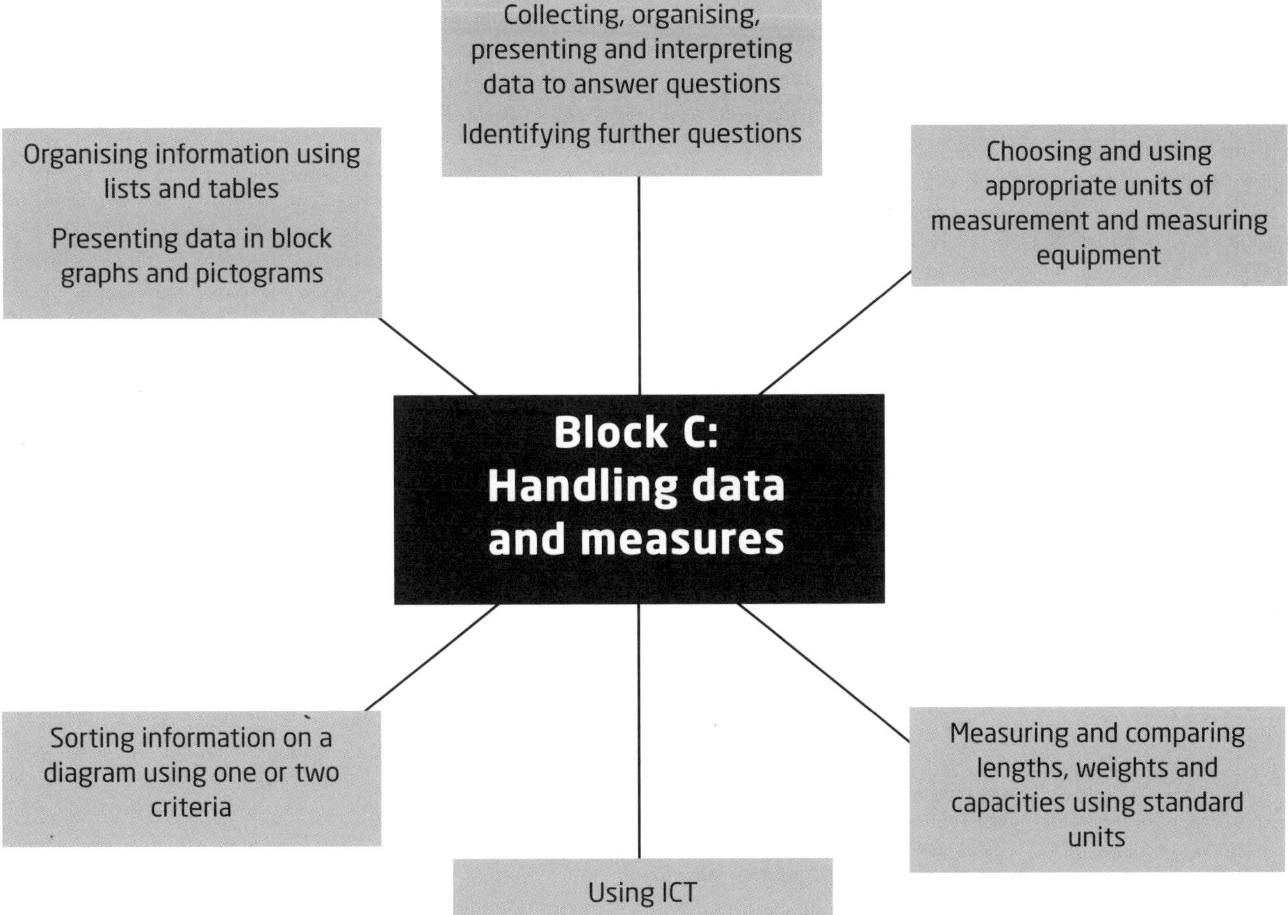

Unit 1 2 weeks

Handling data and measures

Lesson	Strands	Starter	Main teaching activities
1. Review and practise	Use/apply Data	Add/subtract 9 or 11: add/subtract 10 and adjust by 1.	• Follow a line of enquiry; answer questions by choosing and using suitable equipment and selecting, organising and presenting information in lists, tables and simple diagrams. • Answer a question by collecting and recording data in lists and tables; represent the data as block graphs or pictograms to show results; use ICT to organise and present data. **• Use lists, tables and diagrams to sort objects; explain choices using appropriate language, including 'not'.**
2 . Teach and apply	Use/apply Data	As for Lesson 1	As for Lesson 1
3. Teach, practise and evaluate	Use/apply Data	Derive and recall multiplication facts for the 2, 5 and 10 times-tables and the related division facts; recognise multiples of 2, 5 and 10.	As for Lesson 1
4. Review, teach and apply	Use/apply Measures	Read and write two-digit and three-digit numbers in figures and words; describe and extend number sequences and recognise odd and even numbers.	• Follow a line of enquiry; answer questions by choosing and using suitable equipment and selecting, organising and presenting information in lists, tables and simple diagrams. • Estimate, compare and measure lengths, weights and capacities, choosing and using standard units (m, cm, kg, litre) and suitable measuring instruments. • Read the numbered divisions on a scale, and interpret the divisions between them (eg on a scale from 0 to 25 with intervals of 1 shown but only the divisions 0, 5, 10, 15 and 20 numbered); use a ruler to draw and measure lines to the nearest centimetre.
5. Teach and apply	Use/apply Measures	As for Lesson 4	As for Lesson 4
6. Teach, apply and evaluate	Use/apply Measures	As for Lesson 4	As for Lesson 4
7. Review, teach and apply	Use/apply Measures	As for Lesson 4	• Follow a line of enquiry; answer questions by choosing and using suitable equipment and selecting, organising and presenting information in lists, tables and simple diagrams. • Estimate, compare and measure lengths, weights and capacities, choosing and using standard units (m, cm, kg, litre) and suitable measuring instruments. • Read the numbered divisions on a scale, and interpret the divisions between them (eg on a scale from 0 to 25 with intervals of 1 shown but only the divisions 0, 5, 10, 15 and 20 numbered).
8. Apply and evaluate	Use/apply Measures	• Understand that halving is the inverse of doubling and derive and recall doubles of all numbers to 20, and the corresponding halves. • Identify near doubles, from doubles already known (eg 8 + 9, 40 + 41).	As for Lesson 7
9. Review, apply and evaluate	Use/apply Measures	**Use units of time (seconds, minutes, hours, days) and know the relationships between them; read the time to the quarter hour; identify time intervals, including those that cross the hour.**	As for Lesson 7
10. Review, apply and evaluate	Use/apply Measures	As for Lesson 9	As for Lesson 7

BLOCK C Handling data and measures

Speaking and listening objective

- Listen to others in class, ask relevant questions and follow instructions.

Introduction

The first three lessons of this block focus on collecting, organising, presenting and analysing data in tables, lists, pictograms and block charts. The children are encouraged to evaluate the different methods of data handling with regard to their suitability in each case. The rest of the block concentrates on the three measures of length, mass and capacity, where the children are expected to estimate, compare and measure using standard units. Reading scales and interpreting the divisions is regularly revisited throughout this part of the block through demonstrating, modelling and practical measuring. The using and applying aspect of the mathematics is threaded throughout the block and can be identified in each lesson, as can the speaking and listening objective.

Using and applying mathematics

- Follow a line of enquiry; answer questions by choosing and using suitable equipment and selecting, organising and presenting information in lists, tables and simple diagrams.

Lessons 1-3

Preparation

Photocopy the data vocabulary onto A3 card; cut out and laminate the cards. Photocopy both sheets of 'Ways to organise data', 'Pictograms' and 'Sports block graph' onto acetate.

You will need

Photocopiable pages
Copies of 'Favourite food' (page 106) and 'Popular sports' (page 107) for each child.
CD resources
'Organising data vocabulary cards', acetates of 'Ways to organise data', 'Pictograms' and 'Sports block graph' (see General resources).
Equipment
A class 100 square; a 100 square for each child; large sheets of plain paper.

Learning objectives

Starter

- Add/subtract 9 or 11: add/subtract 10 and adjust by 1.
- Derive and recall multiplication facts for the 2, 5 and 10 times-tables and the related division facts; recognise multiples of 2, 5 and 10.

Main teaching activities

2006

- Follow a line of enquiry; answer questions by choosing and using suitable equipment and selecting, organising and presenting information in lists, tables and simple diagrams.
- Answer a question by collecting and recording data in lists and tables; represent the data as block graphs or pictograms to show results; use ICT to organise and present data.
- Use lists, tables and diagrams to sort objects; explain choices using appropriate language, including 'not'.

1999

- Solve a given problem by sorting, classifying and organising information in simple ways.
- Discuss and explain results.

Vocabulary

count, tally, sort, vote, graph, block graph, pictogram, represent, group, set, list, label, title, most popular, least popular, most common, least common

Lesson 1 (Review and practise)

Starter

Rehearse and refine: Rehearse the strategy of adding 9 and 11 to numbers by adding 10 and adjusting by 1, using a class number square. Ask the children to find specific numbers on their individual number squares and add or subtract 9 or 11. Give them a series of instructions, such as: *Find 12, add 9, add 11, add 9, add 20, add 11. Where are you?* Repeat with other starting numbers.

Main teaching activities

Whole class: Explain that the next three lessons are about how to organise and use data. What do the children think that means? If they can't tell you,

show them the 'Organising data vocabulary cards' with Year 1 vocabulary and see whether these assist their thinking. Explain: *Organising data is about showing information in pictures and diagrams, so that we can see the information clearly. We can show data in lists and tables.*

Project the two OHTs of 'Ways to organise data'. For each, ask: *How is the information being shown? What things can you tell me from this list/table? What is the most common/least common? How many people/children were asked/involved?* Ask as many children as possible to tell you an item of information from the data. It might be very simple, such as *The longest word is...*; or more complex, such as *Six more... had... than...*

Group work: Give each mixed-ability group of four children some large sheets of paper. Ask each group to make up a list and then sort it into a table. They need to think of a topic. You could write a few ideas on the board to help them, such as favourite foods, books, sports or pets, or use the children's names or birthdays as in 'Ways to organise data'. Look for a table such as the one shown below as the outcome.

Favourite food

	Sausages	Pasta	Chips	Apples	Fish	Chicken
Sam	✓	✓	✓			✓
Cheryl		✓		✓	✓	✓
Faye	✓		✓			✓
Paul	✓		✓			✓

Review

Ask each group to share their work and explain how they decided on their topics and criteria. Ask the class questions to check whether they are able to extract information from a table. Ask: *Is this a good way to present information? Why?*

Lesson 2 (Teach and apply)

Starter

Reason: Repeat the Starter from Lesson 1, but also include some 'subtract 9' questions, asking the children what they should do (take away 10 and add one because they have taken away one too many).

Main teaching activities

Whole class: Project the OHT of the pictogram showing favourite foods. Ask the children to tell you what it is about and what each picture represents. Explain (adapting as necessary): *This is another way of showing information, it is called a pictogram and each picture represents one person.* Give a few examples of the information the pictogram provides, and then ask the children to discuss with a partner and then share with the class any other information they can see. Ask them questions such as: *How many more voted for pizza than fruit? How many voted for cereals and fish fingers? How many children are in Class 4?*

Ask the class to think of some of their favourite foods. Make a list of the six most popular and then ask the children to vote for one as being the one they prefer above the rest. Make a tally of the votes.

Paired work: Give each pair a copy of the blank pictogram and ask them to make a pictogram according to the tally. Explain that they will need to fill in labels for the foods and numbers and that they can either draw the food or, if they prefer, they can draw a smiley face to represent each child's vote.

Review

Take feedback from the children about the activity, inviting pairs to show their pictograms and share one piece of information. Show the bedtime and birthdays blank pictogram from 'Pictograms' and together complete it using

Differentiation

Less confident learners: Provide adult support if these children need help with completing their pictogram.

More confident learners: Ask these children to explain how they used the information from the tally to fill in their pictogram.

smiley faces according to the information the class gives you. Then discuss by asking such questions as: *What does this pictogram show? Is this a good way to present information? Why?*

Lesson 3 (Teach, practise and evaluate)

Starter

Recall: Recite the two- and ten-times tables together. Now count in multiples of 2 and 10 using fingers; stop the children at various intervals to ask which finger they are on and how many lots of 2 or 10 that is. Ask questions such as 2 × 7, 10 × 6, 12 ÷ 2 and 40 ÷ 10. The children work in pairs to support each other and write the answers on their whiteboards.

Main teaching activities

Whole class: Project the OHT of the first sheet of 'Sports block graph' and the 'Favourite food' pictogram. Ask the children to tell you what is the same and what is different between them. Bring out the fact that instead of pictures, the sports block graph has little boxes to represent the children; these boxes are stacked up to make a block. Focus on the block graph, ask them to tell you as much as they can about it. Ask children who may not find this easy first, so they can contribute before the most obvious facts have been said! Encourage the class to state all possible facts. Ask the children to discuss why this graph is a useful way of telling people about favourite sports. Elicit the response that it is clear, simple and easy to interpret.

Group work: Give mixed-ability groups, of up to four children, copies of both sheets (graph and cards) from 'Sports block graph' and individual copies of the question sheet 'Popular sports' to complete.

Differentiation

Let the children work together in mixed-ability groups. Provide adult support for the less confident members of the group if they need help in completing the activity sheets.

Review

Invite a group to ask the questions that they made up. Ask the other children to answer them, and to describe in detail how they worked them out. Say: *Tell your partner about the ways of showing information that you have learned this week.* Assess whether they have a good understanding of each one.

Lessons 4-6

Preparation

For Lesson 5 write up on the board the activities that the children will do during group work time. Enlarge the cards from CD page 'Measures vocabulary' to A3.

You will need

Photocopiable pages

'Measures activities' (page 143).

CD resources

A copy for each child of the activities for length, from 'Measures activities'; number cards 0-50 from '0-100 number cards', enlarged cards from 'Measures vocabulary' (see General resources).

Equipment

A counting stick; Blu-Tack; strip of paper that is more than a metre long but less than 2 metres; metre sticks marked in 10cm intervals; canes; straws; interlocking cubes; 50cm strip of paper.

Learning objectives

Starter

- Read and write two-digit and three-digit numbers in figures and words; describe and extend number sequences and recognise odd and even numbers.

Main teaching activities

2006

- Follow a line of enquiry; answer questions by choosing and using suitable equipment and selecting, organising and presenting information in lists, tables and simple diagrams.
- Estimate, compare and measure lengths, choosing and using standard units (m, cm, kg, litre) and suitable measuring instruments.
- Read the numbered divisions on a scale, and interpret the divisions between them (eg on a scale from 0 to 25 with intervals of 1 shown but only the divisions 0, 5, 10, 15 and 20 numbered); use a ruler to draw and measure lines to the nearest centimetre.

1999

- Use and begin to read the vocabulary related to length.
- Estimate, measure and compare lengths, using standard units (m, cm); suggest suitable units and equipment for such measurements.

Vocabulary
measure, metre, centimetre, long, short, high, low, tall, wide, narrow, deep, shallow, thick, thin

Lesson 4 (Review, teach and apply)

Starter
Rehearse: Ask a child to pick a number card from 0–50 as a starting number. Ask the children to count in time in ones until you say *Stop*, at which point they count back in ones. Ask the children to pick more cards for other starting numbers. Then ask them to count in tens as you move your finger back and forth on a counting stick, jumping steps occasionally.

Main teaching activities
Whole class: Tell the children that for the next few days they will be thinking about measures. Ask them what they think these words mean: *length*, *weight* and *capacity*. Explain that they will start with length. Hold up the length vocabulary cards (from 'Measures vocabulary') one at a time. Invite the children to read these. The cards can be fixed to the board with Blu-Tack as a reminder of the vocabulary for length. Invite the children to put each word into a sentence to show that they understand its meaning.

Now explain that for this and the next two lessons they will be estimating and measuring length. Hold up the metre stick and ask: *What in this room do you think is about 1 metre long?* Invite the children to make suggestions, then to check by holding the metre stick alongside the items suggested.
Group work: Ask the children to work in groups of about four, with a metre stick. Give each child a copy of the length activities from 'Measures activities'. Read the questions through together. Now ask the children in their groups to work through the activities on the sheet. They can make jottings onto the sheet where they need to record or make a list.

Differentiation
Throughout this unit, place the children in mixed-ability pairs or groups. Children who appear less confident in terms of number skills may do well in work on shapes and measures, where the focus is more spatial. Check that the less confident children are fully focused on the task and are contributing to the work being done.

Review
Invite children from each group to feed back on what they have done. Ask: *Did you estimate which were longer/shorter than a metre? Did you make a good guess?* Now hide the metre sticks, then show the children the strip of paper and ask for a pair to work in front of the other children to cut the paper so that they have a piece about a metre long. Ask the other children: *Do you think they have made a good estimate?* Invite another child to check how close the estimate is by using a metre stick. Discuss how making good estimates will improve with practice.

Lesson 5 (Teach and apply)

Starter
Rehearse: Ask a child to pick two number cards up to 50. Count together from the lower up to the higher number, then back again. Ask the children to do actions (such as clapping) for each multiple of 2, 5 and 10.

Main teaching activities
Whole class: Put out in front of the children the interlocking cubes, metre sticks and canes. Explain that today you would like the children to estimate and measure items in the room and to choose appropriate units for doing this. Ask: *Look at the width of the classroom. Which unit would you choose to measure this? Metre stick? Cane? Straw? Cube? Which would be best? Why do you think that?* Encourage the children to explain why, for example, the cubes would not be suitable (so many would be needed, and there would be the issue of counting accurately how many were used). When children have decided upon a suitable unit, such as metre stick or cane, invite a child to demonstrate how they would measure the width of the classroom using the apparatus. Discuss how there is likely to be a 'bit left over' when measuring.

Group work: Ask the children to work in small groups. Explain that there are the following three activities on the board. They can make a group recording of their results on paper. Ask each group to begin with one of the activities, then to move on to another, until they have covered all three.

- *Which is longer and which is shorter: across the classroom, or along the classroom? Decide which units you will use, then estimate and measure.*
- *How long is it round your reading book? Choose your units, then estimate and measure.*
- *What would you choose to measure how tall the cupboard is? Why? Now estimate and measure.*

Differentiation

Less confident learners: Check that the children make sensible choices of unit and can explain their choice.
More confident learners: If there is time, set a challenge, such as: *How far do you think it is in metres to walk around the edge of the room?* The children can try this out!

Review

Discuss each activity in turn. Ask: *Which unit did you choose? Did you make a sensible choice? Why do you think that?* Encourage the children to explain in sentences, using the correct vocabulary.

Lesson 6 (Teach, apply and evaluate)

Starter

Read and refresh: To reinforce multiples of 2, 5 and 10, use cards up to 100. Hold up one card at a time and ask the children to: clap if it is a multiple of 2, stand up if it is a multiple of 5 and say 'Yeah' if it is a multiple of 10. Discuss why they do all three for a multiple of 10.

Main teaching activities

Whole class: Say: *Metres and centimetres are the units everyone measures with and you will be using these today.* Show the children the metre stick marked in 10 centimetres. Explain that there are 100 centimetres in a metre. Count along the metre stick in tens. Now ask the children to work in small groups, each group with a metre stick marked in 10 centimetres. Invite the children to agree where specific measurements are on the stick. Say, for example: *Where is 10cm? Now point to 30cm.* When the children are confident with this, invite a child to come to the front and to use the metre stick to measure the 50cm strip of paper. Invite the children to estimate how long the paper is. Ask the children to watch what happens. Check that the zero end of the stick is lined up accurately with one end of the paper. Write the measurement on the board and explain that it is 50 centimetres. Ask: *Has he/she made a good measure? How do you know that?*

Group work: Ask the children to estimate and then measure the following things: the height of a chair; the width of a table; the length of a table; the height of a table. Remind them that the measurements are unlikely to be 'spot on' a decade number, and that they will need to think about whether the measurement is just over or just under the nearest 10 centimetres. The children should record their estimates and measures.

Differentiation

Less confident learners: If the children are unsure about how to record the measurements, discuss how they write decade numbers.
More confident learners: Encourage children to measure accurately and to read scales to the nearest division.

Review

Discuss with the children how well they estimated. Invite a child to demonstrate how to measure the height of the chair. Discuss where to read off the measurement on the metre stick. Ask: *Is it about... just over... a bit under...?* Repeat this for other things that the children measured.

Lessons 7-8

Preparation
Check that the dial scale will weigh in 100g increments to 1kg with reasonable accuracy, and adjust if necessary.

You will need
CD resources
Enlarged weight vocabulary cards from 'Measures vocabulary' (see General resources).
Equipment
A counting stick; balances; dial scales; kilogram weights; 100g weights; Plasticine.

Learning objectives

Starter

- Read and write two-digit and three-digit numbers in figures and words; describe and extend number sequences; recognise odd and even numbers.
- Understand that halving is the inverse of doubling and derive and recall doubles of all numbers to 20, and the corresponding halves.
- Identify near doubles, from doubles already known (eg 8 + 9, 40 +41).

Main teaching activities

2006

- Follow a line of enquiry; answer questions by choosing and using suitable equipment and selecting, organising and presenting information in lists, tables and simple diagrams.
- Estimate, compare and measure lengths, weights and capacities, choosing and using standard units (m, cm, kg, litre) and suitable measuring instruments.
- Read the numbered divisions on a scale, and interpret the divisions between them (eg on a scale from 0 to 25 with intervals of 1 shown but only the divisions 0, 5, 10, 15 and 20 numbered); use a ruler to draw and measure lines to the nearest centimetre.

1999

- Estimate, measure and compare masses, using standard units (kg); suggest suitable units and equipment for such measurements.
- Read a simple scale to the nearest labelled division.

Vocabulary

kilogram, half-kilogram, gram, nearly, roughly, about, close to, about the same as, just over, just under

Lesson 7 (Review, teach and apply)

Starter

Refine: Point to jumps of 10 on a counting stick, and count with the children from zero to 100 and back in tens. Repeat, making different jumps (for example, of 30 or 20); ask the children how they knew which number went where. Do this for counting in hundreds from zero to 1000. Ask for a volunteer to use the counting stick as you have been doing for straight counting up and down in ones, tens and then hundreds. As they do this, draw three columns on the board for the ones, the tens and the hundreds numbers. Show the comparisons between 1, 10 and 100, between 2, 20 and 200 and so on, emphasising the fact that the hundreds are ten times bigger than the tens and the tens are ten times bigger than the ones. Do not let the children think that 'adding a zero' to a number makes it ten times bigger.

Main teaching activities

Whole class: Tell the children that during the next two lessons they will be estimating, measuring and comparing weights. Hold up the weight cards from 'Measures vocabulary'. Invite the children to read the words and to explain how these are used in sentences. Pass the kilogram weights around the class so that everyone has the opportunity to hold one and feel its 'weight'. Ask the children to look around the classroom and suggest some things which they think will be heavier, or lighter, than the kilogram weight. Using the bucket balance and the kilogram weight in one pan, invite a child to place one of the objects onto the other pan. Ask: *Did you make a good estimate? Which is heavier? How can you tell that by looking at the balance?* Repeat this for other suggested objects.

Now explain that the kilogram weight is too heavy to measure accurately the weight of lighter objects and that to do this we use grams. Show the children some 100g weights. Again, pass these around the class so that the children can 'feel' the weight. Explain that ten 100g weights weigh the same as 1kg. Ask if anyone can work out how many grams there are in 1kg. Agree that there are 1000g in a kilogram. Ask: *How many grams will a half-kilogram have?*

Now show the children a simple dial scale. Place the kilogram weight onto the scale. Invite a child to point to the position of the dial needle and read off 1kg. Repeat this with a 100g weight.

Group work: Ask the children to work in mixed-ability groups of about four. Tell them to tackle the following two problems, one today and one in the following lesson (it does not matter in which order they do them).

- Ask the children to find things in the classroom that they estimate are heavier, lighter and about the same weight as 100g. They check by weighing. They can record their work in a simple table. This can be repeated for other weights, such as 200g and 500g.

Object	Estimate	Measure
Pencil	Lighter than 100g	Lighter than 100g

- The children make a ball of Plasticine which they estimate weighs about 100g, then check this with a dial scale. Ask them to make Plasticine balls that weigh about 100g, 200g, 300g... to 1kg.

Differentiation

Let the children work together in mixed-ability groups. Check that the less confident learners are taking an active part in both the activities and make sure the more confident learners do not dominate proceedings.

Review

As the main part of this lesson will take more time than usual, the Review is shorter. Ask: *How many grams are there in a kilogram? How many 100g weights weigh the same as a kilogram? How many grams are there in a half-kilogram?* Invite a child to place enough 100g weights onto a dial scale to show a half-kilogram. Now ask: *How many 100g weights do we need to show 600g... 700g... ?* Invite a child to demonstrate with the weights and the dial scale.

Lesson 8 (Apply and evaluate)

Starter

Refresh and reason: Call out numbers to 10 and then, as a challenge, 15, for the children to double and write on their whiteboards. As they do this, ask them for their answers and write them on the board, then discuss the doubles of the related multiples of 10. For example: *6 doubled is 12, 60 doubled is 120 - double 6 and multiply by 10.*

Ask the children to use their skills in doubling to answer simple calculations such as 5 + 6 (double 5 +1) and 20 + 30 (double 20 + 10).

Main teaching activities

Whole class: Recap with the children what they learned in Lesson 7. Repeat the questions from the Review.

Group work: Continue with the work from Lesson 7.

Differentiation

As for Lesson 7.

Review

Review the first problem. Invite children from each group to give examples of items that weighed less, more or about the same as 100g. Ask: *How close were your estimates?* The children may comment that these improved with experience. Praise this response, because it is an important learning point. Review the results of the second problem. Invite children from each group to place one of their balls of Plasticine onto the scales and ask other children to read off how much these weigh. Encourage them to use the language of approximation, such as 'nearly', 'close', 'just over/under'... in their responses.

Lessons 9-10

Preparation
Enlarge and photocopy 'Measures vocabulary' for capacity for classroom use.

You will need
CD resources
0-9 number cards for each child, 'Measures vocabulary' for capacity (see General resources); a copy of 'Litres or millilitres?' per group. Interactive resource 'Measuring jug'.
Equipment
Bottle of water, can of cola or similar, teaspoon, measuring jug, cup, bucket, saucepan, A3 paper, scissors, glue, individual clocks.

Learning objectives

Starter
- Use units of time (seconds, minutes, hours, days) and know the relationships between them; read the time to the quarter hour; identify time intervals, including those that cross the hour.

Main teaching activities
2006
- Follow a line of enquiry; answer questions by choosing and using suitable equipment and selecting, organising and presenting information in lists, tables and simple diagrams.
- Estimate, compare and measure lengths, weights and capacities, choosing and using standard units (m, cm, kg, litre) and suitable measuring instruments.
- Read the numbered divisions on a scale, and interpret the divisions between them (eg on a scale from 0 to 25 with intervals of 1 shown but only the divisions 0, 5, 10, 15 and 20 numbered); use a ruler to draw and measure lines to the nearest centimetre.

1999
- Use and begin to read the vocabulary related to capacity.
- Estimate, measure then compare capacities, using standard units (m, litre); suggest suitable units and equipment for such measurements.
- Read a simple scale to the nearest labelled division, including using a ruler to draw and measure lines to the nearest centimetre.

Vocabulary
litre, half-litre, millilitre, full, half full

Lesson 9 (Teach and apply)

Starter
Read and reason: Give each child a clock. Ask them to find different o'clock times and show you. Repeat for half past and quarter to and quarter past. For this you may need to explain the last two times, for example, that quarter past is quarter of the way round the clock past the o' clock time.

Make up some scenarios. For example: *I left for school at 7 o'clock and got there I hour later, show me the time when I got to school.*

Main teaching activities
Whole class: Tell the children that during the next two lessons they will be estimating, measuring and comparing capacity. Ask them to tell you what they think is meant by 'capacity'. Establish that it is how much something holds and show them in 'real life' – for example, a bottle of water, a can of cola. Ask the children in pairs to think of words to do with capacity, such as *full, litre.* Hold up the capacity cards from 'Measures vocabulary' and ask the children to give themselves a point for any they thought of and then to tell you any that they had thought of that you didn't show. Discuss these. Find out who had the most points. Ask them to make up sentences including the words they thought of.

Discuss how capacity is measured, bringing in the units of litre, half litre and millilitre, using appropriate examples such as large bottles of water, cans of fizzy drinks and teaspoons of 'medicine' respectively as visual aids. Show the scale on a measuring jug and then the interactive resource 'Measuring jug'. Ask the children to tell you all they can about it. Ask questions related to the scale, likening it to a number line. Point to various places and ask how much water there would be at each.

Demonstrate measuring water into a real measuring cylinder, measuring to the amount of a litre. Show the saucepan and ask them to estimate how many litres would fill it, then demonstrate. Repeat for a bucket.

Group work: The children should work in mixed-ability groups of four or five. Ask them to tackle the following two problems, one today and one in the next lesson (it does not matter in which order they do them).

- Make a poster to show appropriate units for different amounts of liquid. The children should cut out the pictures and headings on 'Litres or millilitres?' and arrange them on A3 paper, putting the pictures of things that would be measured in litres under the heading 'litres' and picture of things that would be measured in millilitres under the heading 'millilitres'.
- Provide a plastic beaker or cup, a measuring cylinder and water. The children should estimate how many beakers will make a litre and then try it out, comparing their estimate with the real amount. They repeat with different-sized cups or beakers. They could record their work on a table like the one below.

	Estimate	**Actual**
1st cup		
2nd cup		

Differentiation

Let the children work together in mixed-ability groups. Check that the less confident learners are taking an active part in both the activities and make sure the more confident learners do not dominate proceedings.

Review

Discuss the work the children have done and ask them to tell you what they have learned during the lesson.

Lesson 10 (Review, apply and evaluate)

Starter

Read and reason: Repeat the Starter from Lesson 9 but include digital time for o'clock and half past. Write these on the board and they can show you using their clocks. You will probably need to explain that 3:00 is no minutes past 3, therefore 3 o'clock, and that 3:30 is 30 minutes past and therefore half past 3.

Main teaching activities

Whole class: Review with the children what they learned in Lesson 9.
Group work: Continue with the work from Lesson 9. The children should complete whichever activity they did not tackle in the previous lesson.

Differentiation

As for Lesson 9.

Review

Ask the children to self-assess how well they completed their tasks in the last two lessons. Finally, ask them to tell a partner something that they learned during these two lessons that they didn't know before.

Name ______________________ Date ________________

Favourite food

Pictogram to show Class 4's favourite food

Salad	   
Pizza	        
Fish fingers	       
Fruit	      
Cereal	  
Vegetables	 
	1 2 3 4 5 6 7 8 9

Pictogram to show our favourite food

Name ______________________ Date ______________________

Popular sports

Look at the sports block graph.

Talk with your group. Tell each other some facts from the graph.

Cut out the pictures and numbers that come with the graph.

Look at the graph to work out how many votes each sport has.

Match each sport picture to the number of votes, like this:

13

Answer these questions:

1. Which is the most popular sport? ______________________
2. Which is the least popular sport? ______________________
3. How many children voted altogether? ☐
4. How many more children voted for tennis than for riding? ☐
5. What was the total vote for skiing and swimming? ☐
6. Which is more popular, football or rugby? How do you know? ______________________

____

Make up some questions of your own. Write them here:

1.

____

2.

____

3.

____

Unit 2 2 weeks

Handling data and measures

Lesson	Strands	Starter	Main teaching activities
1. Review and practise	Use/apply Data	**Use units of time (seconds, minutes, hours, days) and know the relationships between them; read the time to the quarter hour; identify time intervals, including those that cross the hour.**	• Follow a line of enquiry; answer questions by choosing and using suitable equipment and selecting, organising and presenting information in lists, tables and simple diagrams. • Answer a question by collecting and recording data in lists and tables; represent the data as block graphs or pictograms to show results; use ICT to organise and present data. **• Use lists, tables and diagrams to sort objects; explain choices using appropriate language, including 'not'.**
2. Review, teach and apply	Use/apply Data	Describe and extend number sequences.	As for Lesson 1
3. Apply	Use/apply Data	As for Lesson 2	As for Lesson 1
4. Teach and apply	Use/apply Data	**Derive and recall all addition and subtraction facts for each number to at least 10, all pairs with totals to 20 and all pairs of multiples of 10 with totals up to 100.**	As for Lesson 1
5. Apply and evaluate	Use/apply Data	Derive and recall multiplication facts for the 2, 5 and 10 times-tables and the related division facts.	As for Lesson 1
6. Review and apply	Use/apply Measures	Read and write two-digit and three-digit numbers in figures and words; describe and extend number sequences and recognise odd and even numbers.	• Follow a line of enquiry; answer questions by choosing and using suitable equipment and selecting, organising and presenting information in lists, tables and simple diagrams. • Estimate, compare and measure lengths, weights and capacities, choosing and using standard units (m, cm, kg, litre) and suitable measuring instruments. • Read the numbered divisions on a scale, and interpret the divisions between them (eg on a scale from 0 to 25 with intervals of 1 shown but only the divisions 0, 5, 10, 15 and 20 numbered); use a ruler to draw and measure lines to the nearest centimetre.
7. Review and apply	Use/apply Measures	Understand that halving is the inverse of doubling and derive and recall doubles of all numbers to 20, and the corresponding halves.	As for Lesson 6
8. Teach and practise	Use/apply Measures	As for Lesson 6	As for Lesson 6
9. Review and apply	Use/apply Measures	As for Lesson 6	As for Lesson 6
10. Apply and evaluate	Use/apply Measures	**Use units of time (seconds, minutes, hours, days) and know the relationships between them; read the time to the quarter hour; identify time intervals, including those that cross the hour.**	As for Lesson 6

Speaking and listening objective

- Ensure everyone contributes, allocate tasks, consider alternatives and reach agreement.

Introduction

The first five lessons of this block focus on collecting, organising, presenting and analysing data in tables, lists, pictograms and block charts. The children are encouraged to evaluate the different methods of data handling with regard to their suitability in each case. The rest of the block concentrates on the three measures of length, mass and capacity, where the children are expected to estimate, compare and measure using standard units. Reading scales and interpreting the divisions is regularly revisited throughout this part of the block through demonstrating, modelling and practical measuring. The using and applying aspect of the mathematics is threaded throughout the block and can be identified in each lesson, as can the speaking and listening objective.

Using and applying mathematics

- Follow a line of enquiry; answer questions by choosing and using suitable equipment and selecting, organising and presenting information in lists, tables and simple diagrams.

Lessons 1-5

Preparation

Make an A3 copy of the 'Up the mountain' gameboard. Copy 'Organising data vocabulary cards' onto A3 card and cut out. Make OHTs of 'Ways to organise data', 'Pictograms' and 'Sports block graph'. Draw smiley faces on some sticky notes. On squared paper, draw horizontal and vertical axes and label them 'Number of children' and 'Colour of paint' respectively, with the title 'Which colour?' Prepare another A1 sheet with vertical and horizontal axes, labelled 'Number of children' and 'Favourite sport', the numbers 1-20 on the vertical axis and the title 'Favourite sports'.

You will need

Photocopiable pages
'Lists and tables' (page 117) and 'Our sports graph' (page 118) for each child.
CD resources
'0-100 number cards', 'Up the mountain' gameboard, 'Up the mountain 2', 'Function machine game' for each child, 'Organising data vocabulary cards', acetates of 'Ways to organise data', 'Pictograms' and 'Sports block graph' (see General resources); 'Lists and tables', 'Which colour?', and 'Our sports graph', support and extension versions.
Equipment
Card clocks; counters; counting stick; a pendulum; class 100 square; individual whiteboards and pens; OHP; sticky notes; A1 squared paper; Blu-Tack.

Learning objectives

Starter

- Use units of time (seconds, minutes, hours, days) and know the relationships between them; read the time to the quarter hour; identify time intervals, including those that cross the hour.
- Describe and extend number sequences.
- Derive and recall all addition and subtraction facts for each number to at least 10, all pairs with totals to 20 and all pairs of multiples of 10 with totals up to 100.
- Derive and recall multiplication facts for the 2, 5 and 10 times-tables and the related division facts.

Main teaching activities

2006
- Follow a line of enquiry; answer questions by choosing and using suitable equipment and selecting, organising and presenting information in lists, tables and simple diagrams.
- Answer a question by collecting and recording data in lists and tables; represent the data as block graphs or pictograms to show results; use ICT to organise and present data.
- Use lists, tables and diagrams to sort objects; explain choices using appropriate language, including 'not'.

1999
- Solve a given problem by sorting, classifying and organising information in simple ways.
- Discuss and explain results.
- Solve a given problem by sorting, classifying and organising information in simple ways.

Vocabulary

count, tally, sort, vote, graph, block graph, pictogram, represent, group, set, list, label, title, most popular, least popular, most common, least common

Lesson 1 (Review and practise)

Starter

Refine, read and rehearse: Blu-Tack the 'Up the mountain' gameboard to the board. Give each child a card clock. Divide the class into two teams and play the first game on 'Up the mountain 2'. As well as asking for times such as 4 o'clock, half past seven or quarter to 6, say: *Find half past 3. Now find one hour later... half an hour earlier.*

Main teaching activities

Whole class: Remind the children of last term's work on organising and using data. Ask: *Can you remember what we mean by 'data' and 'organising and using data'? What words can we think of about this topic?* Write any words they say on the board, and use the vocabulary cards to prompt when necessary. Discuss the meanings of these words. Ask who remembers the ways of organising data that they used in Unit 1. List them: *counting, tallying, sorting, voting and making graphs, such as block graphs and pictograms.* Explain that these are ways we can represent, group or list information. This saves us having to write lots of words, and helps us to see information easily. It also helps us to find out what things are most or least popular and common.

Show the OHTs of 'Ways to organise data', 'Sports block graph' and 'Pictograms' to revise the ways of organising information. For each type of display (list, table, block graph and pictogram), ask questions such as: *How is the information shown here? What does it tell us? What four things can you tell me from this table? Which is the most popular... ? Which is the least common... ? How many people were asked?*

Paired work: Ask the children to work in pairs, making a list and a table and answering some questions about them. Distribute the 'Lists and tables' activity sheet. Demonstrate how to answer the questions, using the examples provided.

Differentiation

Less confident learners: Provide the support version of 'Lists and tables' with a simpler list and table.

More confident learners: Ask children who finish early to make up a table of other things that they like and dislike, and to write some questions about it.

Review

Ask a few pairs to share their work on the photocopiable sheet. They need to explain how they decided which numbers and words to put in their list and table, and how they found the answers to the questions. Now ask other children to show their own lists, tables and questions. Can the class answer their questions?

Lesson 2 (Review, teach and apply)

Starter

Refine and rehearse: Use the pendulum to count with the children on and back in steps of five, then three and four. Encourage them to use fingers, so that when you stop counting they can tell you how many lots of 4 (for example) make 24. Remind them that when they count from zero they are counting in 'lots of' or 'multiples of' the number. Use the counting stick to count in these steps from and back to other small numbers (for example, count in fives from 2 to 77, in threes from 5 to 35 and in fours from 7 to 47).

Main teaching activities

Whole class: The whole-class work will take one lesson and the group work another lesson. Show the 'Pictograms' OHT. Ask: *What is this called? Give me as much information from it as you can.* Tell the children that they are going to solve this problem using a pictogram: *The school caretaker needs to paint the door of our classroom. He has some paints in his shed, but doesn't know which colour to use. He wants your advice. He wants to find out which is the most popular colour. Here are the colour choices: red, yellow, blue, brown and orange.* Give the children some time to talk to a friend and discuss their favourite colour. Make a tally of their choices on the board. Say: *Each smiley face represents one child. How many faces do we need for red?* Invite some children to add the sticky notes with a smiley face on each to your A1 skeleton pictogram. Repeat for the other four colours.

Review

Analyse the class pictogram with the children, asking them to tell you as many facts about it as possible, ask each other questions and come to a conclusion about which paint is most popular.

Lesson 3 (Apply)

Starter

Read and recall: Invite children to take turns to pick a two-digit number card from your pack, and ask the others to write on their whiteboards the number that is one or ten more or less than that number. Encourage any children who are struggling to look at the class 100 square.

Main teaching activities

Group work: Discuss and review the pictogram work in Lesson 2. Explain that today the children will be answering questions from a pictogram and making up their own. Distribute and model the 'Which colour?' CD page. The children could work in mixed-ability pairs; if you prefer them to work in ability groups, use the differentiation on the left.

Differentiation

Less confident learners: Provide adult help to encourage the children to talk about the graph.
More confident learners: Ask children who finish early to make up some questions for the class to answer.

Review

Work through the questions on 'Which colour?'. Invite a few pairs to share the pictograms they made up. Invite more confident children to ask the class their questions. Finally, ask the class to make up some more questions. Assess how confidently they give correct answers.

Lesson 4 (Teach and apply)

Starter

Recall: Write a number up to 10 on the board. Ask the children to write as many addition and subtraction facts for this number as they can in one minute (or two minutes, depending on the number). For example, given 4 they could write: 1 + 3 = 4; 2 + 2 = 4; 4 - 2 = 2; 4 - 1 = 3; 4 - 3 = 1. Discuss their answers, taking one each from several children. Ask less confident children to share their answers first.

Main teaching activities

Whole class: The whole-class work will take one lesson and the group work another lesson. Explain that the children are now going to look at block graphs. Ask: *Who can remember this?* Show the OHT of 'Sports block graph'. Ask the children to tell you as much as they can about it. Encourage them to state all possible facts. Ask children who may find this difficult first, when the more obvious facts have not already been said. If your class is quite competitive, divide them into two teams and play 'Spot the info', using the 'Up the mountain' gameboard and counters. Every time a team spots a new piece of information, they can move their counter two steps closer to the top of the mountain. Ask the children to turn to their neighbours and discuss why this is a useful way to tell people about favourite sports. (Look for: *it is a picture; it is clear and simple; it is easy to interpret.*)

Now say: *We are going to make our own block graph to show our favourite sports.* Collect about six examples of sports the children like. Ask them to choose their favourite one from the list. Give them each a sticky note and ask them to draw a stick picture of themselves playing the sport on it. While they are doing this, write the sport names and appropriate numbers (for the vertical axis) on sticky notes.

Review

Gather the class together. Show them your labels and numbers, and invite children to stick them onto your A1 skeleton graph. Ask them to explain why they have put them in those places. Do the other children agree? Now invite everyone to come to the front and add their stick picture to the correct column, starting from the horizontal axis. Discuss what this graph shows, and ask questions (particularly of the *How many more/less...* type). Encourage the class to ask each other similar questions, perhaps after talking to a friend and making up a question together. Finally, ask: *Which is the most popular sport for this class?*

Lesson 5 (Apply and evaluate)

Starter

Refresh and reason: Recite the two-, five- and ten-times tables with the children. Now count in multiples of 2, 5 and 10, using fingers. Stop the children at various intervals, asking which finger they have reached and how many lots of 2, 5 or 10 that is. Give each child a laminated 'Function machine game'. Ask them to write any numbers from 1 to 10 on the input side and '× 2' in the middle; then, when you say *Go*, to fill in the output side as quickly as possible. Ask them to rub out the outputs and replace × 2 with × 10, then write the new outputs. Repeat with × 5. Finally, to reinforce the link between multiplication and division, call out a few products for the children to tell you or write down the table facts that go with them. For example, call out 20, and they should write 10 × 2 or 2 × 10.

Main teaching activities

Group work: Show the class block graph from Lesson 4. Say: *Today you are going to make your own block graph. You need to help* (name the PE coordinator) *decide what things to buy for the sports cupboard.* Model what the children must do, using large squared paper: *With your partner, you need to choose five sports that we play - or you'd like to play - at school. You need to finish a skeleton graph like the one we used yesterday* (show this) *by adding labels like this* (label the axes and fill in sports and numbers up to 9, as on the 'Our sports graph' activity sheet). Use 1-9 number cards to pick the number of children that choose each sport. *Once you have picked a card, you cannot use it again. Draw blocks of the right height for each sport - so if you pick 5, colour in five squares above that sport.*

Differentiation

Less confident learners: Provide the support version of 'Our sports graph' with pre-labelled axes and five numbers to use.

More confident learners: Provide the extension version with no numbers on the graph. If you think any children may be able to draw the graph on squared paper, let them have a go.

Review

Ask each pair to join with another pair, share their graphs and say four facts that their graph shows. Invite pairs to share their graphs and facts with the class. Let the more confident group ask the class a few of their questions. Recap on this unit by asking questions such as: *Why are lists, tables, pictograms and block graphs useful for showing information? What is the difference between a list and a table? What does a pictogram look like? What about a block graph?*

Lessons 6-10

Preparation

Prepare vocabulary cards for each of the measures from 'Measures vocabulary'. Cut out sets of 'Length cards' and 'Capacity cards'. Enlarge and copy a selection of the pairs of near doubles cards from the 'Near doubles cards'. Before each lesson, set out the equipment ready for use by groups of four. Copy 'Class R's fruit shop 2' instructions onto card, one for each group working on the problem.

You will need

Photocopiable pages

'Class R's fruit shop 1' (page 119) instructions for each group.

Learning objectives

Starter

- Read and write two-digit and three-digit numbers in figures and words; describe and extend number sequences and recognise odd and even numbers.
- Understand that halving is the inverse of doubling and derive and recall doubles of all numbers to 20, and the corresponding halves.
- Use units of time (seconds, minutes, hours, days) and know the relationships between them; read the time to the quarter hour; identify time intervals, including those that cross the hour.

Main teaching activities

2006

- Follow a line of enquiry; answer questions by choosing and using suitable equipment and selecting, organising and presenting information in lists, tables and simple diagrams.
- Estimate, compare and measure lengths, weights and capacities, choosing and using standard units (m, cm, kg, litre) and suitable measuring instruments.

CD resources
A set of 'Near doubles cards', 'Measures vocabulary', 'Lengths', 'Capacities' (see General resources); 'Measuring jugs'; 'Class R's fruit shop 2'. Interactive resource 'Measuring jug'.

Equipment
Digit cards; rulers; metre sticks; strips of coloured paper about 2cm wide; glue; scissors; calculators; Plasticine or dough; two 500g weights; two objects weighing 0.5kg; two scales (kitchen and/or balance); variety of containers, bottles for measuring litres, cartons for amounts in millilitres, measuring jugs; clocks.

- Read the numbered divisions on a scale, and interpret the divisions between them (eg on a scale from 0 to 25 with intervals of 1 shown but only the divisions 0, 5, 10, 15 and 20 numbered); use a ruler to draw and measure lines to the nearest centimetre.

1999

- Use and begin to read the vocabulary related to length, mass and capacity.
- Estimate, measure and compare masses using standard units; suggest suitable units and equipment for such measurements.
- Read a simple scale to the nearest labelled division, including using a ruler to draw and measure lines to the nearest centimetre, recording estimates and measurements as '3 and a bit metres long' or 'about 8 centimetres' or 'nearly 3 kilograms heavy'.

Vocabulary

length, width, height, depth, long, short, tall, high, low, metre, centimetre, ruler, metre stick, tape measure, weight, compare, measuring scale, guess, estimate, nearly, roughly, about, close to, about the same as, just over, just under, balance, scales, lighter, heaviest, weigh, weighs, balances, capacity, full, half full, empty, holds, contains, litre, half litre, millilitre, container

Lesson 6 (Review and apply)

Starter

Rehearse, refresh and read: Practise reading two-digit and three-digit numbers. Ask the children to set out their number cards in order from 0 to 9. While they are getting ready, ask the class simple things like: *Show me four... seven... one more than 8... one less than 4... three more than 9; Double it.* Now ask the children to put a 3 in front of them, then make the 3 into 53, then make 253. Ask them to swap the 2 and the 5. Ask one of the less confident children to read the digits, then invite any child to read the actual number. Repeat several times.

Main teaching activities

Whole class: Say: *Over the next few days you will be solving problems that involve length, weight and capacity.* Explain that you would like them to help your teacher friend Miss Singh to sort out some classroom resources. Her class is going to be working on comparing lengths and she would like them to make strips of paper to different lengths for them to compare. Discuss the vocabulary for length and then display all the words from 'Measures vocabulary'. Ask the children to identify any they hadn't thought of. Sort them into descriptive words, units of measure and measuring equipment, discussing the meaning of each with examples as appropriate. Remind the children that they need to make strips of paper to compare and ask how they might do this. Aim towards measuring different lengths using a ruler. Use a ruler to demonstrate how to measure in centimetres.

Paired work: The children should work in mixed-ability pairs for this activity. Give each pair a selection of 'Lengths', strips of paper, scissors, ruler and metre stick. Make glue available for when they need it. Their task is to cut the strips to the lengths on their cards as accurately as possible. If they have lengths longer then the strips, they need to glue some together.

Differentiation
This could be according to the cards you give the children: some may benefit from measuring multiples of 10cm, others might be able to measure to the nearest centimetre.

Review

Take feedback from the activity, comparing strips. Ask: *Which of these is the longest/shortest? How long do you think this is?* Show a strip that is 20cm in length and say: *This strip is 20cm long. How could you use this to help you find a book that is about 40cm tall? How could you use it to find a book that is about 10cm wide? Show me how you would use it to check that this book is about 23cm tall.*

Lesson 7 (Review and apply)

Starter

Refine and reason: Explain that you will hold up the 'Near doubles cards' you have prepared: *If I hold up 5 and 6, you need to use a double and adjust to find the answer, so you will write down 10 + 1 or 12 - 1.* You will then ask someone what the answer is. The children should write on their whiteboards. Encourage both methods of doubling and adjusting. Use 9 and 10 as an example of a near double where it is quicker to double 10 and subtract than to double 9 and add. Do this for numbers to 20 and some near multiples of 10.

Main teaching activities

Whole class and group work: Say: *Miss Singh was really pleased with the work you did in the last lesson and her class was able to get a really good idea of how to compare length. She wants you to help again.* Recap the work the children did, include vocabulary, show examples of the strips they made and ask them to estimate how long each is. Explain that today Miss Singh wants them to help with something to do with weight. Discuss and sort the appropriate vocabulary as in Lesson 6. Give the children the 'Class R's fruit shop 1' and '2', and model the problem using the teacher's notes. Then ask the children to complete the problem in groups.

Differentiation

Less confident learners: If necessary, provide adult support for these children as they work through the activity sheets.
More confident learners: Encourage these children to explain how they worked out their answers.

Review

Compare the like fruits from two groups. Ask questions such as: *Which of these do you think is the heaviest/lightest? Why? Do you think this apple will be the same weight as the banana? Why/why not?* Put each fruit on the scales to find out. *How many of these fruits do you think will weigh a kilogram?* Use the scales to see how close the children's estimates were.

Lesson 8 (Teach and practise)

Starter

Refine, rehearse and read: Ask the children to follow your instructions, writing and changing two-digit numbers on their whiteboards. They should record all of the numbers. For example: *Write 10. Double it.* (20) *Add 5.* (25) *Add 100.* (125) *Swap the 5 and the 1. What is your number?* (521)

Main teaching activities

Whole class: Say: *There are 3kg of apples in a box. How many kilograms of apples are there in two boxes?* Invite responses and ask: *How did you work that out?* Write the number sentence 3 × 2 = 6 onto the board. Now say: *A bag of sugar weighs 2kg. How many bags will I need to buy so that I have 10kg of sugar?* Again, ask for responses, how the children worked out their answer, and write the number sentence 2 × 5 = 10 onto the board. Discuss how the children can use their mental calculation strategies to solve weight problems.

Individual work: Write some word problems onto the board for the children to solve, such as:

- *There are two parcels to be delivered which weigh 22kg and 15kg. How much do the parcels weigh altogether?*
- *There are five packs of carpet tiles. Each pack weighs 3kg. How much do the packs weigh in total?*
- *A box of books weighs 25kg. Another box weighs 33kg. What is the difference in their weights?*
- (Two-step problem) *There are 12 packets of flour in a stack on the shelves, each weighing 1kg. The shopkeeper puts another 15 packets of flour onto the stack. A customer buys five of the packs. How many kilograms of flour are left?*

Once the children have answered these problems, encourage them to make up some of their own.

Review

Review the problems together. Invite children from each group to explain how they worked out their answers, and which mental strategies they used. Invite a child to write the appropriate number sentence onto the board. Ask: *How did you work this out? Who chose a different way to do this? Is there another way? Which way do you think is best? Why do you think that?*

Differentiation

Less confident learners: You may like to work with these children and discuss each problem and how it could be solved.
More confident learners: You may wish to provide more complex problems for the children to solve.

Lesson 9 (Review and apply)

Starter

Refine, rehearse and read: As for Lesson 8.

Main teaching activities

The following two lessons are about capacity and the activities can be tackled in any order. You may wish to divide the class into two groups, one tackling the practical Lesson 9 activity and the other Lesson 10 and then swap during your next lesson.

Whole class: Remind the children of your friend Miss Singh and ask them to tell you how they helped her. Say: *Miss Singh would like your help again. Her class is going to be working on comparing capacities and she would like you to think of something that might help her class to do this.* Discuss the vocabulary for capacity, include all the words from the vocabulary on the CD. Display the words and ask the children to identify any they haven't thought of. Sort them into descriptive words, units of measure and measuring equipment, discussing the meaning of each with examples as appropriate. Ask the children to tell you what they might be able to do to help Miss Singh's class compare capacities. Encourage them towards saying that they could fill different containers to different capacities.

Show the interactive resource 'Measuring jug' and set the maximum to 1000, explaining that this is 1 litre and that the smaller marks are millilitres. Set the scale to 50. Count in 100s to 1000, and discuss halfway marks, for example, between 100 and 200. Ask them to tell you what these are. Show litre bottles, drinks cartons for millilitre measures and fill the cylinder to these amounts and others, asking the children to write down the measurements on their whiteboards.

Group work 1: The children should work in mixed-ability groups for this activity. Give each group a selection of cards from the 'Capacities' sheet, containers, measuring jugs and access to water. Their task is to estimate and then measure the capacities on the cards.

Group work 2: The children should work in mixed-ability pairs within their groups for this activity. Give each pair a selection of cards from the 'Capacities' sheet as well as a copy of 'Measuring jugs'. Their task is to order the cards from least to most and then mark the levels on the measuring jugs as they think best.

Review

Take feedback from the children about the practical activity, comparing containers: *Which of these has the most/least in? How much do you think is in here? Which containers do you think will hold just a little more than a litre? What do you notice about half a litre and 500ml?* Tell the children that they will be looking at the measuring jug activity in more detail during the following lesson.

Differentiation

Differentiate by providing the children with different capacity cards – some are specific amounts (eg 500ml) while others are not (eg 'Just under 1 litre').

Lesson 10 (Apply and evaluate)

Starter

Read, refresh and reason: Call out analogue and digital times for the children to find on their clocks. Ask questions such as: *My clock is half an hour fast, it says 3:30, what time is it really? I left home at a quarter past ten and walked to the shops. It took an hour. What time did I get there?*

Main teaching activities

Whole class: Recap the main points of Lesson 9, reinforcing vocabulary, sorting the vocabulary cards into descriptive words, units of measure and measuring equipment. Discuss what Miss Singh had asked them to do and take feedback from those who did the measuring activity. Show the interactive resource 'Measuring jug' again; set the maximum to 1000, reminding them that this is 1 litre and that the smaller marks are millilitres. Set the scale to 50. Count in 100s to 1000, and discuss halfway marks as before. Turn the tap by clicking on it and fill the cylinder to a 100 or halfway mark; stop the tap and ask them to write down how full it is. Ask questions such as: *If I added another 100ml, where would my 'water' be?* Repeat this several times. Empty some water out of the cylinder by clicking on the drain tap and ask questions in a similar way to before.

Group work: The children should undertake whichever task they didn't do in Lesson 9.

Review

Repeat the Review from Lesson 9 briefly, and then use the interactive resource 'Measuring jug' and volunteers to demonstrate the work the children did with marking the measuring jugs with the capacities on the cards. Order all the capacity cards, from least to most. Ask the children what they have learned through their measuring work on lengths, weights and capacity.

Differentiation

As for Lesson 9.

Name ______________________ Date ______________

Lists and tables

Make a list of more than 5 odd numbers.

Like this: Now it's your turn. Don't use mine!

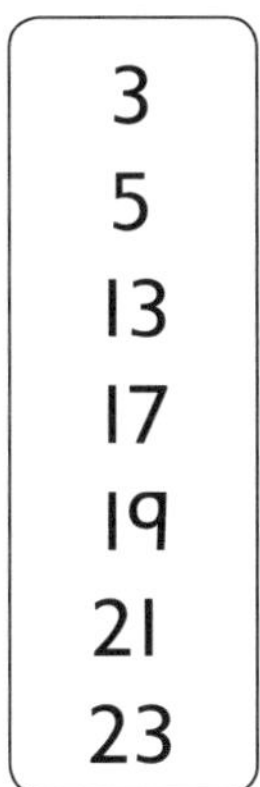

How many numbers are there in your list?

Which is the highest number?

Which is the lowest number?

Make a table to show the colours you both like and the colours you don't like.

Like this:

Sal likes	Rob likes	Sal doesn't like	Rob doesn't like
Red	Blue	Black	Pink
Pink	Black	Brown	Yellow
Blue	Silver	Grey	Purple
Yellow	Orange	Orange	Grey

Now you try:

________ likes	________ likes	______ doesn't like	______ doesn't like

Which colours do you both like?

Which colours do you both not like?

What are your favourite colours?

Name ______________________ Date ______________

Our sports graph

Label the side and bottom boxes. Use these words to help you:

Number of children **Sports**

Choose five sports and write them in the five boxes at the bottom of the graph.
Use 1–9 number cards to pick the number of children that choose each sport.
When you have picked a card, you cannot use it again.
Colour in that number of squares above the sport.

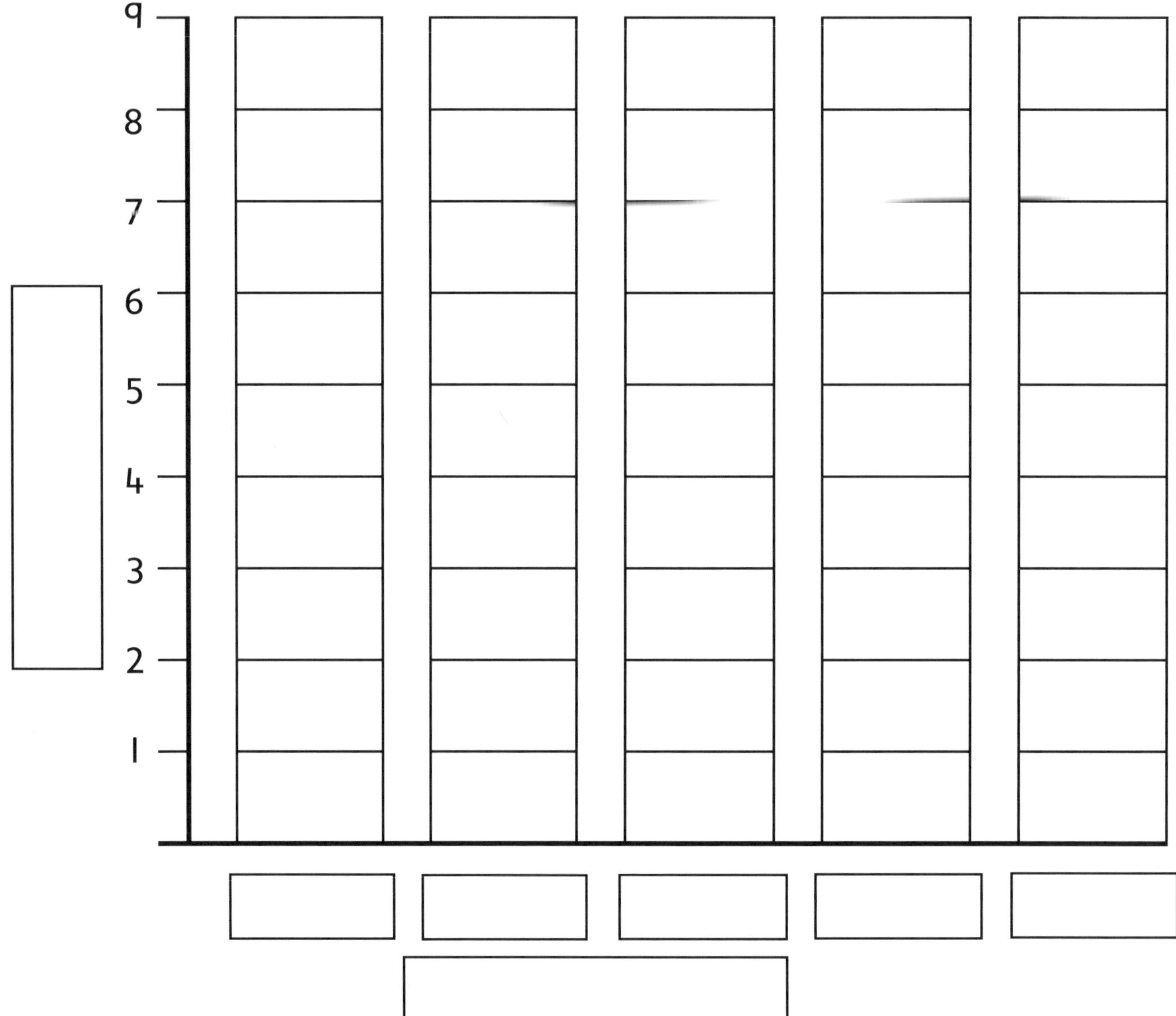

What does your graph tell you?

Write down as many points as you can on the back of this sheet.

Name ______________________ Date ______________

Class R's fruit shop 1

Notes for the teacher or classroom assistant:
Explain to the children that this problem involves your teacher friend Miss Singh, who wants to make a shop in her classroom for her Year R children to use. She'd like your class to help by making some fruit out of Plasticine or play dough.

Give each group 1kg of Plasticine (or another malleable modelling material) and something that weighs 0.5kg (such as a 500g weight or jar of coffee).

Model exactly what you expect the children to do:
- Break the Plasticine into four pieces.
- Pick up the 0.5kg weight. Take a piece of Plasticine to make an apple and compare it with the weight (without actually weighing it). Take from or add to the Plasticine to make what you estimate to be less than 0.5kg. When you think you are about right, make the apple. Repeat this for the orange and banana. For the melon, you need to estimate more than 0.5kg.
- You must use all the Plasticine. Adjust the amounts until you are happy that all the model fruits have the correct weight.

After you have modelled this part of the activity, ask the children to have a go.

When they have done this, stop the children and model how to read 500g or 0.5kg on a set of kitchen scales. They need to use the scales to measure the weight of their model fruit. If you have a group of children who are not able to use top pan scales, they can use balance scales, putting their fruit on one side and the 500g weight on the other.

Unit 3 2 weeks

Handling data and measures

Speaking and listening objective

- Explain their views to others in a small group; decide how to report the group's views to the class.

Introduction

The first five lessons of this block focus on collecting, organising, presenting and analysing data in tables, lists, pictograms and block charts. The children are encouraged to evaluate the different methods of data handling with regard to their suitability in each case. They are given the opportunity to apply their knowledge in this area to solve problems, so making handling data purposeful to them. The rest of the block concentrates on the three measures of length, mass and capacity, where the children are expected to estimate, compare and measure using standard units. Reading scales and interpreting the divisions is regularly revisited throughout this part of the block through demonstrating, modelling and practical measuring. The using and applying aspect of the mathematics is threaded throughout the block and can be identified in each lesson, as can the speaking and listening objective.

Lesson	Strands	Starter	Main teaching activities
1. Review and practise	Use/apply Data	**Use units of time (seconds, minutes, hours, days) and know the relationships between them; read the time to the quarter hour; identify time intervals, including those that cross the hour.**	• Follow a line of enquiry; answer questions by choosing and using suitable equipment and selecting, organising and presenting information in lists, tables and simple diagrams. • Answer a question by collecting and recording data in lists and tables; represent the data as block graphs or pictograms to show results; use ICT to organise and present data. **• Use lists, tables and diagrams to sort objects; explain choices using appropriate language, including 'not'.**
2. Review, teach and apply	Use/apply Data	Describe and extend number sequences.	As for Lesson 1
3. Apply and evaluate	Use/apply Data	As for Lesson 2	As for Lesson 1
4. Review, teach and practise	Use/apply Data	**Derive and recall all addition and subtraction facts for each number to at least 10.**	As for Lesson 1
5. Apply and evaluate	Use/apply Data	Derive and recall multiplication facts for the 2, 5 and 10 times-tables and the related division facts.	As for Lesson 1
6. Review and practise	Use/apply Measures	• Read and write two-digit and three-digit numbers in figures and words. **• Explain what each digit in a two-digit number represents, including numbers where 0 is a place holder.**	• Follow a line of enquiry; answer questions by choosing and using suitable equipment and selecting, organising and presenting information in lists, tables and simple diagrams. • Estimate, compare and measure weights choosing and using standard units (kg) and suitable measuring instruments. • Read the numbered divisions on a scale, and interpret the divisions between them (eg on a scale from 0 to 25 with intervals of 1 shown but only the divisions 0, 5, 10, 15 and 20 numbered).
7. Teach and apply	Use/apply Measures	**State the subtraction corresponding to a given addition, and vice versa.**	As for Lesson 6
8. Teach and apply	Use/apply Measures	Understand that halving is the inverse of doubling and derive and recall doubles of all numbers to 20, and the corresponding halves.	As for Lesson 6
9. Teach and apply	Use/apply Measures	As for Lesson 1	As for Lesson 6
10. Practise and evaluate	Use/apply Measures	As for Lesson 6	As for Lesson 6

Using and applying mathematics

- Follow a line of enquiry; answer questions by choosing and using suitable equipment and selecting, organising and presenting information in lists, tables and simple diagrams.

Lessons 1-5

Preparation

Make an A3 copy of the 'Up the mountain' gameboard. Copy 'Organising data vocabulary cards' onto A3 card and cut out.

You will need

Photocopiable pages
'Table information' (page 128) for each pair.
CD resources
'0-100 number cards', 'Up the mountain' gameboard, 'Up the mountain 2', 'Function machine game' for each child, 'Organising data vocabulary cards', 'Sports block graph' (see General resources); copies of 'Which colour?'
Equipment
Blue-Tack, card clocks; counters; counting stick; a pendulum; class 100 square; sticky notes; dice.

Learning objectives

Starter

- Use units of time (seconds, minutes, hours, days) and know the relationships between them; read the time to the quarter hour; identify time intervals, including those that cross the hour.
- Describe and extend number sequences.
- Derive and recall all addition and subtraction facts for each number to at least 10.
- Derive and recall multiplication facts for the 2, 5 and 10 times-tables and the related division facts.

Main teaching activities

2006

- Follow a line of enquiry; answer questions by choosing and using suitable equipment and selecting, organising and presenting information in lists, tables and simple diagrams.
- Answer a question by collecting and recording data in lists and tables; represent the data as block graphs or pictograms to show results; use ICT to organise and present data.
- Use lists, tables and diagrams to sort objects; explain choices using appropriate language, including 'not'.

1999

- Solve a given problem by sorting, classifying and organising information in simple ways.
- Discuss and explain results.

Vocabulary

count, tally, sort, vote, graph, block graph, pictogram, represent, group, set, list, label, title, most/least popular, most/least common

Lesson 1 (Review and practise)

Starter

Read and refresh: Blu-Tack the 'Up the mountain' gameboard to the board. Give each child a card clock. Divide the class into two teams and play 'Up the mountain 2', game 1. As well as asking for times such as 8 o'clock, half past three, quarter to 9 and quarter past 11, say: *Find quarter past 7. Now find one hour later... half an hour earlier. My clock shows 2:30. It is 15 minutes slow. What time should it show?*

Main teaching activities

Whole class: Remind the children of the work they did on organising and using data in Units 1 and 2. Ask: *Can you remember what we mean by 'data' and 'organising and using data'? What words can we use about this topic?* Write any words they say on the board, and use the vocabulary cards to prompt when necessary. Discuss the meanings of these words. Ask who remembers the ways of organising data: counting, tallying, sorting, voting and making graphs, such as block graphs and pictograms. Recap that these are ways we can represent, group or list information, that they save us having to write lots of words and help us to see information easily.

Focus on lists and tables. As a class, make up some categories for lists, for

example, food, shapes, colours, and ask the children to think of examples to go in each. During their paired activity they will focus on tables.
Paired work: The children should work in pairs. Give each pair a copy of 'Table information'. Discuss the example. There are an additional three sets of information. The children should choose two to put into two tables and then make up questions from them for the rest of the class to answer during the Review.

Differentiation

Less confident learners: This group should work on one set of information. Provide them with a table frame.
More confident learners: This group should work on all the sets, making three tables in all.

Review

Ask two pairs to work together to ask each other questions from their tables. They should then choose the best two questions to ask everyone.

Lesson 2 (Review, teach and apply)

Starter

Recall: Use the pendulum to count with the children on and back in steps of five, then three and four. Encourage them to use their fingers, so that when you stop counting they can tell you how many lots of 4, for example, make 24. Include corresponding divisions saying, for example: *What would I divide 24 by to give 4?*

Main teaching activities

Whole class: The class will be focusing on pictograms and completing a similar activity to that in Block C, Unit 2, Lesson 2. Today's lesson is a whole-class lesson. Remind them of the school caretaker's problem and the paint by showing 'Which colour?'. Say that today they are going to solve another problem using a pictogram: *Ivan Apple owns a fruit shop. He needs to order some more fruit but doesn't know which type to ask for. He wants your advice. He wants to find out which are the most popular fruits.* Give the children some time to talk to a friend and discuss their favourite fruit. Make a tally of their choices on the board. Draw a labelled skeleton pictogram. Say: *Each smiley face represents one child. How many faces do we need for apples?* Focus on one fruit at a time and invite some children to draw smiley faces onto your skeleton pictogram according to the tally results. Repeat for the other fruits. Keep this for the next lesson.

Review

Analyse the class pictogram with the children, asking them to tell you as many facts about it as possible. Say: *Ivan Apple wants to order four different fruits.* Come to a conclusion about which fruits he should order.

Lesson 3 (Apply and evaluate)

Starter

Read and rehearse: Invite the children to take turns to pick a two-digit number card from your pack, and ask the others to write on their whiteboards the number that is one or ten more or less than that number. Next ask them to add 9/11, 19/21 by adding 10/20 and adjusting. Encourage any children who are struggling to look at the class 100 square.

Main teaching activities

Whole class: Discuss and review the pictogram work in Lesson 2. Explain that today the children will be making up their own pictogram based on a problem similar to the last one.
Group work: They need to imagine that Ivor Potato owns a vegetable shop and needs to find out what vegetables to order. Together, generate a list of eight vegetables. The children should make up the numbers 'voted' by throwing two dice and finding the total. They should then make up a pictogram to show the information. Remind them to add labels and a title. Once they have completed their pictogram they should make up statements from it to share during the Review.

Differentiation

Less confident learners: Provide a skeleton pictogram for these children to use.
More confident learners: Ask these children to generate numbers by multiplying the dice numbers together.

Review

Invite the children to show their pictograms and share their information statements. Assess their work and how confident they are in talking about it.

Lesson 4 (Review, teach and practise)

Starter

Refine and reason: Write a number up to 10 on the board. Ask the children to write as many addition and subtraction facts for this number as they can in one minute. Repeat a few times and then progress to numbers from 11 to 20, giving them two minutes this time. For example, given 14 they could write: 11 + 3 = 14; 12 + 2 = 14; 14 - 12 = 2; 14 - 11 = 3; 14 - 13 = 1. Discuss their answers, taking one each from several children. Ask less confident children to share their answers first so that they can put forward the most obvious facts.

Main teaching activities

Whole class: As in Lessons 2 and 3, the whole-class work will take one lesson and the group work another (in Lesson 5). Explain that the children are now going to look at block graphs. Ask: *Who can remember this?* Show the OHT of 'Sports block graph' and remind them that they have seen this before (in Block C, Unit 1). Ask the children to tell you as much as they can about it. Encourage them to state all possible facts.

Say: *We are going to make our own block graph to show our favourite animals.* Collect about six examples of animals that the children like. Ask them to choose their favourite one from the list. Give them each a sticky note and ask them to draw a picture of their chosen animal. While they are doing this, write the animal names and appropriate numbers (for the vertical axis) on sticky notes and draw a skeleton graph on the board.

Gather the class together. Show them your labels and numbers, and invite children to stick them onto your skeleton graph. Encourage them to explain why they have put them in those places. Do the other children agree? Now invite everyone to come to the front and add their picture to the correct column, starting from the horizontal axis. Remember to keep the graph for the next lesson.

Review

Discuss what this graph shows, and ask questions (particularly of the *How many more/less...* type). Encourage the class to ask each other similar questions, perhaps after talking to a friend and making up a question together. Finally, ask: *Which is the most popular animal for this class?*

Lesson 5 (Apply and evaluate)

Starter

Rehearse, recall and reason: Recite the two-, five- and ten-times tables with the children. Now count together in multiples of 2, 5 and 10, using fingers. Stop the children at various intervals, asking which finger they have got to and how many lots of 2, 5 or 10 that is. As you do this, ask questions related to corresponding divisions, for example: *What do we divide 30 by to get 5?* Give each child a laminated 'Function machine game', pen and cloth. Ask them to write any numbers from 1 to 10 on the input side and '× 2' in the middle; then, when you say *Go*, to fill in the output side as quickly as possible. Ask them to rub out the outputs and replace × 2 with × 10, then write the new outputs. Ask children who do this quickly to repeat with × 5.

Main teaching activities

Whole class: Show the class block graph from Lesson 4. Say: *Today you are going to make your own block graph. You need to help Anne Emu, the pet shop owner, decide what to order for her pet shop.*

Group work: Model what the children must do, using large squared paper. Say: *In your group, you need to choose six animals that would make good pets. You need to finish a skeleton graph like the one we used yesterday by adding labels like this* (label the axes and fill with some animals and numbers up to 12). *Make up the numbers using dice as before: throwing two and adding the numbers up for your total. Draw blocks of the right height for each animal - so if you pick 5, colour in five squares above that animal.*

Differentiation

Less confident learners: Provide a skeleton graph for this group to use.
More confident learners: These children could total three dice and extend their vertical axis to 18.

Review

Ask each pair to join with another pair, share their graphs and state four facts that their graph shows. Invite some pairs to share their graphs and facts with the class. Let the more confident group ask the class a few of their questions.

Recap on this unit by asking questions such as: *Why are lists, tables, pictograms and block graphs useful for showing information? What is the difference between a list and a table? What does a pictogram look like? What about a block graph?*

Lessons 6-10

Preparation

Cut the 'Measures vocabulary' words into individual word cards, and then enlarge and photocopy 'Measures vocabulary' for length, weight and capacity for classroom use. Cut up the 'Capacity cards', 'Weight cards' and 'Length cards' activities onto cards to give to groups of children. Cut some 10cm strips of paper, copy 'Reading scales' and 'Drawing scales' onto acetate.

You will need

Photocopiable pages
'Capacity cards' (page 129) and 'Weight cards' (page 130); 'Reading scales' (page 131) and 'Drawing scales' (page 132) for each pair of children.
CD resources
0-9 number cards (from '0-100 number cards') for each child, 'Measures vocabulary', 'Addition and subtraction cards' (see General resources); copies of 'Length cards'. Interactive resources 'Measuring jug'and 'Weighing scales'.
Equipment
Containers of different capacities: spoons, cups... as uniform non-standard units; container with an elastic band around it, approximately at the mid-point; containers with scales in litres; containers with scales in 100ml; cardboard clock for each child; water; weighing scales; 5kg bag of potatoes; 1kg bag of sugar; packet of sweets/crisps; different items for weighing; 100g weight; rulers; metre sticks; 10cm strips.

Learning objectives

Starter

- Read and write two-digit and three-digit numbers in figures and words.
- Explain what each digit in a two-digit number represents, including numbers where 0 is a place holder.
- State the subtraction corresponding to a given addition, and vice versa.
- Understand that halving is the inverse of doubling and derive and recall doubles of all numbers to 20, and the corresponding halves.

Main teaching activities

2006

- Follow a line of enquiry; answer questions by choosing and using suitable equipment and selecting, organising and presenting information in lists, tables and simple diagrams.
- Estimate, compare and measure lengths, weights and capacities, choosing and using standard units (m, cm, kg, litre) and suitable measuring instruments.
- Read the numbered divisions on a scale, and interpret the divisions between them (eg on a scale from 0 to 25 with intervals of 1 shown but only the divisions 0, 5, 10, 15 and 20 numbered); use a ruler to draw and measure lines to the nearest centimetre.

1999

- Use and begin to read the vocabulary related to capacity.
- Estimate, measure and then compare capacities, using standard units (m, litre); suggest suitable units and equipment for such measurements.
- Read a simple scale to the nearest labelled division, including using a ruler to draw and measure lines to the nearest centimetre.

Vocabulary

length, weight, capacity, compare, measuring scales, guess, estimate, nearly, roughly, about, close to, about the same as, just over, just under, ruler, metre stick, tape measure, metre, centimetre, balance, scales, kilogram, half kilogram, gram, container, full, half-full, empty, litre, half-litre, millilitre

Lesson 6 (Review and practise)

Starter

Refine: Ask the children to write single-digit numbers on their whiteboards and give them instructions to follow. For example: *Write three, double it, add five, add nine. How did you do that? Double it, what is your number? What is the zero there for? Add four, add eleven. How did you do that?*

Main teaching activities

Whole class: Say: *Today we are going to begin a series of lessons on measures. What do I mean by measures?* Blu-Tack three A3 sheets of paper with the headings 'length', 'weight' and 'capacity' onto the board. *Tell me the words you know that can be put under these headings.* Ask for verbal feedback only; don't write anything on the board as yet. As the children give their suggestions, ask such questions as: *What would we measure using that unit? What would we measure using a metre stick?* Tell them that today's lesson will concentrate on vocabulary and the rest of the week will be more practical. Organise the class to work in mixed-ability groups of four for the week.

Group work: Give each group three sheets of A4 paper and ask them to take a sheet each and write one of the measures headings on each piece. Give each group a set of vocabulary cards. Ask them to sort these cards into groups according to the measure they are associated with and place them on the appropriate sheet of paper. Once they have done this, each child should write down all or some of the words (depending on their ability) and make a vocabulary poster.

Differentiation

Let the children work together in mixed-ability groups. Check that the less confident learners are taking an active part in both the activities and make sure the more confident learners do not dominate proceedings.

Review

Invite groups of children to show their posters and check that the words they have written on them are where they should be. Add the words they have sorted to your A3 sheets. Display some of these posters, so that the children can make reference to them during the week.

Lesson 7 (Teach and apply)

Starter

Refresh and refine: Begin by holding up some of the 'Addition and subtraction cards' and ask the children to write the corresponding number sentences on their whiteboards and show you. Repeat this a few times. Move on to writing numbers on the board and asking the children to make up two corresponding number sentences for each. For example, you write 6 4 10, they write 6 + 4 = 10 and 10 - 4 = 6. Repeat this with different numbers.

Main teaching activities

Whole class: Recap the work the children did in the previous lesson on vocabulary. Discuss general words relating to length, weight and capacity, plus units and equipment. For a selection of the words given, invite the children to give an example of how they could be used in a sentence. Pin up the capacity vocabulary cards as a reminder, saying: *Today we are going to focus on capacity.* Discuss this in more detail, asking for examples of units to measure large and small amounts. Remind them that the standard units for measuring capacity are litres and millilitres. On the board, write: *1 litre = 1000 millilitres.*

Now show the children two containers of different sizes and ask: *Which one holds more? Which holds less? Why do you think that? How can you check your estimate?* Establish that they would need some form of measuring jug. Invite a child to check the capacity of each of the containers using a measuring jug.

Use the interactive resource 'Measuring jug' to demonstrate as in previous units, asking appropriate questions.

Group work: The children should work in mixed-ability groups of three or four to tackle one of the activities from the 'Capacity cards'. Ensure that activities are covered. The groups will feed back to the others during the Review. The instructions on the cards can be written on the board for ease of reference.

Differentiation
If the less confident learners find the activity sheet difficult to read and understand, suggest that a confident reader reads the instructions on the cards to the whole group. Then encourage the children to explain to each other what they have to do.

Review
Invite children to explain how they carried out the activities and recorded their work. Ask them to evaluate the effectiveness of their chosen recording. Discuss how the children can become more accurate in estimating by learning from previous experience.

Lesson 8 (Teach and apply)

Starter
Rehearse, refine and recall: The children will each need a set of 0–9 number cards for this activity. Call out numbers from one to 15 and ask the children to show you their doubles, for example, you call out 12, they show you 24. Move on to multiples of five to 50, for example, you call out 35 and they show you 70, and then tens to 100. Hold up some number cards to 50 for the children to add together. Expect them to use the strategy of near doubles to work out the answer. For example, if you hold up 15 and 16, they show you 31 and explain how they got that answer by doubling and adjusting. Repeat for near multiples of 10.

Main teaching activities
Whole class: Recap Lesson 7 and ask: *How many millilitres are there in a litre? So how many 100 millilitres are there in a litre? How much is half a litre in millilitres?* Explain that today the children will be doing a similar activity but focusing on weight. Discuss this in more detail, recapping the necessary vocabulary from 'Measures vocabulary'. Pin up these words as a reminder. Ask for examples of units to measure large and small amounts. Remind the children that the standard units for measuring weight are grams and kilograms. On the board, write: *1kg = 1000 grams.*

Use the interactive resource 'Weighing scales' to demonstrate as in previous units, weighing some of the items on the screen, and asking appropriate questions. Show the potatoes, sugar and crisps, and ask: *Which is the heaviest? Which is the lightest? Why do you think that? What do you think they each weigh? How can you check your estimate?* Establish that the children would need some form of measuring scale. Invite a child to check the weight of each item using the scales.

Group work: The children should work in the same groups as Lesson 7 to tackle one of the activities on 'Weight cards'. Ensure that all are covered. The groups will feed back to the others during the Review.

Review
Repeat the Review from Lesson 6 for these activities. Again, ask the children to evaluate the effectiveness of their chosen recording method. Discuss how the children can become more accurate in estimating by learning from previous experience.

Differentiation
As for Lesson 7.

Lesson 9 (Teach and apply)

Starter
Refresh, read and reason: Each child will need a clock. Ask them to find different times: o'clock, half past, quarter past and quarter to. Solve problems such as: *My clock says half past seven. It is half an hour fast. What time is it really? My watch says 3 o'clock. It is 15 minutes slow. What time is it really?*

Main teaching activities
Whole class: Invite children from each group to recap on what they did in Lesson 8, including vocabulary and units. Ask questions such as: *How*

many grams are there in 1kg? So how many 100 grams are there in 1kg? How much is half a kilogram in grams? Say that today they will be doing a similar activity but focusing on length. Discuss this in more detail, recapping the necessary words from 'Measures vocabulary'. Pin these words up as a reminder. Ask for examples of units to measure lengths. Remind them that the standard units for measuring length are centimetres and metres; ask if they know of any others, for example, kilometres and millimetres. On the board, write: *1m = 100cm.* Demonstrate measuring centimetres as in previous units, asking appropriate questions as you do. Ask the children to think of things in the classroom that would be measured in metres. Together, measure these items using a metre stick. Discuss the measurement as the number of metres, and the number of centimetres left over and write, for example, 1m 40cms.

Group work: The children should work in the same groups as in Lessons 7 and 8 to tackle one of the activities on 'Length cards'. Ensure that all activities are covered. Each group will feed back to the others during the Review.

Differentiation

As for Lesson 7.

Review

Repeat the Review from Lessons 6 and 7 for these activities.

Lesson 10 (Practise and evaluate)

Starter

Rehearse and refine: As for Lesson 6.

Main teaching activities

Whole class: Tell the children that today they will practise reading scales. Ask: *What do I mean by reading scales?* Show a ruler, weighing scales and a measuring jug. Ask: *Why do you think we need scales?* Talk to a partner and chat about when in real life people would need to read scales. Take feedback. Give some examples, such as making a cake, when you need specific amounts that are weighed out. Tell them that some of the scales they will be reading are similar to ones they have used this week and some are different. Put the acetate of 'Reading scales' on the OHP. Show one picture at a time. Ask the children what they think the item is measuring - length, weight or capacity - and why. Then look at the units and ask whether this confirms their thoughts. Discuss how scales are used to work out measurements. Discuss the units. Can the children tell the size or amount by the unit?

Group work: The children will need to work in pairs or small groups on 'Reading scales' and 'Drawing scales'. Put a copy of 'Reading scales' on the OHP again and demonstrate what the children should do. Give them five minutes or so and then draw the class together and ask some children to come to the front and explain how they read two or three of the scales. Then explain 'Drawing scales', which asks the children to draw on the measurement according to the amount written.

Differentiation

This should be through peer support. Work with any groups of children that need your help.

Review

Put the two acetates of 'Reading scales and 'Drawing scales' on the OHP and work through each, asking the children to mark and correct their own work. Choose one measuring scale and make up a word problem that would include it, for example: *This measuring jug shows that there is 500ml of orange squash in it. There was a litre; some has been poured into a glass. How much has been poured into a glass?* Ask children to self-assess what they have learned from the last five lessons on measurements.

Name ______________________ Date ______________

Table information

Here is some information about favourite colours in a class.
Here is the same information in a table.

Favourite colours

5 children like blue
6 children like red
8 children like yellow
3 children like brown
4 children like white
5 children like green

Favourite colours						
	Blue	**Red**	**Yellow**	**Brown**	**White**	**Green**
Children	5	6	8	3	4	5

Make tables for favourite animals, fruit and sport.

Favourite animals

9 children like dogs
9 children like cats
4 children like hamsters
3 children like mice
7 children like rabbits
2 children like fish

Favourite fruit

12 children like bananas
4 children like apples
2 children like oranges
4 children like plums
8 children like grapes
5 children like kiwi fruit

Favourite sport

2 children like tennis
2 children like running
3 children like cycling
12 children like football
6 children like rugby

Name ____________________ Date ____________________

Capacity cards

Capacity card 1

Estimate the order of capacities for four different containers. Check your estimate by measuring using a measuring jug. Decide how to record the estimate and results.

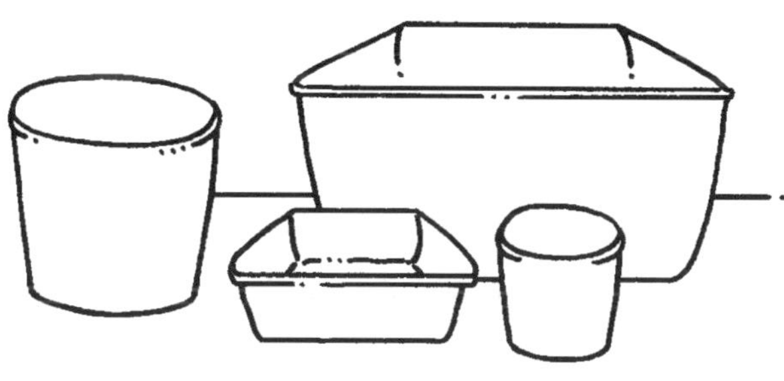

Capacity card 2

Put an elastic band around a container. How many millilitres of water do you think will be needed to fill the container to the elastic band mark? Check by pouring. Record the estimate and measure. Now move the elastic band to a different place. Repeat the activity.

Capacity card 3

Find some containers which you estimate will hold about 2 litres. Check by pouring water from these into a container with a scale marked in litres.

Decide how to record your results.

Capacity card 4

Choose some containers. For each one, decide whether to measure its capacity in millilitres or litres. Estimate and then measure the capacity by filling and pouring. Record your estimate and measure.

Name ______________________ Date ______________

Weight cards

Weight card 1

Take four different objects. Estimate their weights and put them in order. Then check the estimate by weighing. Decide how to record the estimate and results.

Weight card 2

Put one 100g weight on the scales. Estimate how many cubes you need to add to make 200g. Find out using the scales. Decide how to record your estimate and results.

Weight card 3

Find some objects that you estimate will weigh about $\frac{1}{2}$ kg. Check by weighing. Decide how to record your results.

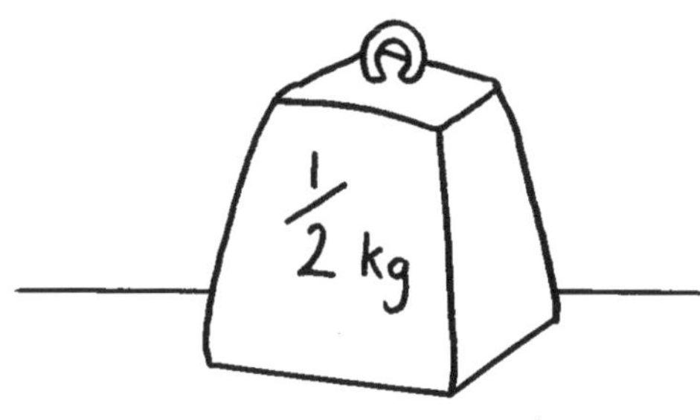

Weight card 4

Find two different objects that you would weigh in grams and two that you would weigh in kg. Estimate and then measure their weights. Record your estimates and measures.

Name ______________________ Date ______________

Reading scales

What do these scales say?

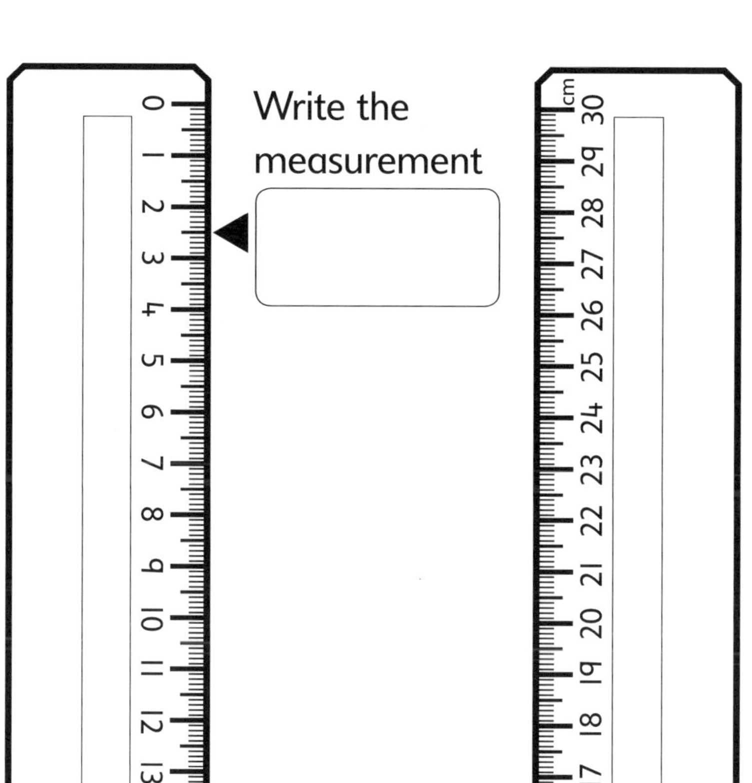

Write the measurement

Write the measurement

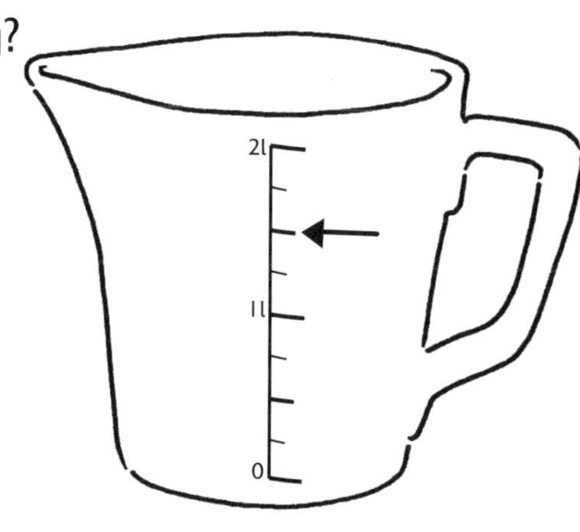

Write the measurement

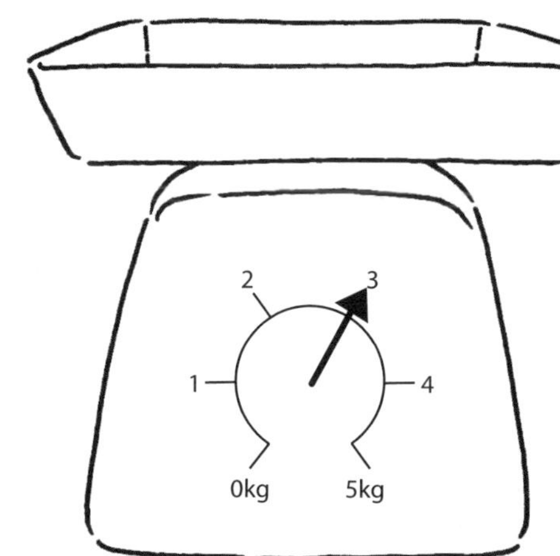

Write the measurement

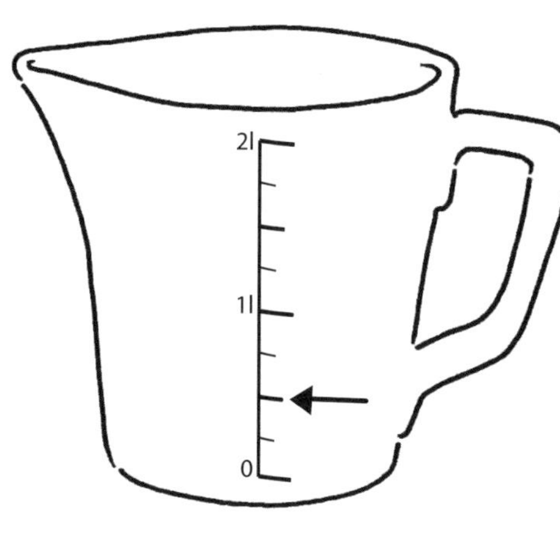

Write the measurement

Name ______________________ Date ______________________

Drawing scales

Draw an arrow to show 20cm

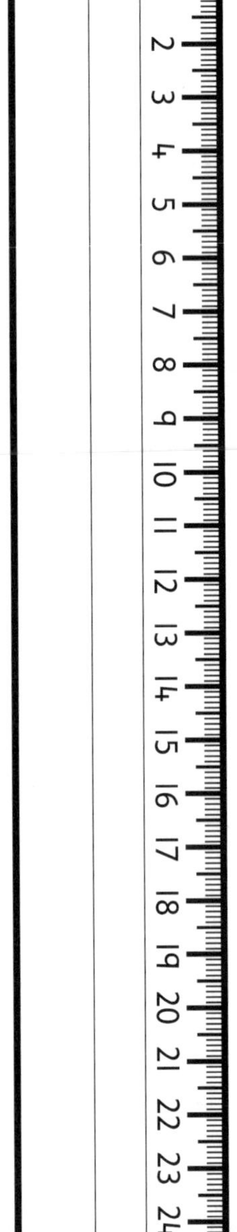

Draw an arrow to show 15cm

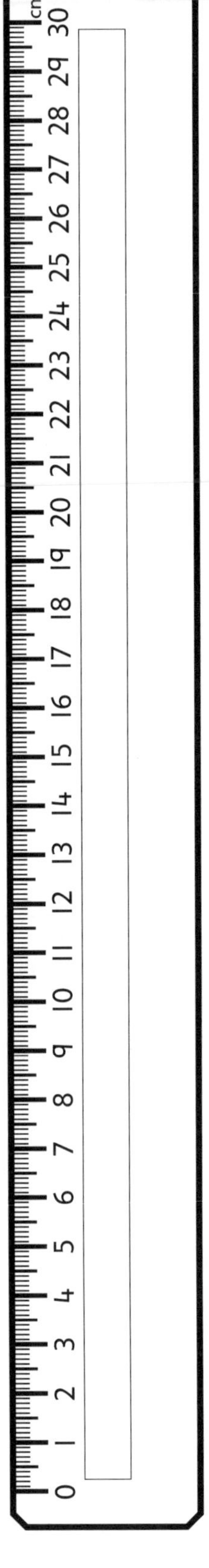

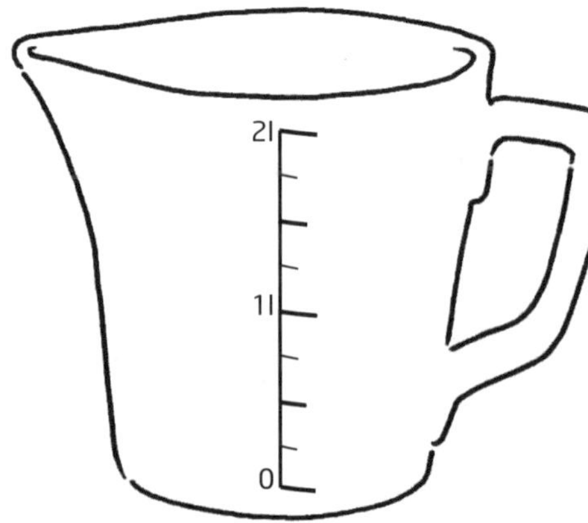

Draw an arrow to show just less than $\frac{1}{2}$ litre

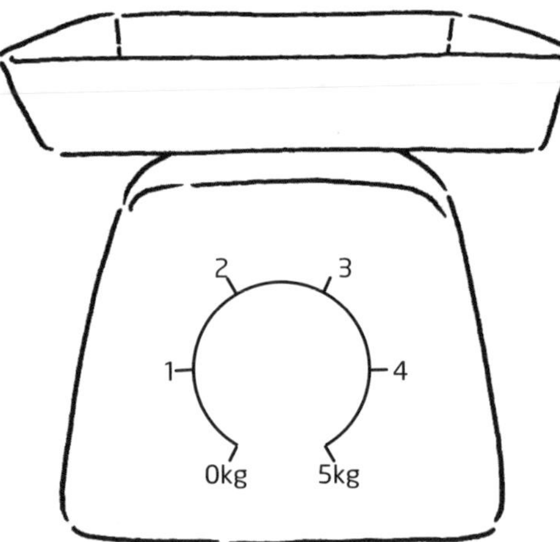

Draw an arrow to show $2\frac{1}{2}$ kg

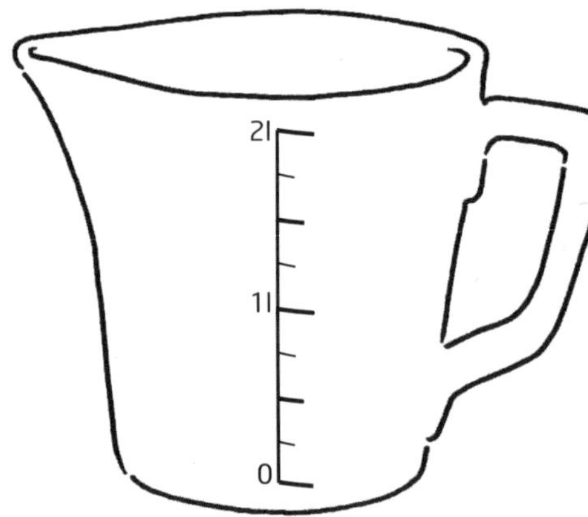

Draw an arrow to show 1l 500ml

Calculating, measuring and understanding shape

Key aspects of learning
- Problem solving
- Reasoning
- Evaluation
- Social skills
- Communication

Expected prior learning

Check that children can already:
- solve problems involving counting, adding or subtracting, doubling or halving
- use practical and informal written methods for addition and subtraction of a one-digit number or a multiple of 10 to and from a one or two-digit number
- estimate, measure and compare objects, choosing suitable uniform non-standard or standard units and instruments
- use vocabulary related to time; order days of the week and months; read the time to the hour and half hour
- visualise and use everyday language to describe the position of objects and direction and distance when moving them.

Objectives overview

The text in this diagram identifies the focus of mathematics learning within the block.

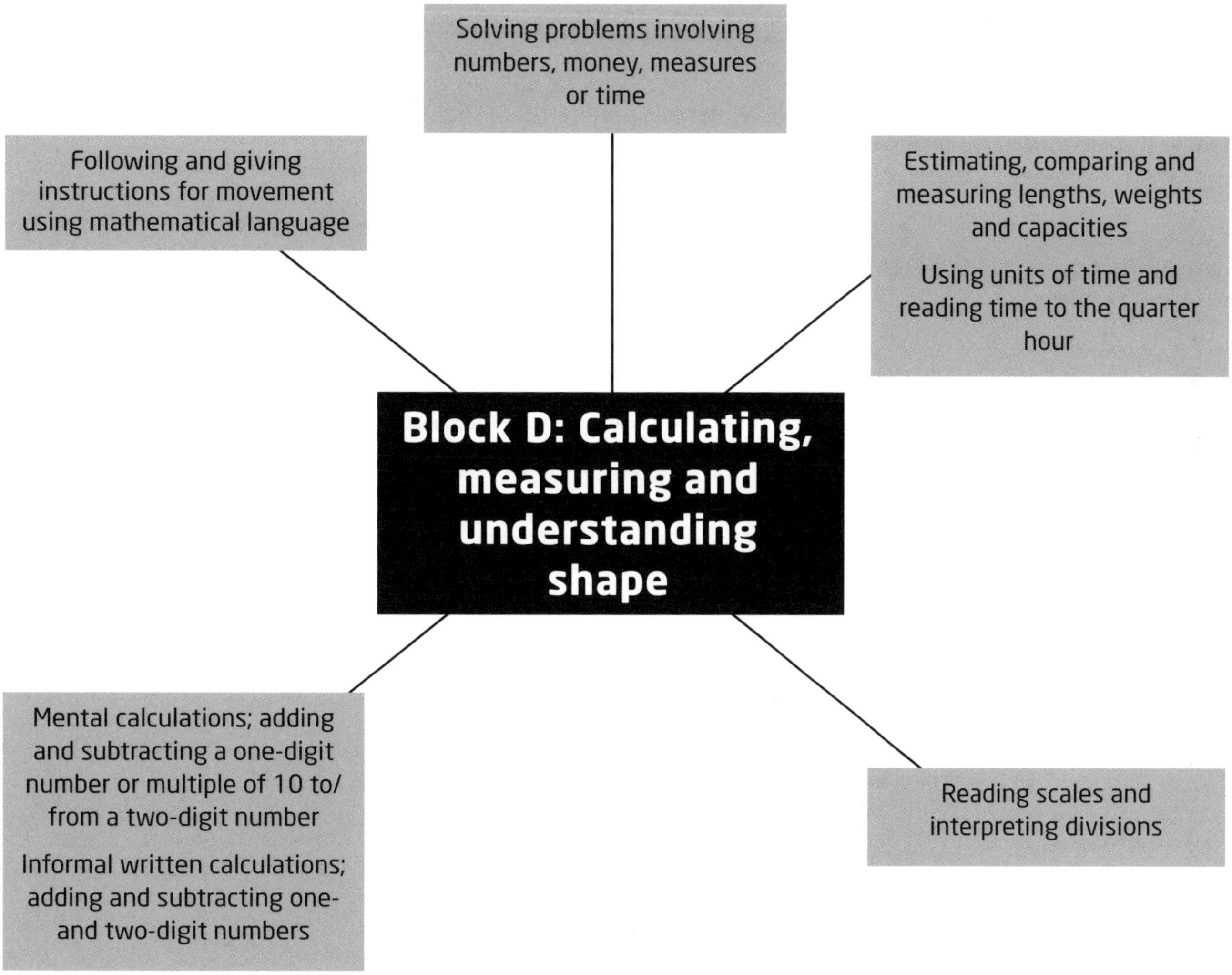

Block D: Calculating, measuring and understanding shape

Solving problems involving numbers, money, measures or time

Following and giving instructions for movement using mathematical language

Estimating, comparing and measuring lengths, weights and capacities

Using units of time and reading time to the quarter hour

Mental calculations; adding and subtracting a one-digit number or multiple of 10 to/ from a two-digit number

Informal written calculations; adding and subtracting one- and two-digit numbers

Reading scales and interpreting divisions

Unit 1 2 weeks

Calculating, measuring and understanding shape

Lesson	Strands	Starter	Main teaching activities
1. Review	Use/apply Calculate	**Derive and recall all addition facts for each number to at least 10.**	• Solve problems involving addition, subtraction, multiplication or division in contexts of numbers, measures or pounds and pence. **• Add or subtract mentally a one-digit number or a multiple of 10 to or from any two-digit number; use practical and informal written methods to add and subtract two-digit numbers.**
2. Teach and practise	Use/apply Calculate	Derive and recall multiplication facts for the 2, 5 and 10 times-tables and the related division facts.	As for Lesson 1
3. Teach, practise and evaluate	Use/apply Calculate	As for Lesson 2	As for Lesson 1
4. Review and practise	Use/apply Measure	**Use the symbols +, –, ×, ÷ and = to record and interpret number sentences involving all four operations; calculate the value of an unknown in a number sentence (eg ❑ ÷ 2 = 6, 30 – ❑ = 24).**	• Solve problems involving addition, subtraction, multiplication or division in contexts of numbers, measures or pounds and pence. • Estimate, compare and measure lengths, choosing and using standard units (m, cm) and suitable measuring instruments. • Read the numbered divisions on a scale, and interpret the divisions between them (eg on a scale from 0 to 25 with intervals of 1 shown but only the divisions 0, 5, 10, 15 and 20 numbered).
5. Review, teach and practise	Use/apply Measure	As for Lesson 4	As for Lesson 4
6. Practise and evaluate	Use/apply Measure	Add/subtract 9 or 11: add/subtract 10 and adjust by 1.	As for Lesson 4
7. Review, teach and practise	Use/apply Measure	Derive and recall multiplication facts for the 2, 5 and 10 times-tables and the related division facts; recognise multiples of 2, 5 and 10.	• Solve problems involving addition, subtraction, multiplication or division in contexts of numbers, measures or pounds and pence. **• Use units of time (seconds, minutes, hours, days) and know the relationships between them; read the time to the quarter hour; identify time intervals, including those that cross the hour.**
8. Teach, practise and evaluate	Use/apply Measure	As for Lesson 7	As for Lesson 7
9. Review and apply	Use/apply Shape	**• Visualise common 2D shapes and 3D solids; identify shapes from pictures of them in different positions and orientations; sort, make and describe shapes, referring to their properties.**	• Solve problems involving addition, subtraction, multiplication or division in contexts of numbers, measures or pounds and pence. • Follow and give instructions involving position, direction and movement.
10. Teach, apply and evaluate	Use/apply Shape	As for Lesson 9	As for Lesson 9

Unit 1 2 weeks

Speaking and listening objective

- Listen to others in class, ask relevant questions and follow instructions.

Introduction

Lessons 1 to 3 in this block rehearse, consolidate and progress from work in Block C concerning addition and subtraction strategies. The children are expected to work on problems involving money. Lessons 4 to 6 involve working with length, weight and capacity, again through solving problems and building on skills that they have been taught in Block C and also in Year 1. Lessons 7 and 8 are the first real introduction that the children have to the subject of time in Year 2. They have had opportunities in starter activities to rehearse what they learnt in Year 1 and this is built on during these two lessons. Lessons 9 and 10 focus on position, direction and movement. Threaded throughout this entire block is the using and applying objective of solving problems involving numbers, money, measures and time. The speaking and listening objective is actively encouraged during whole class and group work when the children are asked to contribute to discussion and to respond to what others say in a large group or in paired work.

Using and applying mathematics

- Solve problems involving addition, subtraction, multiplication or division in contexts of numbers, measures or pounds and pence.

Lessons 1-3

Preparation

Make a laminated copy of 'Coin cards and labels' for each child. Provide a mixture of plastic coins in a small container and at least 12 shopping cards for each group of three children. Set up a shop counter with toys or similar items, labelled with some of the prices from 'Price labels (pence)'.

You will need

CD resources

Number cards 0-10 from '0-100 number cards', a copy of the 'Function machine game' for each child, 'Spider charts for multiplying', a set of 'Coin cards and labels', a set of 'Price labels (pence)', a set of 'Price labels (£.p)', a copy of 'Addition and subtraction vocabulary' cards (see General resources); 'Shopping cards 1' and '2'.

Equipment

0-10 number line; Blu-Tack; plastic coins, real coins and large card coins; small containers; ten different toys, fruits or similar; a Unifix pendulum; a counting stick.

Learning objectives

Starter

- Derive and recall all addition facts for each number to at least 10.
- Derive and recall multiplication facts for the 2, 5 and 10 times-tables and the related division facts.

Main teaching activities

2006

- Solve problems involving addition, subtraction, multiplication or division in contexts of numbers, measures or pounds and pence.
- Add or subtract mentally a one-digit number or a multiple of 10 to or from any two-digit number; use practical and informal written methods to add and subtract two-digit numbers.

1999

- Extend understanding of the operations of addition and subtraction. Use and begin to read the related vocabulary.
- Find a small difference by counting up from the smaller to the larger number.
- Recognise all coins and begin to use £.p notation for money. Find totals, give change and work out which coins to pay.
- Choose and use appropriate operations and efficient calculation strategies (eg mental, mental with jottings) to solve problems.

Vocabulary

money, coin, penny, pence, pound, £, spend, pay, change, total, addition, subtraction, difference between, equal to (also see 'Addition and subtraction vocabulary' sheet)

Lesson 1 (Review)

Starter

Recall: Hold up number cards 0-10 at random, and ask the children to write the number that goes with each to make 10. They can use their fingers to check and/or make jumps along a 0-10 number line. Repeat for other totals below 10, such as 8, 3, 5 or 9.

Main teaching activities

Whole class: Say: *During the next few lessons you will be adding and subtracting money.* Ask the children to tell you some words related to addition and subtraction. As they do so, show the appropriate 'Addition and subtraction vocabulary' cards and stick them on the board. Next, ask them which coins we use in our money system. Again, hold up a coin label, large card coin and real coin for each value. Attach these to the board.

Show the children your shop display. Go through the items, showing the price labels and asking how much each costs. Then ask, for example: *How much would it cost to buy a bunch of bananas and a pineapple?* Discuss strategies for calculating. Encourage rounding and adjusting; putting the largest number first and counting on; partitioning; making a 10; and counting along a number line – whichever is most appropriate for the problem.

Group work: Model the activity. *You will be working on your own today, but sharing cards and money with two others. You need to pick two shopping cards and work out the total you will spend, record the strategy you used, then find the smallest number of coins that you can use to pay. Last of all, you need to write down which coins you used.*

Differentiation

Less confident learners: Give this group shopping cards up to 14p from 'Shopping cards 1', so that their totals are less than 30p.

More confident learners: Ask this group to total three amounts.

Review

Invite a few children to give examples of their work and explain the strategies they used to find the totals. For each strategy, ask: *How else could you have found that total? Which is more efficient?* For example, for 24p + 46p, you might compare: *I put 46p in my head and counted on 20, then 4* with *I know 4 and 6 is 10, so I added 20p, 40p and 10p.* Check that the children can use the addition strategies they have been taught in previous units to add amounts of money.

Lesson 2 (Teach and practise)

Starter

Rehearse: Use the 'Spider charts for multiplying' to practise multiplying by 10. Then give each child a copy of the 'Function machine game'. Ask the children to write random numbers up to 10 on the input side and write 10 in the middle. When you say *Go* they multiply each number by 10 and write the answer on the output side. Ask children who are struggling to write only two or three numbers on the left. Go through the answers. Repeat for multiplying by 2. If there is time, repeat both with new input numbers.

Main teaching activities

Whole class: Using your shop display, hold up a pair of items and ask the children to find the difference between their prices. Encourage them to count up from the smaller to the larger number. Draw a number line as a visual reminder and talk through the steps. For example, using a book (35p) and a horn (46p): 35p to 40p is 5p, and 46p is another 6p. 5p and 6p is 11p. The difference in price is 11p. Record: 5p + 6p = 11p.

Group work: As for Lesson 1, but instead of adding up prices the children can work individually to find the difference between the prices on pairs of shopping cards.

Differentiation

Less confident learners: Give this group only the shopping cards to 14p from 'Shopping cards 1'.

More confident learners: These children can find bigger differences. Give them two piles of cards: one set of cards to 14p and the other set as normal from 'Shopping cards 2'. They should take one card from each pile.

Review

Ask some children whom you would like to assess to explain their work and demonstrate their use of the number line. Then demonstrate how to use the same strategy for finding change from £1 and £2.

Lesson 3 (Teach, practise and evaluate)

Starter

Refine: Repeat from Lesson 2, but first use a counting stick to count in twos and tens. Stop at different interval marks to ask how many lots of 2 or 10 your finger is on, and how many that is altogether.

Main teaching activities

Whole class: Explain that today the children will be changing amounts of pence into pounds and pence, then working with these amounts to find totals and change. Announce that there has been an increase in the cost of all the items on your shop counter. Take off the pence labels and replace them with a selection of pounds and pence ones. As you do this, challenge the children to work out each price increase. For example: *The pineapple was 50p. Now it is £1.10. How much has it gone up?*

When you have found the price increase for each item, write some of the new prices on the board. Explain that when an amount such as £2.34 is written, the number just after the £ sign is the number of pounds and the numbers after the dot are pence. The dot separates the pounds from the pence. Point to the other new prices you have written and for each, ask how many pounds there are and how many pence. Ask: *How many pence are there in a pound... in £2... in £4?* As a challenge, find out who can tell you how many pence there are in each price on the board.

Hold up two items with their new labels - for example, a pineapple at £1.10 and a bunch of bananas at £1.40. Ask how much they will cost altogether and invite someone to explain their strategy for addition. Then say: *If I give the shopkeeper £3, how much change will I be given?* Use a number line to find the answer by counting on.

Paired work: Give each pair of children a pile of £.p price label cards. They pick two, work out the total cost and record their strategy, then work out the change from £3.00 and record their strategy.

Differentiation

Less confident learners: Ask this group to use one price card that is a multiple of 10p, and to work out the change from £2.

More confident learners: This group can work out the change from £5.

Review

Invite some children to demonstrate their work and their strategies. Ask all the children to turn to a partner and tell them some of the things they have learned so far during this unit, and whether they have a good understanding of what they have done. Encourage them to discuss whether they used: rounding and adjusting; putting the largest number first and counting on; partitioning; making a 10; counting along a number line. After a few minutes, ask selected pairs to share their thoughts and then to do a self-assessment of how confident they feel about these strategies by putting their thumbs up, down or sideways.

Lessons 4-6

Preparation

Decide which eight length words from the 'Measures vocabulary' CD page you think are the most important and cut these out. Do the same for weight and capacity.

You will need

Photocopiable pages

'Measures activities' (page 143).

CD resources

'Measures vocabulary' (see General resources). Interactive resources 'Measuring scales' and 'Measuring jug'.

Equipment

Metre stick, strips of 1cm length paper (one for you and one per child), Plasticine, a 1kg weight, balance scales, measuring jug, water, 100 square for each child.

Learning objectives

Starter

- Use the symbols +, -, ×, ÷ and = to record and interpret number sentences involving all four operations; calculate the value of an unknown in a number sentence (eg □ ÷ 2 = 6, 30 - □ = 24).
- Add/subtract 9 or 11: add/subtract 10 and adjust by 1.

Main teaching activities

2006

- Solve problems involving addition, subtraction, multiplication or division in contexts of numbers, measures or pounds and pence.
- Estimate, compare and measure weights and capacities, choosing and using standard units (kg, litre) and suitable measuring instruments.
- Read the numbered divisions on a scale, and interpret the divisions between them (eg on a scale from 0 to 25 with intervals of 1 shown but only the divisions 0, 5, 10, 15 and 20 numbered).

1999

- Use and begin to read the vocabulary related to length.
- Estimate, measure and compare lengths, using standard units (m, cm); suggest suitable units and equipment for such measurements.

Vocabulary

length, measure, metre (m), centimetre (cm), long, short, high, low, tall, wide, narrow, deep, shallow, thick, thin, ruler, metre stick, gram (g), kilogram (kg), half-kilogram, light, heavy, scales, balance, weight, capacity, litre (l), millilitre (ml), half-litre, full, half-full, empty, contains, container

Lesson 4 (Review and practise)

Starter

Read and reason: Write up a missing number sentence, such as 6 + □ = 10. Ask the children to write the missing number on their whiteboards and then to explain how they worked it out. Repeat with different additions and subtractions, putting the symbol in different positions. Make some simple, as in the example, and some more challenging, such as □ + 25 = 42.

Main teaching activities

Whole class: Tell the children that for the next few days they will be thinking about measures. Ask them what they think the word means. Establish that length, weight and capacity are important in this. Give each child one of the measures words. It may be necessary for you to pair some of the children; if so, mixed-ability pairs would be best. Ask them to look at their card, read it to a neighbour and tell them whether it is a word relating to length, weight or capacity. Give the children a few minutes to get into three groups according to which measure they are holding. In these groups, they should each make up a sentence for one of the other children's words. Get together as a class and ask some children to share their sentences.

Focus on length for the rest of the lesson. Remind the children of what they did in Block C a week or so ago on this subject, and discuss the units they used. Show a metre stick and discuss things that are longer/shorter than this. Ask which units are used for lengths that are smaller and show the 10cm strip, explaining what it is and then asking them to tell you things that are shorter/longer than 10cm.

Individual work: The children should work as a class for this activity. They each need a piece of Plasticine. Ask them to make five 'worms' of different lengths. Then, ask them to order these from shortest to longest before grouping them according to whether they think they are shorter or longer than 10cm. Let them use a 10cm strip to check whether they are correct.

Differentiation

Less confident learners: Provide adult support if necessary, to help the children make, order and measure their Plasticine 'worms'.

More confident learners: Ask these children to discuss how they estimated the length of the different Plasticine strips.

Review

Take feedback from the children about this activity. For example: *How many worms were longer/shorter than 10cm?* Discuss the word 'estimating' and ask them how they used this skill during their work: grouping without the 10cm strip. Find out how their estimating is progressing by collecting some of the worms and putting them together to make longer ones. Do this until you have five longer worms. Order them and say: *Can you estimate how many 10cm strips they are in length? Are any longer than a metre?*

Lesson 5 (Review, teach and practise)

Starter

Read and reason: As for Lesson 4.

Main teaching activities

The focus of the next two lessons is weight and capacity. Discuss each term and find out how much the children remember, including the units to be used (kg, g, l, ml) and the equipment. Encourage them to think first, then share with a partner and then the rest of the class. Show the interactive resources 'Measuring scales' and 'Measuring jug' and discuss the differences. Focus on the scales. Begin with the jug, which goes up in 10s to 100, practise counting in tens and ask addition and subtraction questions. For example: *I filled this to 80ml, then poured out 9ml, how much is left? I filled this*

to 20ml, then added 5ml and then 6ml, how much is in it now? Repeat, adapting as necessary with the scales which go up in 100s to 1000 (1kg).
Group work: There are two activities for the children to work on, one during this lesson and one during the next (it doesn't matter in which order). These are the weight and capacity activities from 'Measures activities'.

Review
Take feedback from each group, discussing what they found easy/difficult about their task and what they learned or reinforced.

Differentiation
Let the children work in mixed-ability groups. If the less confident learners find the activity sheet difficult to read and understand, suggest that a confident reader reads the sheet to the whole group. Then encourage the children to explain to each other what they have to do.

Lesson 6 (Practise and evaluate)

Starter
Refresh: Give each child a 100 square. Ask them to find the number 4 and add 11 by adding ten and then one. Discuss the 100 square and therefore the way to do this. Continue this activity by asking them to add/subtract 9 in this way. Check after every few instructions, to make sure the class is together; this will allow any who have been left behind to catch up.

Main teaching activities
Whole class: Recap with the children what they learned about in their last lesson.
Group work: The children continue with their mixed-ability work from the previous lesson, doing whichever activity they didn't do then.

Review
Take feedback from each group, discussing what they found easy/difficult about their task and what they learned or reinforced this time. Finish by giving the children the measures words and asking them to explain what each means. This can be used as an assessment opportunity.

Differentiation
As for Lesson 5.

Lessons 7-8

Preparation
Photocopy CD page 'Measures vocabulary' for time onto A3. Cut out each clock from sheet 1 of 'Clocks' for each pair of children.

You will need
Photocopiable pages
'Time differences' (page 144) and 'Units of time' (page 145).
CD resources
'Measures vocabulary' for time, the first page of 'Clocks' (see General resources); support and extension versions of 'Time differences'. Interactive resource 'Clocks'.
Equipment
A geared clock for you; individual small clocks for the children.

Learning objectives

Starter
- Derive and recall multiplication facts for the 2, 5 and 10 times-tables and the related division facts; recognise multiples of 2, 5 and 10.

Main teaching activities
2006
- Solve problems involving addition, subtraction, multiplication or division in contexts of numbers, measures or pounds and pence.
- Use units of time (seconds, minutes, hours, days) and know the relationships between them; read the time to the quarter hour; identify time intervals, including those that cross the hour.

1999
- Use and begin to read the vocabulary related to time.
- Suggest suitable units to estimate or measure time.
- Use units of time and know the relationships between them (second, minute, hour, day, week).

Vocabulary
day, week, fortnight, month, year, weekend, second (s), minute (min), hour (h), half an hour, quarter of an hour

Lesson 7 (Review, teach and practise)

Starter

Recall: Ask the children to write any number from 0 to 10 to the left of their whiteboard. In the middle, they write ×10. When you say *Go*, they work out the answer and write on the right. Repeat with other numbers before working with ×2 in the middle.

Main teaching activities

Whole class: Say: *For the next two lessons we will be thinking about time.* Ask the children to think of all the words they know to do with time and to tell their neighbour. Blu-Tack the 'Measures vocabulary cards' to the board one by one and ask them to put their hands up each time a word they thought of is shown. As a class, sort the words into groups, discussing why they belong where they do. Go over the units of time and their equivalents. For example, 60 minutes = one hour using the 'Units of time' photocopiable page.

Each child needs a small clock and should copy what you do next: using a geared clock, move the hands in a clockwise direction and show o'clock times. Ask the children to say them. Repeat for half past times. Call out different o'clock and half past times and ask them to find them on their clocks. (If you prefer you can use the interactive resource 'Clocks' and randomly generate the times.) Say: *If we start the lesson at 10 o'clock* (show 10 o'clock) *and it finishes at 11 o'clock* (move the hands to show 11 o'clock), *we will know from the clock how long our lesson took. How long did it take?* Repeat with other such examples.

Paired work: Write up some times on the board such as: 6 o'clock, 9 o'clock, 10 o'clock, half past seven and demonstrate the 'Time differences' photocopiable sheet. You will need two clocks. Choose two times and set the first time on one and the second time on another. Calculate how long it is between the two times and then make up two related sentences.

Differentiation

Less confident learners: These children use the support version of 'Time differences' and concentrate on o'clock times and whole hours.

More confident learners: These children use the extension version of 'Time differences' which includes quarter past and quarter to times.

Review

Invite each group to give the other groups their first two sentences and for the other children to work out the difference in times. Ask: *How did you work that out? Who has a way of doing this without using a clock?* Encourage the children to explain their methods, such as counting on in ones for hours, then half hours.

Lesson 8 (Teach, practise and evaluate)

Starter

Read and rehearse: Practise counting in fives using a clock. Display the clock on the Interactive resource and remind the children that there are five minutes from one number to the next. Point at the numbers 1, 2, 3, and so on, and expect the children to count 5, 10, 15... Then point at random numbers - for example, 5, then 2, then 9, asking the children to tell you how many that is: 25, 10, 45. Make the link to multiplication facts for the five-times table.

Main teaching activities

Whole class: Recap what the children did in the previous lesson: time vocabulary, units of time, time differences, o'clock and half-past times. Say: *Today we will be thinking about digital time.* Discuss what this means: time in numbers only. Ask the children to tell you where they see these times: TV, clocks, DVD players, and so on. Show your real or interactive clock and discuss the hour numbers and the minute marks. Talk about the fact that there are five minutes from one hour number to the next and that these show the minutes past the o'clock time. Say: *At 4 o'clock there are no minutes past the hour so the digital time would be 4:00.* Repeat and then progress on to half-past times in the same way.

Paired work: Give the pairs a set of 'Clocks' cards, they should order them from earliest to latest and stick them onto A3 paper. Once they have, they should label each time with the digital equivalent.

Differentiation
If necessary, provide adult support for less confident learners, to help them label the clocks on their A3 sheets of paper.

Review
Take feedback from the children about their paired work. Finish by showing clock times on one of your clocks and asking the children to write the digital equivalent on their whiteboards.

Lessons 9-10

Preparation
Make an A3 copy of the 'Position vocabulary' sheet on card and cut out the cards.

You will need
Photocopiable pages
'3D shapes' (page 60) and '2D shapes' (page 61).
CD resources
Enlarged 'Position vocabulary cards' (see General resources).
Equipment
A collection of 2D and 3D shapes; Compare Bears or similar counting toys.

Learning objectives

Starter

- Visualise common 2D shapes and 3D solids; identify shapes from pictures of them in different positions and orientations; sort, make and describe shapes, referring to their properties.

Main teaching activities

2006

- Solve problems involving addition, subtraction, multiplication or division in contexts of numbers, measures or pounds and pence.
- Follow and give instructions involving position, direction and movement.

1999

- Use mathematical vocabulary to describe position, direction and movement: describe, place, tick, draw or visualise objects in given positions.

Vocabulary
position, over, under, underneath, above, below, top, bottom, side, on, in, outside, inside, around, in front, behind, front, back, before, after, beside, next to, opposite, apart, between, middle, edge, centre, corner, along, through, to, from, towards, away from, clockwise, anti-clockwise, slide, roll, whole turn, half turn, quarter turn

Lesson 9 (Review and apply)

Starter
Refresh: Give each child a 2D shape; use a mixture of regular and irregular shapes. Call out some names and properties and ask the children to stand up if their shape has the property or name that you say (for example: triangle; pentagon with equal sides; six sides; symmetrical).

Main teaching activities
Whole class: Explain that today the children are going to think about the positions of objects. Give each child a shape, using a mixture of 2D and 3D shapes. Hold up each 'Position vocabulary card' in turn, and ask the children with a particular shape to put it in a place that is appropriate to that word (for example, ask whoever has a cube to put it somewhere that shows what is meant by *underneath*). Ask those children to explain what they did.
Paired work: Give each pair three or four position vocabulary cards and a counting toy. They need to make up a story about their toy that involves the words on the cards, then practise acting it out. Explain that some of them will act out their stories to the class later.

Differentiation
Check that less confident learners have the opportunity to take an active part in the discussions during the paired activity, and that more confident learners do not dominate proceedings.

Review
Choose those children whom you wish to assess to act out their stories first. If you have time, invite others to share their stories.

Lesson 10 (Teach, apply and evaluate)

Starter

Refresh and refine: Repeat the starter from Lesson 9 but include some counting. For example, ask the children to stand up if their shape has the property or name that you say. When they are standing, ask how many sides there are altogether on their shapes. This will involve counting in steps of 3, 4 and 5, which they need to practise. For any hexagons or octagons, let them have a go, using a number line as appropriate.

Main teaching activities

Whole class: Recap with the children what they did in Lesson 9, asking them to turn to a partner and together to think of as many position words as they can. Say: *Today we are going to think about moving things around.* Ask them to think of words to do with this. Show the movement vocabulary cards and ask them to describe what they mean as a 'think, pair, share' activity.

Group work: The children's task is similar to the last lesson, the difference being that they should use three or four direction cards to make up their story with their counting toy. Leave 'movement' out of the selection that you give to the children. After they have made up their story, encourage them to act it out.

Review

Choose volunteer pairs to act out their stories first. After this, ask them to think of how they can also add some of the position words they thought of last time in their story. Give them a few minutes to think and take feedback. Ask them to tell each other one thing they have learned over the last two lessons and then share with the class.

Differentiation

As for Lesson 9.

Name ______________________ Date ______________

Measures activities

Length

Find six things in the classroom that you estimate to be longer than a metre.

Find six things in the classroom that you estimate to be shorter than a metre.

Find something that you know is exactly a metre long.

Make three piles: things that you think are longer than 1 m, things that you think are shorter than 1 m, and things that are exactly 1 m.

Use a metre stick to measure each length.

Discuss within your group how good your estimating was.

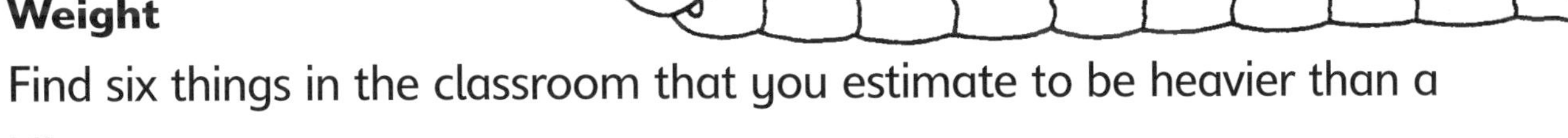

Weight

Find six things in the classroom that you estimate to be heavier than a kilogram.

Find six things in the classroom that you estimate to be lighter than a kilogram.

Find something that you know weighs exactly a kilogram.

Make three piles: things that you think are heavier than 1 kg, things that you think are lighter than 1 kg, and things that are exactly 1 kg.

Compare each thing with a 1 kg weight, using balance scales.

Discuss within your group how good your estimating was.

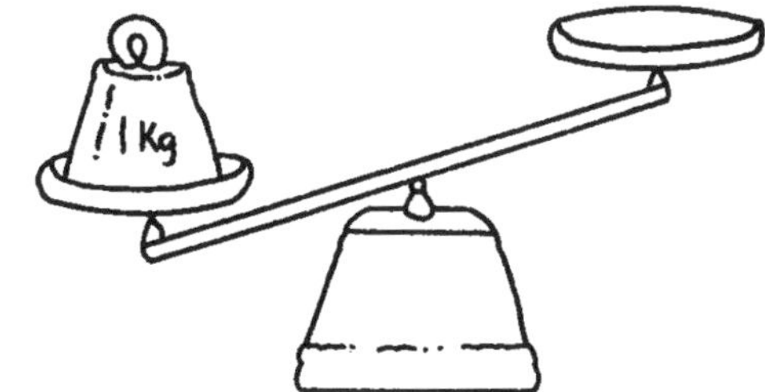

Capacity

Find four things in the classroom that you estimate will hold more than a litre.

Find four things in the classroom that you estimate will hold less than a litre.

Find something that you know will hold exactly a litre.

Make three piles: things that you think hold more than 1 litre, things that you think hold less than 1 litre, and things that hold exactly 1 litre.

Use water and a litre measuring jug to measure each capacity.

Discuss within your group how good your estimating was.

Name ______________________ Date ______________

Time differences

Work in pairs. You will need one clock each.

Choose two clock times. Make the first time on one of your clocks and the other time on the other clock.

Work out how long it is between the two times.

Make up some sentences using the two times and the time difference.

Record your work.

Do this five times. (The first example has been done for you.)

1st time	2nd time	Difference	Sentence
12, 1, 2, 3, 4, 5, 6, 7, 8, 9, 10, 11	12, 1, 2, 3, 4, 5, 6, 7, 8, 9, 10, 11	3 hours	I had my tea at 6 o'clock. I went to bed at 9 o'clock. This was 3 hours after tea.
12, 1, 2, 3, 4, 5, 6, 7, 8, 9, 10, 11	12, 1, 2, 3, 4, 5, 6, 7, 8, 9, 10, 11		
12, 1, 2, 3, 4, 5, 6, 7, 8, 9, 10, 11	12, 1, 2, 3, 4, 5, 6, 7, 8, 9, 10, 11		
12, 1, 2, 3, 4, 5, 6, 7, 8, 9, 10, 11	12, 1, 2, 3, 4, 5, 6, 7, 8, 9, 10, 11		
12, 1, 2, 3, 4, 5, 6, 7, 8, 9, 10, 11	12, 1, 2, 3, 4, 5, 6, 7, 8, 9, 10, 11		
12, 1, 2, 3, 4, 5, 6, 7, 8, 9, 10, 11	12, 1, 2, 3, 4, 5, 6, 7, 8, 9, 10, 11		

Name ______________________ Date ______________

Units of time

Which units of time would we use to measure these?

Yawning	A day at school	Playtime
We would measure this in: ____________	We would measure this in: ____________	We would measure this in: ____________
The weekend	Summer holidays	Monday
We would measure this in: ____________	We would measure this in: ____________	We would measure this in: ____________
A plant growing	Coughing	Birthday party
We would measure this in: ____________	We would measure this in: ____________	We would measure this in: ____________
A trip to the cinema	Sleeping	Eating a meal
We would measure this in: ____________	We would measure this in: ____________	We would measure this in: ____________

Unit 2 2 weeks

Calculating, measuring and understanding shape

Speaking and listening objective

- Listen to others in class, ask relevant questions and follow instructions.

Introduction

Lessons 1 to 3 in this block rehearse, consolidate and progress mental addition and subtraction strategies in the context of money and length. Lessons 4 to 6 involve working with length, weight and capacity, concentrating on measuring scales and estimating. Lessons 7 and 8 focus on analogue and digital time, building on the children's experiences during Unit 1, and several starter activities. Lessons 9 and 10 focus on position, direction and movement using whole, half and quarter turns, both clockwise and anti-clockwise. The children are introduced to the right angle representing a quarter turn. Threaded throughout this entire block is the using and applying objective of solving problems involving numbers, money, measures and time. There are also frequent opportunities to add or subtract a single-digit number or a multiple of 10 to or from any two-digit number mentally and to use practical and informal written methods to add and subtract two-digit numbers. The speaking and listening objective is actively encouraged during whole-class and group work when the children are asked to contribute to discussion and to respond to what others say in whole-class or pair work.

Lesson	Strands	Starter	Main teaching activities
1. Review, teach and apply	Use/apply Calculate	**Derive and recall all addition and subtraction facts for each number to at least 10, all pairs with totals to 20 and all pairs of multiples of 10 with totals up to 100.**	• Solve problems involving addition, subtraction, multiplication or division in contexts of numbers, measures or pounds and pence. **• Add or subtract mentally a one-digit number or a multiple of 10 to or from any two-digit number; use practical and informal written methods to add and subtract two-digit numbers.**
2. Review, teach and apply	Use/apply Calculate	As for Lesson 1	As for Lesson 1
3. Review and evaluate	Use/apply Calculate	Order two-digit numbers and position them on a number line; use the greater than (>) and less than (<) signs.	As for Lesson 1
4. Review, teach and practise	Measure	Read and write two-digit and three-digit numbers in figures and words; describe and extend number sequences and recognise odd and even numbers.	• Estimate, compare and measure lengths, choosing and using standard units (m, cm) and suitable measuring instruments. • Read the numbered divisions on a scale, and interpret the divisions between them (eg on a scale from 0 to 25 with intervals of 1 shown but only the divisions 0, 5, 10, 15 and 20 numbered).
5. Review, teach and practise	Measure	• As for Lesson 4 • Estimate a number of objects; round two-digit numbers to the nearest 10.	As for Lesson 4
6. Review, teach, practise and evaluate	Measure	As for Lesson 5	As for Lesson 4
7. Review, teach and practise	Measure	• Understand that halving is the inverse of doubling and derive and recall doubles of all numbers to 20, and the corresponding halves. • Identify near doubles using doubles already known (eg 8 + 9, 40 + 41).	**• Use units of time (seconds, minutes, hours, days) and know the relationships between them; read the time to the quarter hour; identify time intervals, including those that cross the hour.**
8. Teach, practise and evaluate	Measure	**State the subtraction corresponding to a given addition, and vice versa.**	As for Lesson 7
9. Review, teach and apply	Shape	As for Lesson 4	• Recognise and use whole, half and quarter turns, both clockwise and anti-clockwise; know that a right angle represents a quarter turn. • Follow and give instructions involving position, direction and movement.
10. Review, teach, apply and evaluate	Shape	As for Lesson 4	As for Lesson 9

Using and applying mathematics

- Solve problems involving addition, subtraction, multiplication or division in contexts of numbers, measures or pounds and pence.

Lessons 1-3

Preparation

Make an A3 copy of 'How to solve a problem' as a poster. Sort a mixture of plastic coins into a small container for each group of three children. Display the ten items as if on a shop counter and label them with prices from 'Price labels (pence)' and 'Price labels (£.p)'. Make enough shopping cards for at least 12 per group. Prepare 50cm, 1m, 1.5m and 2m lengths of ribbon or string. Make cards from 'Measures and money cards' for each pair or group, by ability (see Differentiation on page 148). Make OHTs of 'Recording sheet 1', 'Recording sheet 2' and 'Measures and money cards'; cut up the latter.

You will need

Photocopiable pages
'Measures and money problems' (page 155) for each child.
CD resources
'0-100 number cards', a set of 'Coin cards and labels', 'Price labels (pence)' and 'Price labels (£.p)' for each child, 'Addition and subtraction vocabulary' cards, an A3 copy of 'How to solve a problem', a set of 'Measures and money cards' for each pair or group (see General resources); OHTs of 'Recording sheet 1' and 'Recording sheet 2'; support and extension versions of 'Measures and money problems'; 'Shopping cards 1', '2' and '3'.
Equipment
Blu-Tack; plastic and real coins; small containers; ten different toys, food items or similar; a pendulum; a counting stick; ribbon or string.

Learning objectives

Starter

- Derive and recall all addition and subtraction facts for each number to at least 10, all pairs with totals to 20 and all pairs of multiples of 10 with totals up to 100.
- Order two-digit numbers and position them on a number line; use the greater than (>) and less than (<) signs.

Main teaching activities

2006

- Solve problems involving addition, subtraction, multiplication or division in contexts of numbers, measures or pounds and pence.
- Add or subtract mentally a one-digit number or a multiple of 10 to or from any two-digit number; use practical and informal written methods to add and subtract two-digit numbers.

1999

- Extend understanding of the operations of addition and subtraction.
- Use the related vocabulary.
- Partition into '5 and a bit' when adding 6, 7, 8 or 9, then recombine.
- Partition additions into tens and units, then recombine.
- Bridge through 10, then 20, and adjust.
- Find totals, give change and work out which coins to pay.
- Use mental addition and subtraction, simple multiplication and division to solve simple word problems involving numbers in 'real life', money or measures, using one or two steps.

Vocabulary

money, coin, penny, pence, pound, £, spend, pay, change, total, addition, subtraction, difference, equal

Lesson 1 (Review, teach and apply)

Starter

Recall and rehearse: Hold up a number from 0 to 10. Ask the children to write the number that adds to it to make 10 on their whiteboards. Ask for other pairs to make 10. Use fingers and jump along a number line to check. Repeat for 20 and then other totals below 20. See how many pairs of numbers the children can find to make the total in one minute.

Main teaching activities

Whole class: Explain that for the next few sessions, the children will practise mental addition and subtraction using money and length. Ask them to tell you words about addition and subtraction; as they do so, show the vocabulary cards and stick them on the board. Now ask them which coins we use; as they do so, hold up the labels and coins. Show the children the ten labelled items. Ask what each item costs. Ask questions such as: *How much does a bunch of bananas and a pineapple cost altogether?* Discuss strategies for calculating; encourage the children to use rounding and adjusting, counting on from the largest number, partitioning or counting along a number line.
Group work: Distribute the 'Recording sheet 1', one copy to each child. Model how they are going to use it. *You will be working on your own today, but sharing cards and money with two others. You need to have two piles of*

Differentiation

Less confident learners: Give this group shopping cards only to 50p.
More confident learners: Ask this group to pick three shopping cards (a mixture of the two types).

shopping cards: one for pence and the other for pounds and pence. Pick two cards, one from each pile, and work out the total you will spend. Record how you worked it out, then find the least number of coins that you need to pay. Write down what these coins are.

Review

Invite a few children to give examples of their work and explain their strategies. For each strategy, ask for an alternative and let the class decide which is more efficient.

Lesson 2 (Review, teach and apply)

Starter

Refresh: Draw a number line on the board with 20 divisions. Mark on 11, then jump up in ones to 20. Ask: *How many jumps? What goes with 11 to make 20?* Repeat a few times. Swing a pendulum and call out a number; as it swings the other way, the children call out the complement to make 20.

Main teaching activities

Whole class: Repeat the activity from Lesson 1, but use ribbon or string. *Today we are going to solve money problems that involve length. I would like to buy 2m of ribbon.* (Show this.) *Each metre costs 50p. How much will I spend? I have 10p, 20p and 50p coins in my purse. What coins could I use to pay for my ribbon? Is there another way? Think of as many ways as you can. If I have a £2 coin in my purse, how much change will I need? I want to buy 4m of ribbon. I have £1.80 in my purse. Do I have enough to buy the ribbon? How much more do I need? Which of these lengths of ribbon can be put together to make 4m? I have lengths of 50cm, 1m, 1m 50cm and 2m.* Repeat with similar scenarios and questions.
Group work: Provide the 'Measures and money cards' sheet 1, and a copy of 'Recording sheet 2' for each pair. Model how the children use these. *Work with a friend. You have two piles of cards: one to tell you what you are going to buy, the other to tell you how much money you have. You need to work out how much you will spend and then decide whether you have enough money. If you do, work out how much you will have left over; if you don't, work out how much more you need.* Work through two or three examples.

Review

Write a problem on the board based on the measures and money cards, such as: *Suzie needs some rope. She buys 5m. Each metre costs £1.25. How much does she spend? She gives the shopkeeper seven pound coins. How much change is she given?* Ask the children what they must do to solve the problem. Ask questions such as: *What is the problem asking you to find out? Which words tell us that? How can you work out how much she spent? Is there another way?* Show the poster of 'How to solve a problem' and work through each point for this problem. Invite some children to talk through problems they solved, sharing their methods and relating them to the poster. Use questions as above to assess the children's problem-solving skills.

Differentiation

Less confident learners: Provide the 'Measures and money cards' sheet 2, with money to £1. Work with this group, reading the problems and giving guidance.
More confident learners: Provide the 'Measures and money cards' sheet 3, with larger amounts of money.

Lesson 3 (Apply and evaluate)

Starter

Read and reason: Give each child a number card at random from 0–100. Ask five children to come to the front and stand with their numbers held up, ordered from lowest to highest. Invite other children to stand in the place appropriate to their number. Ask the class to check that they are standing in the right places and explain why. When the line is ten children long, ask the original five to sit down and another five to go to the places appropriate to their numbers. Repeat until everyone has had a go. Ask questions such as: *Who is holding the number closest to 34? Who is holding an odd number between 20 and 30?*

Main teaching activities

Whole class: Explain that this lesson is about solving 'real-life' problems. The children will be thinking about how to solve two-step problems and the best strategies to use. Discuss strategies for addition and subtraction, particularly: partitioning and recombining; adding 10 or 20 and then adjusting; using the inverse operation. Ask the children what they must do to solve a problem. Show the poster of 'How to solve a problem' and write a problem from the Review of Lesson 2 on the OHP. Work through it using the strategies above and ask if anyone can think of other strategies. Discuss which strategy is most efficient.

Paired/individual work: Ask the children to work individually or with a partner on the 'Measures and money problems' photocopiable sheet, finding the best strategy to answer each problem. Model an example from the sheet.

Differentiation

Less confident learners: Provide the support version of 'Measures and money problems' with simpler quantities. Work with this group: take them through the problems step by step, give guidance and discuss their strategies.

More confident learners: Provide the extension version with more complex quantities.

Review

Invite some children to explain how they solved their problems. Question them carefully about the steps they used and why they chose particular strategies. Ask how they could check their answers. Encourage them to think about using the inverse operation. Demonstrate this using arrow diagrams.

Lessons 4-6

Preparation

Cut out two 10cm strips of paper about 2cms wide per child.

You will need

Photocopiable pages

'How long am I?' (page 156) and 'What weight am I?' (page 157).

CD resources

'What capacity am I?'. Interactive resources 'Weighing scales' and 'Measuring jug'.

Equipment

Metre stick, one ruler per child, six different objects per group, 500g per group, weighing scales, measuring jugs, six different containers of water per group, 2l pop bottle filled with water per group.

Learning objectives

Starter

- Read and write two-digit and three-digit numbrs in figures and words; describe and extend number sequences; recognise odd and even numbers.
- Estimate a number of objects; round two-digit numbers to the nearest 10.

Main teaching activities

2006

- Estimate, compare and measure lengths, weights and capacities, choosing and using standard units (m, cm, kg, litre) and suitable measuring instruments.
- Read the numbered divisions on a scale, and interpret the divisions between them (eg on a scale from 0 to 25 with intervals of 1 shown but only the divisions 0, 5, 10, 15 and 20 numbered); use a ruler to draw and measure lines to the nearest centimetre.

1999

- Use and begin to read the vocabulary related to length.
- Estimate, measure and compare lengths, using standard units (m, cm); suggest suitable units and equipment for such measurements.

Vocabulary

measure, metre, centimetre, long, short, high, low, tall, wide, narrow, deep, shallow, thick, thin, ruler, metre stick, gram, kilogram, half-kilogram, light, heavy, scales, balance, weight, litre, millilitre, half-litre, full, half-full, empty, contain, container

Lesson 4 (Review, teach and practise)

Starter

Read and refine: Write a three-digit number on the board and ask the children to read it and then write it on their whiteboards. Tell them to treat the number as individual digits and encourage them to make as many two-digit numbers as they can, writing them down. Take feedback and then ask them to order those numbers from smallest to largest. Discuss which are odd and even, and which are multiples of 2, 5 and 10. Repeat with another three-digit number.

Main teaching activities

Whole class: Say: *For the next three lessons we will be reminding ourselves of what we did in Block C with measures, and thinking especially about scale. Today we will work with length.* Ask the children to work together in twos to think of vocabulary words to do with length. Take feedback, sort these into words for: units, equipment, descriptive. Discuss the different units by asking: *What would we use to measure someone's height, the length of a book and the length of your fingernail?*

Show a metre stick and choose a volunteer. Ask the class to estimate the volunteer's height and then measure them. Repeat with a few children, expecting estimates to get better.

Demonstrate how to measure a line, discuss the scale markings and point to a few, asking such questions as: *What is this length? If I drew a line double/half that length, how long would it be? If it was 1/10cm longer/shorter, what length would that be? How do you work out the numbers between the ones that are shown on the scale? If this scale carried on, what other numbers would be marked?*

Paired/individual work: The children should work individually or in pairs within groups of about four in order to share equipment and ideas. They each need a copy of 'How long am I?', 10cm strips of paper and a ruler. For each line, they should use the 10cm strip of paper to help them estimate and then the ruler to actually measure. They should record as shown on the sheet.

Differentiation

The lines are differentiated; all children should have the opportunity to try to measure each as accurately as possible. Some may answer to the nearest centimetre, some may be more accurate.

Review

Take feedback from the activity. Ask the children to give you their estimates from one of the lines. Write five of these on the board and order them from shortest to longest and then compare each with the actual length.

Lesson 5 (Review, teach and practise)

Starter

Refine, read and rehearse: Repeat the starter from Lesson 4. Then ask the children to round the numbers to the nearest 10.

Main teaching activities

Whole class: Recap the work from Lesson 4, paying particular attention to the types of scale used and the estimating and actual measuring. Say that they will be doing something similar today but concentrating on weight. Ask the children to work together in twos, and to think of vocabulary words to do with weight. Take feedback, sort these into words for: units, equipment, description. Discuss the different units by asking: *What would we use to weigh a person/elephant? How about a potato/glass?*

Show the children the interactive resource 'Weighing scales' and discuss the marks. Add some weights to the pan and ask such questions as: *What is this weight? If I added another 100g, what weight would that be? If it was 1/10/100 grams heavier/lighter, what weight would that be? How do you work out the numbers between the ones that are shown on the scale?*

Show your objects and ask the children to estimate how much they think they might weigh, one at a time, and then compare with the actual weight using the scales. Discuss why it is difficult to make a sensible estimate: you really need to hold the item.

Group work: The children should work in mixed-ability groups of about four. Each group needs a 500g weight and six objects. Their task is to estimate the weights of the objects by comparing with the 500g weight (ask them to estimate to the nearest 100g). They should record on 'What weight am I?'.

Differentiation

Check that less confident learners are taking an active part in the estimating activity, and that more confident learners are not being allowed to dominate the group discussions.

Review

Ask individuals to help you to weigh the items so that they can complete the actual weights on their recording grid. Ask them to work out the differences between their estimates and the actual weights, and find out which groups were closest for each item.

Lesson 6 (Review, teach, practise and evaluate)

Starter

Refine, read and rehearse: As for Lesson 5.

Main teaching activities

Whole class: Recap the work from Lesson 5. Tell the children they will be doing something similar today but concentrating on capacity. Ask them to work together in twos, to think of vocabulary words and then sort them into: units, equipment, description. Discuss the different units by asking: *What would we use to measure water in a teaspoon? How about a bath?*

Show them the interactive resource 'Measuring jug' and discuss the marks. Add some liquid and ask such questions as: *What is this capacity? If I added another 100ml, what would that be? If there was 1/10/100ml more/less, what would that be? How do you work out the numbers between the ones that are shown on the scale? If this scale carried on, what other numbers would be marked?*

Show some of the containers and ask the children to estimate how much they think they might be, one at a time, and then compare with the actual capacity using a measuring jug. Discuss why it is difficult to make a sensible estimate: you need something to compare it with.

Group work: The children should work in mixed-ability groups of about four. Each group needs a two-litre bottle of water and six containers. Their task is to estimate the capacity of the containers by comparing with the two-litre bottle. Ask them to estimate to the nearest 100ml. They should record on the 'What capacity am I?' activity sheet.

Review

As a class, ask individuals to help you to measure the items so that they can complete the actual capacities on their recording grid. Ask them to work out the differences between their estimates and the actual capacities. Find out which groups were closest for each.

Differentiation

As for Lesson 5.

Lessons 7-8

Preparation

Copy and laminate the gameboard and copy and cut out the cards and spinners from 'Dartboard doubles' game; copy the 'Up the mountain' gameboard onto A3, and make laminated A4 copies; copy and laminate the 'Analogue and digital time cards' and 'Addition and subtraction cards'.

You will need

CD resources

An A3 copy of 'Up the mountain' and a copy for each group, plus 'Up the mountain 2', time vocabulary cards from 'Measures vocabulary', 'Dartboard doubles' game, 'Analogue and digital time cards', 'Addition and subtraction cards' (see General resources). Interactive resource 'Clocks'.

Equipment

An analogue card clock for each child; a real digital clock; dice; counters.

Learning objectives

Starter

- Understand that halving is the inverse of doubling and derive and recall doubles of all numbers to 20, and the corresponding halves.
- Identify near doubles using doubles already known (eg 8 + 9, 40 + 41).
- State the subtraction corresponding to a given addition, and vice versa.

Main teaching activities

2006

- Use units of time (seconds, minutes, hours, days) and know the relationships between them; read the time to the quarter hour; identify time intervals, including those that cross the hour.

1999

- Use and begin to read the vocabulary related to time.
- Suggest suitable units to estimate or measure time.
- Use units of time and know the relationships between them (second, minute, hour, day, week).

Vocabulary

time, month, year, weekend, second, minute, hour, half an hour, quarter of an hour, o'clock, half past, quarter past, quarter to, digital, analogue, clock, watch, hands, January, February...

Lesson 7 (Review, teach and practise)

Starter

Recall and refresh: Play the 'Dartboard doubles' game. Adapt the instructions for the class to play in two or three teams.

Main teaching activities

Whole class: Explain that the next two lessons are about time. Give each child a card clock. Ask the children to give you some facts about it. Look for: *The numbers going round from 1 to 12 show us what the hour is; the minute hand shows us parts of an hour, such as 'o'clock' (hand on 12), 'half past' (hand on 6), 'quarter past' (hand on 3) or 'quarter to' (hand on 9); the little marks in between the numbers are minutes; there are five minutes from one number to the next.*

Ask the children to put a finger on the 12, then move to the 1. *How many minutes is that?* Carry on so that the children are counting in fives. Ask them to put the hour hand on the 12. Count round in fives again; when you reach 3, ask how many minutes past the o'clock that is. Write on the board '15 minutes past 12'. Ask them how else we can say that, reminding them that the minute hand has gone a quarter of the way round. (Quarter past 12.)

Show the digital clock and say: *How would you see this time on a digital clock or a video/DVD recorder? The hour number goes first and then the number of minutes past, so you will see 12:15.* Repeat this for 30 minutes past 12, 45 minutes past 12 and 1 o'clock. Link quarter past 12 to 12:15, and link 15 to three lots of 5, or 5 × 3.

Call out analogue and digital times from the cards for the children to show on their clocks, such as: *3:45, quarter past 6, 2:30, 15 minutes past 11.* Divide the class into two teams to play 'Up the mountain'. Call out a time, wait until everyone has shown it (the children can help each other) and then throw a dice. If an even number is thrown, the first team moves up the mountain; if an odd number is thrown, the second team moves. Expecting all the children to show the time will ensure that they all participate.

Review

Ask the children to show you how confident they are with times by showing a thumbs up, down or level sign. Talk about the vocabulary of time. Show the time vocabulary cards or write them on the board, asking the children to explain what they mean.

Lesson 8 (Teach, practise and evaluate)

Starter

Recall: Show the 'Addition and subtraction cards' and ask the children to write the corresponding addition or subtraction. For example, if you show 12 + 7 = 19 they should write 19 - 7 = 12. Ask them to explain their responses and demonstrate with jumps of 1 along a number line.

Main teaching activities

Whole class: Recap Lesson 7 and ask the children to play 'Up the mountain' again to help them practise finding analogue and digital times.

Group work: Put the children into mixed-ability groups of four to play as two pairs. Model the game using the appropriate instructions.

Review

Ask the children to give a thumbs-up sign if they think they can find times more quickly now than they could before. Make a note of any who cannot, so that you can target them specifically with oral and mental starter activities related to time. Set the children some problems that they can answer using their clocks, such as: *My clock says 1 o'clock, but it is half an hour slow. Show me what time it really is. My clock says half past six, but it is 15 minutes fast. What time is it really?*

Differentiation

Check that more confident learners do not dominate proceedings in the 'Up the mountain' activity.

Lessons 9-10

Preparation
Photocopy 'Position vocabulary' onto A3 card and cut out the cards.

You will need
CD resources
'Position vocabulary' cards (see General resources), an OHT of 'Amazing race' (see General resources).
Equipment
Individual whiteboards and pens; an OHP; a Roamer or similar floor robot; the NNS ICT program *Unit the Robot.*

Learning objectives

Starter
- Read and write two-digit and three-digit numbers in figures and words; describe and extend number sequences and recognise odd and even numbers.

Main teaching activities
2006
- Recognise and use whole, half and quarter turns, both clockwise and anti-clockwise; know that a right angle represents a quarter turn.
- Follow and give instructions involving position, direction and movement.

1999
- Use mathematical vocabulary to describe position, direction and movement.
- Recognise whole, half and quarter turns, to the left or right, clockwise, anticlockwise.

Vocabulary
over, under, underneath, above, below, top, bottom, side, outside, inside, around, in front, behind, front, back, beside, next to, opposite, between, middle, edge, centre, corner, direction, clockwise, anticlockwise, whole turn, half turn, quarter turn, right angle, straight line

Lesson 9 (Review, teach and apply)

Starter
Refresh and reason: Hold up a triangle and ask how many sides it has. Ask a child to write the number on the board. Show two triangles and ask: *How many sides altogether?* Ask the child at the board to write that number. Repeat for up to ten triangles. Ask the children what they notice. (They are counting in threes.) Repeat for quadrilaterals. Can the children predict what will happen with pentagons? Try it and see.

Main teaching activities
Whole class: Explain that today, the children will revise their work on positions of objects, then think about moving and turning them. Ask them to give you some position vocabulary. As they do so, hold up the vocabulary cards. Ask them to use their whiteboards: *Draw a circle under a line. Draw a square over a circle. Draw a pentagon beside a triangle.*

Write these words on the board: 'clockwise', 'anticlockwise', 'whole turn', 'half turn', 'quarter turn', 'right angle', 'straight line'. Point to the words and say: *Who can tell me what a turn is? Can you show me? What is a quarter turn? What type of angle does it make? Which direction is clockwise? What about anticlockwise? Everyone stand up. Turn clockwise for a quarter of a turn. Turn anticlockwise to make a right angle turn. Turn anticlockwise to make a turn the size of a straight line.*

Group work: Demonstrate the program *Unit the Robot* with a floor robot. Let groups of children have a turn at this program. If a PC is not available, choose an adult or a child to be the 'robot' and orally 'program' them with instructions to move around the classroom.

Review
Discuss how the children got on with the computer program. Invite some children to 'program' a human robot (an adult or child) to get around the classroom by moving and turning. Assess whether they know the necessary vocabulary and use it correctly.

Differentiation
Less confident learners: Encourage peer buddying for any child who is having difficulty.
More confident learners: Ask the children for more complicated programming.

Lesson 10 (Review, teach, apply and evaluate)

Starter

Refresh and reason: As for Lesson 9.

Main teaching activities

Whole class: Revisit the vocabulary of direction and movement. Ask: *Who can tell me what a turn is? Can you show me? What is a quarter turn? What angle does a quarter turn make? Which direction is clockwise... anticlockwise? Give the children card clocks. Show me 12 o'clock. Move the minute hand a quarter turn clockwise. What time does that say? Now move it a half turn clockwise. What time is that? Make a whole turn anticlockwise. What time is that?* Repeat with the children moving. *Now everyone stand up. Turn clockwise for a quarter turn...* and so on.

Now project the OHT of 'Amazing race' and ask the children to tell you how to move a counter through the maze.

Paired work: The children work in pairs to design a maze on A3 paper with right-angled turns (both clockwise and anticlockwise) and straight-on moves, then give each other instructions to steer a toy car through the maze.

Differentiation

Check that less confident learners are taking an active part in designing a maze, and that more confident learners are not being allowed to dominate the activity.

Review

Ask the class to give directions through each of the mazes. Ask the children to make a right angle with their hands. Ask them to look around the room and point to any right angles they can see. Ask: *What shapes have right angles?* Discuss right angles in real life: in objects, shapes and turns.

Name ______________________ Date ________________

Measures and money problems

Solve these problems.

Show what you did.

For example:

Ben found some string.

He found 8cm in his cupboard.

He found 7cm under his bed.

He wanted 20cm. How much more did he need?

I did this: 5 + 3 + 5 + 2 = 10 + 5 = 15

15 to 20 is 5.

My answer is: 5cm

Now you try:

Sally found some ribbon.

She found 18cm in her cupboard.

She found 19cm in her pocket.

She wanted 50cm.

How much more did she need?

I did this:

My answer is:

Tyrone spent 75p on some rope and 90p on some string.

He gave the shopkeeper £5.

How much change did he need?

I did this:

My answer is:

Hyatt found some ribbon.

She found 29cm in her bedroom.

She found 39cm in her pocket.

She used 60cm.

How much did she have left over?

I did this:

My answer is:

Kulvinder bought 5 metres of rope.

The rope cost 50p a metre.

He had £2.

How much more money did he need?

I did this:

My answer is:

Shelley needed 1m of wool.

Her mother gave her a piece 30cm long.

Her sister gave her a piece 49cm long.

How much more did she need?

I did this:

My answer is:

Name ______________________ Date ______________________

How long am I?

Line	Estimate	Actual
1		
2		
3		
4		
5		
6		
7		
8		
9		
10		

7.

8.

9.

10.

1. ______

2. ____________

3. ______________

4. ____________________

5. __________________________

6. ______________________________

Name ______________________ Date ______________

What weight am I?

Object	Estimate	Actual
1		
2		
3		
4		
5		
6		

Calculating, measuring and understanding shape

Speaking and listening objective

- Listen to others in class, ask relevant questions and follow instructions.

Introduction

Lessons 1 and 2 in this block rehearse, consolidate and progress mental addition and subtraction strategies in the context of money. Lessons 3 and 4 are based on estimating and measuring, with a focus on reading scales and making reference to number lines. These lessons build on work carried out more extensively in Block C Unit 3. Lessons 5 to 9 focus on analogue and digital time, building on the children's experiences during Unit 2 and also in several starter activities. Lesson 10 focuses on direction and movement using whole, half and quarter turns, both clockwise and anti-clockwise. This lesson makes the link to time and the movement on an analogue clock. Threaded throughout this entire block is the using and applying objective of solving problems involving numbers, money, measures and time. There are also frequent opportunities to add or subtract a single-digit number or a multiple of 10 mentally, to or from any two-digit number and to use practical and informal written methods to add and subtract two-digit numbers. The speaking and listening objective is actively encouraged during whole-class and group work when the children are asked to contribute to discussion and to respond to what others say in whole-class or pair situations.

Lesson	Strands	Starter	Main teaching activities
1. Review, teach and apply	Calculate Use/apply	**Derive and recall all addition and subtraction facts for each number to at least 10, all pairs with totals to 20 and all pairs of multiples of 10 with totals up to 100.**	• Solve problems involving addition, subtraction, multiplication or division in contexts of numbers, measures or pounds and pence. • **Add or subtract mentally a one-digit number or a multiple of 10 to or from any two-digit number; use practical and informal written methods to add and subtract two-digit numbers.**
2. Teach, apply and evaluate	Calculate	As for Lesson 1	As for Lesson 1
3. Review, teach and practise	Calculate	Read and write two-digit and three-digit numbers in figures and words; describe and extend number sequences and recognise odd and even numbers.	• Estimate, compare and measure lengths, choosing and using standard units (m, cm) and suitable measuring instruments. • Read the numbered divisions on a scale, and interpret the divisions between them (eg on a scale from 0 to 25 with intervals of 1 shown but only the divisions 0, 5, 10, 15 and 20 numbered); use a ruler to draw and measure lines to the nearest centimetre.
4. Apply and evaluate	Measure	Estimate a number of objects; round two-digit numbers to the nearest 10.	As for Lesson 3
5. Review and practise	Measure	As for Lesson 1	**Use units of time (seconds, minutes, hours, days) and know the relationships between them; read the time to the quarter hour; identify time intervals, including those that cross the hour.**
6. Review, practise and evaluate	Measure	**Visualise common 2D shapes and 3D solids; identify shapes from pictures of them in different positions and orientations; sort, make and describe shapes, referring to their properties.**	As for Lesson 5
7. Review, teach and practise	Measure	As for Lesson 6	As for Lesson 5
8. Teach and practise	Measure	**Derive and recall all addition and subtraction facts for each number to at least 10.**	As for Lesson 5
9. Teach, apply and evaluate	Shape	• Add/subtract 9 or 11: add/subtract 10 and adjust by 1. • Add/subtract 19 or 21: add/subtract 20 and adjust by 1.	As for Lesson 5
10. Review, teach, apply and evaluate	Shape	As for Lesson 6	Recognise and use whole, half and quarter turns, both clockwise and anti-clockwise; know that a right angle represents a quarter turn.

Using and applying mathematics

- Solve problems involving addition, subtraction, multiplication or division in contexts of numbers, measures or pounds and pence.

Lessons 1-2

Preparation
Copy 'How much change?' onto an OHT.

You will need
Photocopiable pages
An OHT of 'How much change?' (page 168).
CD resources
An A3 copy of 'Flip-flap for 20', 'Price labels (pence)' and 'Price labels (£.p)' for each group, 'How to solve a problem' poster, 'Flip-flap for 10' for each child (see General resources); 'Change problems', support, extension and template versions. Interactive resource 'Money'.
Equipment
Coins.

Learning objectives

Starter

- Derive and recall all addition and subtraction facts for each number to at least 10, all pairs with totals to 20 and all pairs of multiples of 10 with totals up to 100.

Main teaching activities

2006

- Solve problems involving addition, subtraction, multiplication or division in contexts of numbers, measures or pounds and pence.
- Add or subtract mentally a one-digit number or a multiple of 10 to or from any two-digit number; use practical and informal written methods to add and subtract two-digit numbers.

1999

- Recognise all coins and begin to use £.p notation for money.
- Find totals, give change, and work out which coins to pay.
- Use mental calculation strategies.

Vocabulary

lots of, groups of, times, multiply, multiplied by, multiple of, repeated addition, array, row, column, equal groups of, repeated subtraction, divide, divided by

Lesson 1 (Review, teach and apply)

Starter

Refresh and reason: Show the children your A3 'Flip-flap for 20' unfolded and ask how many ladybirds they can see. Fold it so that when you hold it up, they can see one ladybird. Ask: *If you can only see one and there are 20 altogether, how many can you see?* Fold it so that they can see 12: *Now how many can you see? How many can I see?* Repeat several times. Give each child a copy of 'Flip-flap for 10'. Ask the children to imagine that each snail means ten snails. Ask them to show you 40, 60, 20 and so on. Now ask questions such as: *If I can see 70, show me how many you can see.*

Main teaching activities

Whole class: Show the children the coins we use; ask them to identify the different coins and say what each is worth. Hold up some of the 'pence' price label cards and ask them which coins they could use to make each amount. Ask a child to explain, for example, how you could swap three pennies for one 2p coin and a penny. After a couple of goes with the children calling out or raising hands, ask them to write the answers on their whiteboards. Move on to doing the same thing with the '£.p' labels. Remind the children that the number after the £ sign is the pounds and the number after the decimal point is the pence. If you prefer, use the interactive resource 'Money' to demonstrate this activity.

Tell the children that you have £1. Choose a volunteer to be the shopkeeper, who picks a 'pence' card and tells you what it is. Say: *That is the amount I have spent. I am going to give my pound to the shopkeeper. What change does s/he need to give me?* Allow some thinking time, then check the children's answers by counting up on a number line on the board. Ask the children which coins you should use. Repeat for a different card.

Group work: Ask the children to work in groups of three or four. Each group needs a pile of price label cards ('pence' and '£.p') face down, and a container with coins including £1 and £2. They take turns to pick a card, read the amount they will spend and decide how many whole pounds to give the shopkeeper; then the group work out the change together using a number line.

Differentiation
Less confident learners: Provide price label cards with amounts to £1, and real coins for the children to use. If possible, move them on to finding change from £2.
More confident learners: Encourage the children to find change from £5 and £10.

Review
Invite a few children, particularly any whom you wish to assess, to show what they did in the group activity. Ask questions such as: *How are you going to find out the change? What amount will you count on from? What is the first amount you will count to? What next? What is the total change?* You or a more confident child could draw the answers on a number line.

Lesson 2 (Teach, apply and evaluate)

Starter
Refine: Repeat the Starter from Lesson 1, but spend longer on using the 'Flip-flap for 10' to explore the multiples of 10.

Main teaching activities
Whole class: This lesson is about real-life money problems. Ask: *When do we have problems to solve that involve money?* Talk about shopping and how we might ask ourselves: 'Can I afford both of those?' Recap on what we need to do when solving a problem. Write the stages of problem solving (see the 'How to solve a problem' poster) on the board. Stick the problem-solving poster on the wall. Work through the three problems on the OHT of 'How much change?' Ask questions about the process as you go along. For example, when considering the first problem, ask questions such as: (1) *What is the problem asking us to find? Which words tell us that?* (2) *What information do we need to find the answer? Do we need to know which shop I was in? Do we need to know how much the mango cost?* (3) *What do we have to do? Would it help to count on from 59p to £1?* (4) *What is the answer? Does that make sense? How can we check it? Would it help to add our answer to the cost of the mango and see if that makes £1?*

Focus on addition strategies for totalling two amounts by asking such questions as: *What is 34p + 48p? What number facts might you use to help you to work this out? How many do you need to add to 34 to get to the next multiple of 10? How might you partition 8 to help you?*
Paired work: Ask the children to work in pairs on the 'Change problems' activity sheet. Talk it through with them first.

Differentiation
Less confident learners: Provide these children with the support version of 'Change problems'.
More confident learners: These children can be given the extension version of the activity sheet.

Review
Invite a few children, particularly any whom you wish to assess, to show what they did to find the answers to the problems. Ask questions similar to those in the review for Lesson 1. Also recap addition and subtraction strategies by asking: *Show me how you could work out the answer to 47p + 29p. What about 72p + 48p? Can you work out your answer in a different way? Which way do you find most helpful? Why?* Repeat with subtractions. *Find the missing number:* 12 + □ - 25 = 58.

Lessons 3-4

You will need
CD resources
'Estimating activities'. Interactive resources 'Weighing scales' and 'Measuring jug'.
Equipment
Individual whiteboards and pens; mug, bag of potatoes, string, ruler, metre stick. For each group: string, rulers, loose potatoes.

Learning objectives

Starter

- Read and write two-digit and three-digit numbers in figures and words; describe and extend number sequences; recognise odd and even numbers.
- Estimate a number of objects; round two-digit numbers to the nearest 10.

Main teaching activities

2006

- Estimate, compare and measure lengths, weights and capacities, choosing and using standard units (m, cm, kg, litre) and suitable measuring instruments.
- Read the numbered divisions on a scale, and interpret the divisions between them (eg on a scale from 0 to 25 with intervals of 1 shown but only the divisions 0, 5, 10, 15 and 20 numbered); use a ruler to draw and measure lines to the nearest centimetre.

1999

- Read a simple scale to the nearest labelled division.
- Use and begin to read the vocabulary related to length.
- Estimate, measure and compare lengths, using standard units (m, cm); suggest suitable units and equipment for such measurements.

Vocabulary

measure, metre, centimetre, long, short, high, low, tall, wide, narrow, deep, shallow, thick, thin, ruler, metre stick, gram, kilogram, half-kilogram, light, heavy, scales, balance, weight, litre, millilitre, half-litre, full, half-full, empty, contain, container

Lesson 3 (Review, teach and practise)

Starter

Rehearse and read: Ask the children to write 5 on their whiteboards, next ask them to follow your instructions, for example, make it 30 more, take away 5, add 100, double it, take away 100. After a few instructions, ask them to read the new number and show you their boards, adjusting if necessary.

Main teaching activities

Whole class: Tell the children that the next two lessons will focus briefly on measures and reading scales. Say that they will be using their experiences from the work done in Block C to help them.

Discuss the different measures, including vocabulary, units and equipment. Write up 100cm = ?, ? = 1kg, ?l = ?ml on the board and ask the children to complete the statements. Then repeat for other measurements, eg ½m = ?, 500ml = ? Show a metre stick and ask: *What can you see in the classroom that is longer than 1 metre; what is shorter? Tell me two lengths that make one metre. Can you tell me another two lengths?* Draw a ruler on the board and ask questions regarding the scale. Draw a line on the screen and ask the children to estimate the length of that line, using the ruler as a guide. Measure it and compare estimates. Repeat a few times.

Ask the children to draw a line on a piece of paper using a ruler and then give their line to a partner. The partner should estimate the length of the line and then measure it. Repeat this a few times, allowing the children to work at their own pace. Take feedback from this activity.

Move on to weight. Show the children the interactive resource 'Weighing scales' and focus on the scale adding and taking away different weights. Ask questions such as: *Can you tell me two weights that make 1 kilogram? Can*

you tell me another two weights? Repeat for capacity, using the interactive resource 'Measuring jug'.

Review

Briefly recap on the units of measure. Draw a line similar to the one below and ask: *About how long do you think this line is? How could you measure it?* Demonstrate how to do this using string and a ruler.

Show the mug and ask: *Which of these amounts is the estimate of the capacity of the mug?*

1 metre   1 litre   1 kilogram   1 centimetre   ¼ kilogram   ¼ litre

Show the bag of potatoes and ask the same question.

Tell the children that they will be doing a few practical tasks during the next lesson that will help to reinforce this.

Lesson 4 (Apply and evaluate)

Starter

Rehearse, refine and read: Repeat the Starter from Lesson 3, but this time include rounding as well. For example, ask the children to round to the nearest 10, take away 1.

Main teaching activities

Whole class: Briefly recap the vocabulary, units and measuring equipment for each measure. Say that today the children will be working, in groups, through an activity sheet which will reinforce the work they have been doing on estimating, measuring and reading scales.

Group work: The children should work in mixed ability groups of about four. Demonstrate the first activity from the CD page 'Estimating activities'. Ask them to tell you what they think they should do for the other two activities. Ask the groups to start on different activities, so all will be covered. Encourage them to measure as accurately as they can.

Review

Take feedback from the children about the activities, asking them to evaluate their estimating skills. Draw a number line on the board like the one below, with an arrow pointing to 50, and ask: *Who can come and draw an arrow to show where the number 125 belongs? What about 25, 75, 110?*

Draw this scale and say: *Here is a scale which shows the weight of a letter.*

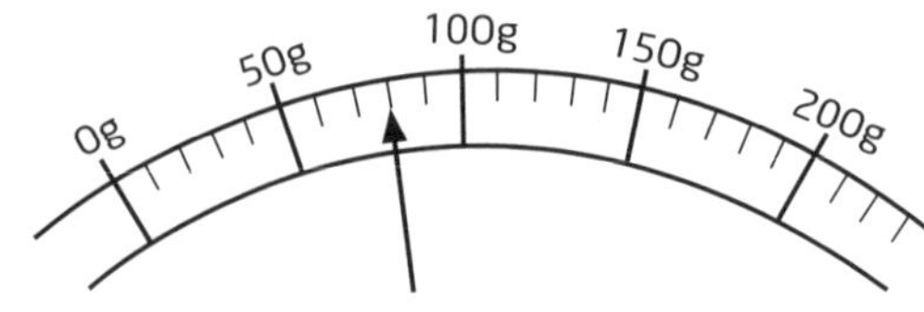

Ask: *How much does the letter weigh?*

Repeat the question for different weights and then, if you have time, repeat for capacity. Ask: *How do you work out the numbers not shown on a scale?*

Differentiation

If the less confident learners find the activity sheet difficult to read and understand, suggest that a confident reader reads the sheet to the whole group. Then encourage the children to explain to each other what they have to do.

Lessons 5-6

Preparation
If you haven't already done this, copy the 'Up the mountain' gameboard onto A3 paper for whole-class use. Enlarge and photocopy 'Measures vocabulary' for time, 'Months of the year cards' and 'More time vocabulary' onto card. Group the time vocabulary cards into days of the week, months, seasons, general words and comparisons.

You will need
CD resources
'0-100 number cards', 'Up the mountain gameboard', 'Measures vocabulary' for time, 'Months of the year cards', 'Templates for irregular shapes 1' and '2', 'Templates for regular shapes' and 'More time vocabulary' (see General resources).
Equipment
Three or four counters; dice; individual whiteboards, pens and cloths; tape recorder.

Learning objectives

Starter
- Derive and recall all addition and subtraction facts for each number to at least 10, all pairs with totals to 20 and all pairs of multiples of 10 with totals up to 100.
- Visualise common 2D shapes and 3D solids; identify shapes from pictures of them in different positions and orientations; sort, make and describe shapes, referring to their properties.

Main teaching activities
2006
- Use units of time (seconds, minutes, hours, days) and know the relationships between them; read the time to the quarter hour; identify time intervals, including those that cross the hour.

1999
- Suggest suitable units to estimate or measure time.

Vocabulary
Monday, Tuesday... Sunday, January, February... December, spring, summer, autumn, winter, day, week, fortnight, month, year, weekend, birthday, holiday, morning, afternoon, evening, night, midnight, bedtime, dinnertime, playtime, today, yesterday, tomorrow, before, after, next, last, now, soon, early, late, quick, quicker, quickest, quickly, fast, faster, fastest, slow, slower, slowest, slowly, old, older, oldest, new, newer, newest, takes longer, takes less time

Lesson 5 (Review and practise)

Starter
Recall: You will need the number cards to 20, the cards with multiples of 10 to 100, and the 'Up the mountain' gameboard. Divide the children into three or four teams. Pick a number card, show it to the class and expect all the children to write on their whiteboards the number that goes with it to make 20 or, if a multiple of 10, 100. The children can support each other in this activity. When everyone has written their answer and they are all correct, throw the dice and whichever number thrown matches the team number, that is, one for Team 1, two for Team 2, and so on, they move a place up the mountain. If you throw a 5 or 6, everyone moves up two spaces.

Main teaching activities
Whole class: Say: *This week you will be thinking about time. Today and tomorrow we are concentrating on how we measure time. Let's start by thinking about the words that we know that are to do with time. What vocabulary would we use for this topic?* Listen to the children's suggestions and talk about when they would use each one. Don't show the vocabulary cards just yet.

Say*: I'm going to hold up a vocabulary card now and I would like you to think about the other words that would go with it.* Show one of the days of the week cards. After the children have told you that this is a day and what the others are, give one card to each of seven children and ask the class to order them. Ask them to tell you something that happens on each day of the week, either in their home life or their school life. Repeat this with the months of the year, bringing in birthdays, seasons and holidays.

Show the cards that say: 'day', 'week', 'fortnight', 'month', 'year', 'weekend', 'morning', 'afternoon', 'evening', 'night', 'midnight', 'bedtime', 'dinnertime', 'playtime', 'today', 'yesterday', 'tomorrow' and ask the children what they think is meant by these words.

Mix up all the vocabulary cards that you have shown and randomly choose four of them. Show them to the children. Ask them to turn to a partner and make up a short story that uses all four words correctly. Give them an example: words: *week, evening, tomorrow, bedtime. My mum said that tomorrow my bedtime can be later than normal, because in the evening we are going to the circus. The circus came to town last week and will be going in a few days. I'm very excited about seeing it.*

Group work: The children should work in pairs or small groups. Give four vocabulary cards to each group and ask them to make up a story to include each word. They can either jot down their ideas or simply remember them.

Differentiation

Check that less confident learners take an active part in the story-telling activity, and that more confident learners do not dominate proceedings.

Review

Ask each group to share their stories. If you have any facilities for doing so, you could make audio recordings for the future. Discuss whether any of the vocabulary words were difficult to use, and invite all of the children to think about ways in which these could be incorporated into sentences.

Lesson 6 (Review, practise and evaluate)

Starter

Refresh: Give each child a shape cut from 'Templates for irregular shapes' and 'Templates for regular shapes'. Call out the properties of shapes to do with number of sides, corners and lines of symmetry, and their names. Ask the children to stand if their shape matches the properties or names that you are calling out.

Main teaching activities

Whole class: Recap on the vocabulary that the children thought about in Lesson 5 and then show them the comparison and measure type words: 'before', 'after', 'next', 'last', 'now', 'soon', 'early', 'late', 'quick', 'quicker', 'quickest', 'quickly', 'fast', 'faster', 'fastest', 'slow', 'slower', 'slowest', 'slowly', 'old', 'older', 'oldest', 'new', 'newer', 'newest', 'takes longer', 'takes less time'. Ask the children to work with a partner. Give each pair one of the first eight words and ask them to make up a sentence using it. Listen to each pair's ideas.

Group work: Show the five sets of cards that have got the three or four linked words (eg 'quick', 'quicker', 'quickest', 'quickly'). Give each pair one of these and ask them to make up a story which uses each word. Give them an example first: *My friend is a fast runner. She ran a race and was faster than anyone else. She is the fastest runner in our class.*

Differentiation

As for Lesson 5.

Review

Listen to each pair's story. Recap the vocabulary used during the lesson. As: *What have you learned today? What did you find difficult/easy?*

Lessons 7-9

Preparation

Copy the 'Up the mountain' gameboard onto A3 paper for whole-class use. Copy and cut out the 'Analogue and digital time cards' and the 'Time "follow me" cards'. Copy 'Race against time' onto card. Cut out the problem cards and laminate the game board if possible.

You will need

CD resources

'Analogue and digital time cards', an 'Up the mountain gameboard'

Learning objectives

Starter

- Visualise common 2D shapes and 3D solids; identify shapes from pictures of them in different positions and orientations; sort, make and describe shapes, referring to their properties.
- Derive and recall all addition and subtraction facts for each number to at least 10.
- Add/subtract 9 or 11: add/subtract 10 and adjust by 1.
- Add/subtract 19 or 21: add/subtract 20 and adjust by 1.

Main teaching activities

2006

- Use units of time (seconds, minutes, hours, days) and know the

for each group, 'Time "follow me" cards', 'Race against time' instructions, gameboard and problem cards (see General resources). Interactive resource 'Clocks'.

Equipment
Dice; counters; clocks; paper; hundred squares; small cubes and dice.

relationships between them; read the time to the quarter hour; identify time intervals, including those that cross the hour.

1999

- Read the time to the hour, half hour or quarter hour on an analogue clock and a 12-hour digital clock, and understand the notation 7:30.

Vocabulary

hour, minute, second, o'clock, half past, quarter to, quarter past, clock, watch, hands, digital/analogue clock/watch, timer

Lesson 7 (Review, teach and practise)

Starter

Refine and rehearse: Give each child a piece of paper and ask them to fold it. Give criteria as in Lesson 6 to do with the properties of the shapes. If they fit your criteria, ask the children to stand up. Ask them to fold their paper again and repeat what you have just done.

Main teaching activities

Whole class: Introduce this series of three lessons by looking at the vocabulary of clock times from 'Analogue and digital time cards'. Ask the children to try to give you a sentence using each word. Next, give each child a clock. As you did last term, ask them to look at it and give you some facts about it. Look for answers like: *The numbers go round from one to 12. Those numbers show us what the hour is. If the minute hand is on the 12, it is something o'clock. If the minute hand is on the six, it is half past something. If the minute hand is on the three, it is quarter past something. If the minute hand is on the nine, it is quarter to something. The little marks in between the numbers are minutes. There are five minutes from one number to the next.*

Focus on the last two points. Ask the children to put a finger on the 12, then move to the 1. Ask how many minutes that is. Then repeat, with a finger on the 2, and so on so that the children are counting in fives from zero to 60. Use the clock as a sort of spider chart. Count round in fives again, and when you get to the 3 ask how many minutes past the o'clock position that is. Make the link with it being three lots of 5. Also make the link between saying, for example, *12:15 and quarter past 12*. Do the same at 6 and 9. Each time, link with how many minutes, lots of 5 and the digital and analogue ways of representing them. Finally, go to the 12 and ask the children how many minutes, making the link to: *12 lots of 5, which is 60, the number of minutes in an hour; 1:00, which is where you will be 60 minutes after 12 o'clock; its analogue version of 1 o'clock.*

Call out some times for the children to find on their clocks. Make these a mixture of analogue and digital times, eg *3:45, quarter past 6, 2:30.* Remind the children of the game they played last term, called 'Up the mountain'. Divide the class into two teams, one 'even' and the other 'odd'. Call out a time, wait until everyone has found it (the children can help each other) and then throw a dice. If an even number is thrown the even team moves up the mountain, if an odd number is thrown the odd team moves. The winning team is the one that gets to the top of the mountain first.

Review

Ask the children how this game has helped them in their learning about time. Give them a clock each, and finish the session by asking them some problems, such as: *My clock says quarter past 6, but it is one hour slow. Show me what time it is really. My clock says quarter to 10, but it is half an hour fast. What time is it really?*

Lesson 8 (Teach and practise)

Starter

Read, recall and reason: Write this statement on the board: □ + □ = 3. Ask the children to write on their whiteboards four number sentences to make the statement true. Give them about a minute and then ask them to show you. Write on the board their answers beginning with 0 + 3 = 3 and then 3 + 0 = 3 beside it, 1 + 2 = 3 and 2 + 1 = 3 beside it. Repeat this with □ + □ = 4 and then 5, 6 and 7. Again, write what they have and any they have missed on the board systematically. Ask them what they notice. Aim for using the same numbers twice but in a different order. Move on to subtraction: 3 - □ = □. Write these on the board beside the corresponding additions. Again repeat with 4, 5, 6 and 7. Ask what they notice, aiming towards the inversion aspect and also the fact that the numbers can't be swapped to give the same answer.

Main teaching activities

Whole class: Call out various o'clock, quarter past, half past and quarter to times for the children to find on their clocks. Mix these analogue times with digital. For each time, after they have found it, invite some children to write the analogue and digital times on the board. After they have had lots of practice, tell the children that they will be playing a matching game similar to one they did last term. They will practise matching digital and analogue times and clock faces. Demonstrate the 'Up the mountain' game, as played in Block D, Unit 1 but using 'Analogue and digital time cards'.

Review

Play the 'follow me' game using 'Time "follow me" cards'. Give pairs or small groups of children a few cards. Play once and then talk through the sequence, then play again.

Lesson 9 (Teach, apply and evaluate)

Starter

Rehearse and refine: Give each child a 100 square. Say a starting number for them to put their fingers on. Then ask them to add 9, add 11, add 19, take away 21, add 9 and then tell you where they are. Repeat this a few times with different starting numbers and instructions. Next, ask them to do the same thing but visualise the 100 square in their heads.

Main teaching activities

Whole class: Begin by generating some random times using the interactive resource 'Clocks' and asking children what the times say. Then ask them to find different times on their clocks; ask some problems similar to those random ones in Lesson 7's Review. Choose a theme, such as Sports Day, and make up problems: *It is now 2 o'clock. The race starts in an hour. What time does it start? The race started at half past 1. It took Sam one and a half hours to finish. At what time did he finish?*

Group work: Tell the children that they will be playing another game. This time they have to solve problems to get across the board. Demonstrate the 'Race against time' game. Encourage the children to work in mixed-ability groups. Provide clocks for each group.

Review

Discuss the problems described on the 'Race against time' cards, inviting children to come to the front to explain how they solved them. Ask the children to talk to each other about some of the things they have learned to do with time. Take some whole-class feedback.

Differentiation

If the less confident learners find the problem cards for the 'Race against time' game difficult to read and understand, suggest that a confident reader reads the cards to the whole group.

Lesson 10

You will need

CD resources
'2D shapes vocabulary', '3D shapes vocabulary', 'Can you see the right angle?', '3D' and '2D' shape cards, 'Position vocabulary' (see 'General resources').
Equipment
Cards, clocks.

Learning objectives

Starter

- Visualise common 2D shapes and 3D solids; identify shapes from pictures of them in different positions and orientations; sort, make and describe shapes, referring to their properties.

Main teaching activities

2006
- Recognise and use whole, half and quarter turns, both clockwise and anti-clockwise; know that a right angle represents a quarter turn.

1999
- Recognise whole, half and quarter turns, to the left or right, clockwise or anti-clockwise; know that a right angle is a measure of a quarter turn, and recognise right angles in squares and rectangles.
- Use mathematical vocabulary to describe position, direction and movement.

Vocabulary

hour, minute, o'clock, half past, quarter to, quarter past, clock, clockwise, anticlockwise, whole turn, half turn, quarter turn, right angle, straight line

Lesson 10 (Review, teach, apply and evaluate)

Starter

Read and refresh: Ask the children to think of as many shapes as they can and to draw them on their whiteboards. They should then turn to a partner and describe the properties of some of them for their partner to guess. Give each child a shape card. Hold up a shape vocabulary card and ask children with any shape that links to it to stand up and explain why they are standing. Repeat for as many vocabulary cards as possible.

Main teaching activities

Whole class: The children will be focusing on movement and direction. Ask them to explain what is meant by these terms. Show the vocabulary cards and ask the children to work in pairs to put each word into a sentence. You may wish to designate particular words to different pairs, in order to ensure that all words are covered. Take feedback. Ask them to look at their clocks and to find half past five. Ask them to tell you in which direction the hands move (clockwise). Ask them to move the minute hand a quarter turn in that direction, show you where it is and say the new time. Explain that a quarter turn is 15 minutes. Repeat for different positions and different directions, for example, begin on quarter past and move a quarter turn anticlockwise. Repeat for half turns and equate these to 30 minutes. For each, ask for the time. Discuss right angles and ask them to place the hands on their clock to show different right angles, eg between 6 and 9, 2 and 5. Make the link that a quarter turn is the same size as a right angle. Repeat for half turns. Link to this being the same as two quarter turns/right angles.
Paired work: Demonstrate the children's activity using an example similar to those on their CD page 'Can you see the right angle?'. This is a visual activity so some children who have difficulty with number work may excel in this.

Differentiation

This can be through peer support.

Review

Take feedback. Together, point out right angles in the classroom. Ask: *What do we use every day that has four right angles?* (The corners of books or paper.) *How can we use these to help us check those other right angles in the classroom?* Finish by recapping the vocabulary and different turns, asking the children to physically make these turns.

Name ______________________ Date ________________

How much change?

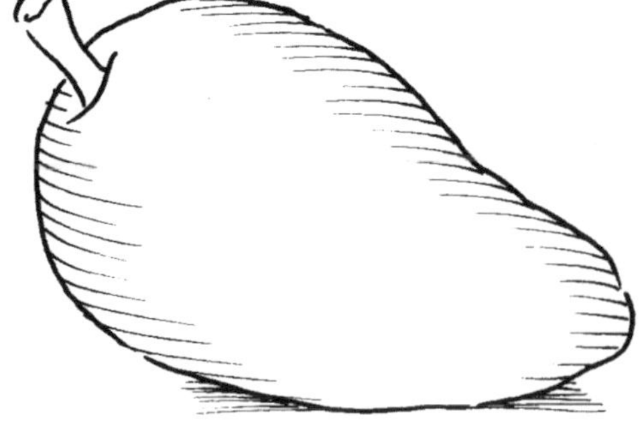

I was in the greengrocer's and I saw a nice-looking mango.

I asked my mum if she would buy it for me.

She gave me a pound. It cost 59p.

How much change should I get?

Which three coins could I be given as change?

I was in the corner shop and I decided to buy a bag of crisps and a bottle of water.

The crisps were 45p.

The water was 65p.

I gave the shopkeeper £2.

How much change should I get?

Which three coins could I be given?

I was in the newsagent's and I bought two comics.

One was £1.20 and the other was £1.10.

I gave the shopkeeper £3.

How much change should I get?

Which two coins could I be given?

Securing number facts, relationships and calculating

Key aspects of learning
- Enquiry
- Problem solving
- Reasoning
- Information processing
- Motivation

Expected prior learning

Check that children can already:

- solve problems involving doubling or halving, combining groups of 2, 5 or 10, or sharing into equal groups
- count on or back in ones, twos, fives and tens and use this knowledge to derive the multiples of 2, 5 and 10 to the tenth multiple
- recall the doubles of all numbers to at least 10
- use the vocabulary of halves and quarters in context.

Objectives overview

The text in this diagram identifies the focus of mathematics learning within the block.

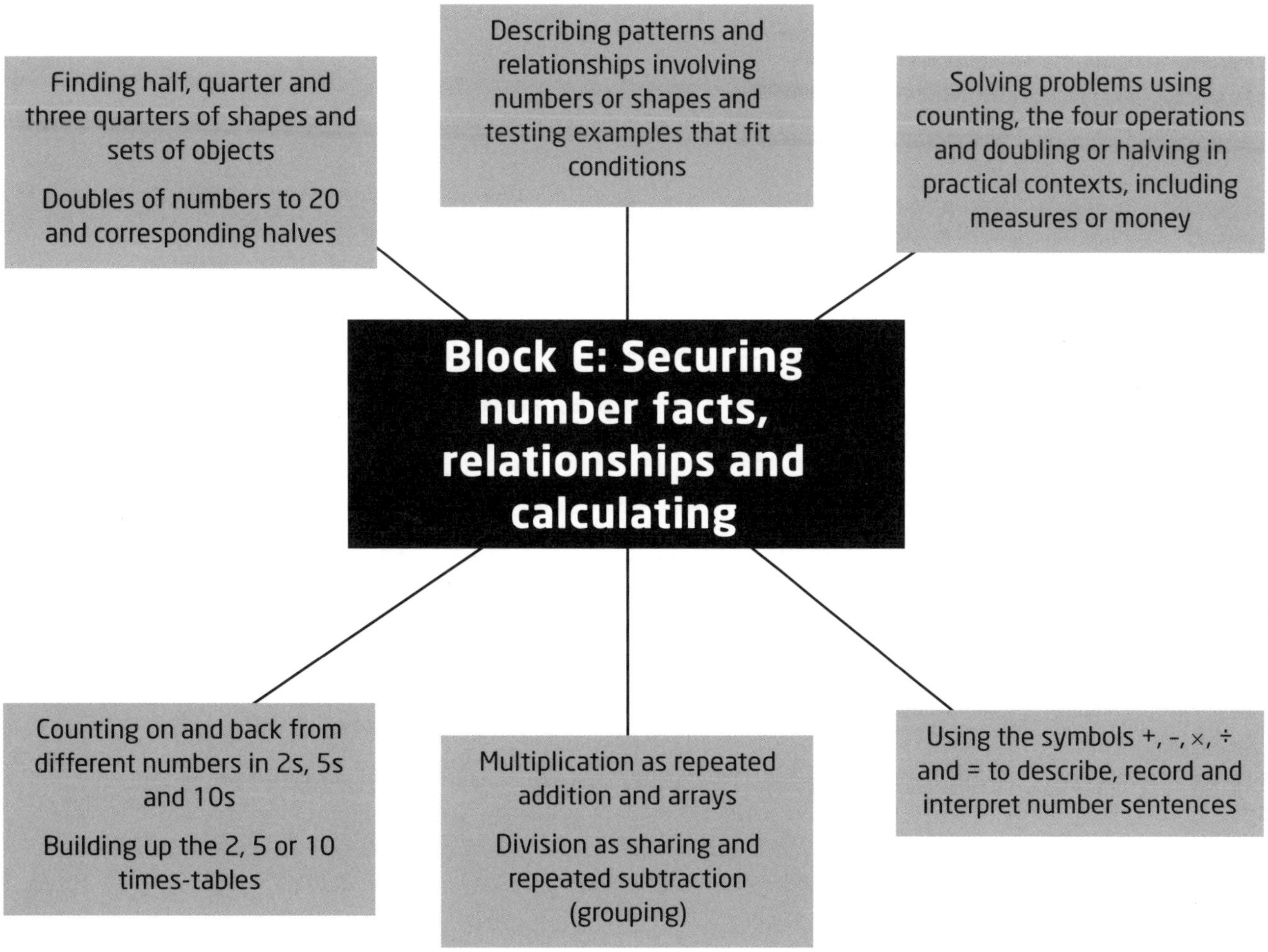

Finding half, quarter and three quarters of shapes and sets of objects

Doubles of numbers to 20 and corresponding halves

Describing patterns and relationships involving numbers or shapes and testing examples that fit conditions

Solving problems using counting, the four operations and doubling or halving in practical contexts, including measures or money

Block E: Securing number facts, relationships and calculating

Counting on and back from different numbers in 2s, 5s and 10s

Building up the 2, 5 or 10 times-tables

Multiplication as repeated addition and arrays

Division as sharing and repeated subtraction (grouping)

Using the symbols +, –, ×, ÷ and = to describe, record and interpret number sentences

Unit 1 3 weeks

Securing number facts, relationships and calculating

Lesson	Strands	Starter	Main teaching activities
1. Review, teach and practise	Use/apply Calculate	Read and write two-digit and three-digit numbers in figures and words; describe and extend number sequences and recognise odd and even numbers.	• Identify and record the information or calculation needed to solve a puzzle or problem; carry out the steps or calculations and check the solution in the context of the problem. • Represent repeated addition and arrays as multiplication, and sharing and repeated subtraction (grouping) as division; use practical and informal written methods and related vocabulary to support multiplication and division, including calculations with remainders.
2. Teach and practise	Use/apply Calculate	As for Lesson 1	As for Lesson 1
3. Review, teach and practise	Use/apply Calculate	Derive and recall multiplication facts for the 2, 5 and 10 times-tables and the related division facts; recognise multiples of 2, 5 and 10.	As for Lesson 1
4. Teach and practise	Use/apply Calculate	As for Lesson 3	As for Lesson 1
5. Teach, apply and evaluate	Use/apply Calculate	As for Lesson 3	As for Lesson 1
6. Review and apply	Use/apply Calculate	**Derive and recall all addition and subtraction facts for each number to at least 10, all pairs with totals to 20 and all pairs of multiples of 10 with totals up to 100.**	As for Lesson 1
7. Apply and evaluate	Use/apply Calculate	Derive and recall multiplication facts for the 2, 5 and 10 times-tables and the related division facts; recognise multiples of 2, 5 and 10.	As for Lesson 1
8. Review and practise	Use/apply Calculate	As for Lesson 7	• Identify and record the information or calculation needed to solve a puzzle or problem; carry out the steps or calculations and check the solution in the context of the problem. **• Use the symbols +, -, ×, ÷ and = to record and interpret number sentences involving all four operations; calculate the value of an unknown in a number sentence (eg □ ÷ 2 = 6, 30 - □ = 24).**
9. Teach and apply	Calculate Knowledge	As for Lesson 7	• Identify and record the information or calculation needed to solve a puzzle or problem; carry out the steps or calculations and check the solution in the context of the problem. • Understand that halving is the inverse of doubling and derive and recall doubles of all numbers to 20, and the corresponding halves. **• Use the symbols +, -, ×, ÷ and = to record and interpret number sentences involving all four operations; calculate the value of an unknown in a number sentence (eg □ ÷ 2 = 6, 30 - □ = 24).**
10. Teach, practise and evaluate	Calculate Knowledge	Read and write two-digit and three-digit numbers in figures and words.	As for Lesson 9
11. Review, teach and practise	Counting	Add/subtract 9 or 11: add/subtract 10 and adjust by 1.	Find one half, one quarter and three quarters of shapes and sets of objects.
12. Teach and apply	Counting	Order two-digit numbers and position them on a number line.	As for Lesson 11
13. Teach and apply	Counting	As for Lesson 12	As for Lesson 11
14. Teach and apply	Counting	As for Lesson 11	As for Lesson 11
15. Practise and evaluate	Counting	**Derive and recall all pairs of numbers with totals to 20.**	As for Lesson 11

Speaking and listening objectives

- Listen to talk by an adult, remember some specific points and identify what they have learned.
- Adopt appropriate roles in small or large groups and consider alternative courses of action.

Introduction

This block contains 15 lessons, the first 7 of which focus on multiplication and division and the basic understanding that the children need in order to progress in this area. During these lessons, the children will be using the symbols ×, ÷ and = as a way of recording their work. The eighth lesson focuses on using symbols to record and interpret number sentences. Lessons 9 and 10 concentrate on doubling and its inverse of halving, deriving and recalling doubles of all numbers to 20, and the corresponding halves. The final part of this block concentrates on fractions. Throughout the block, the children identify and record information or calculations needed to solve problems and carry out the steps or calculations needed to find solutions. In several lessons there is a focus on checking results. The objectives related to multiplication facts for the two-, five- and ten-times tables, the related division facts and recognising multiples of 2, 5 and 10 are the focus of many of the starter activities and are integrated into the lessons on multiplication and division and doubling and halving. The speaking and listening objectives (see left) are an integral part of each lesson.

Using and applying mathematics

- Identify and record the information or calculation needed to solve a puzzle or problem; carry out the steps or calculations and check the solution in the context of the problem.

Lessons 1-5

Preparation

Photocopy 'Multiplication and division vocabulary' onto A3 card and cut out the vocabulary cards.

You will need

Photocopiable pages

'Things to multiply' (page 182), 'Jumping up and down' (page 183) and 'Array for maths!' (page 202) for each child.

CD resources

'0-100 number cards', a 'Function machine game' for each child, 'Multiplication and division vocabulary' cards (see General resources); 'Things to multiply', 'Array for maths!' and 'Jumping up and down', support and extension versions, ITP Grouping.

Equipment

Multilink cubes or other counting equipment, number cards from 10 to 50.

Learning objectives

Starter

- Read and write two-digit and three-digit numbers in figures and words; describe and extend number sequences and recognise odd and even numbers.
- Derive and recall multiplication facts for the 2, 5 and 10 times-tables and the related division facts; recognise multiples of 2, 5 and 10.

Main teaching activities

2006

- Identify and record the information or calculation needed to solve a puzzle or problem; carry out the steps or calculations and check the solution in the context of the problem.
- Represent repeated addition and arrays as multiplication, and sharing and repeated subtraction (grouping) as division; use practical and informal written methods and related vocabulary to support multiplication and division, including calculations with remainders.

1999

- Understand the operation of multiplication as repeated addition or as describing an array, and begin to understand division as grouping or sharing.
- Use and read the related vocabulary.
- Use the ×, ÷ and = signs to record mental calculations in a number sentence, and recognise the use of a symbol such as □ to stand for an unknown number.

Vocabulary

lots of, groups of, times, multiply, multiplied by, multiple of, repeated addition, array, row, column, equal groups of, repeated subtraction, divide, divided by

Lesson 1 (Review, teach and practise)

Starter

Read and refresh: Give the children some single-digit and two-digit numbers to write as numerals. Show them some single-digit and two-digit number cards to write as words. Now ask them to write a number and change it: *Write 4, make it 24, now add 10* (34), *change the 4 to a 7* (37), *add 3* (40), *take away two tens* (20), *add 100* (120), *double the tens number* (140), *add 9* (149). Repeat for a different start number.

Main teaching activities

Whole class: Tell the children that they are going to learn about multiplication and division. They will begin by learning to multiply and divide by 2, 10 and 5. Do they know what 'multiplication' and 'division' mean? Together group the multiplication and division vocabulary cards into two groups, one for each operation, explaining what each word means.

Write 2 × 6 on the board. Choose six children to help you. Give each child two Multilink cubes. Ask: *How many Multilink cubes does Sam have? How many does Aisha have? How many do they have altogether? Yes, six lots of 2 is 12. Two times 6 or 2 multiplied by 6 is 12.*

Write 2 + 2 + 2 + 2 + 2 + 2 = 12. Ask: *What have I written? Yes, an addition, because multiplication is like addition. Two times 6 is the same as 2 + 2 + 2 + 2 + 2 + 2. Let's count in multiples of 2 six times and see if we get the same answer.* Repeat this multiplication of 2 by other numbers below 10. Move on to multiplying by 10 as above. This links with counting in multiples of numbers, and also with division as repeated subtraction (which the children will think about later). Finish by demonstrating multiplying by 5.

Group work: Ask the children to work in pairs, using counting apparatus to carry out the multiplications on 'Things to multiply'.

Review

Write a multiplication on the board, such as 2 × 6. Ask what two times 6 or six lots of 2 means as a repeated addition. As they tell you, draw circles, then tell the children that this is called an array. Now loop the circles:

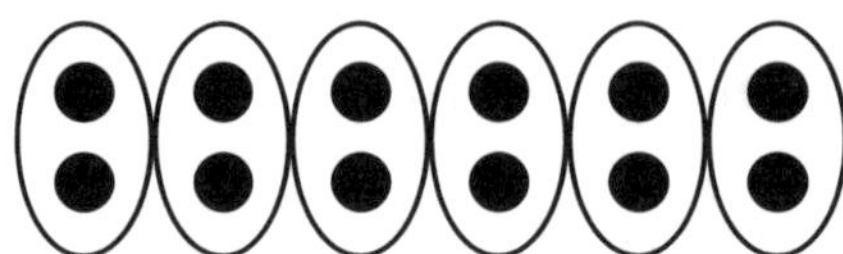

2 + 2 + 2 + 2 + 2 + 2
2 × 6

Repeat for six times two or two lots of six: 6 + 6. Draw and loop circles, referring to the term 'arrays' and write the calculations: 6 + 6 and 6 × 2. Ask the children what they notice – that six times 2 and two times 6 have the same answer.

Differentiation

Less confident learners: Provide the support version of 'Things to multiply', where objects are used throughout.
More confident learners: Provide the extension version that moves on quickly to thinking about multiples.

Lesson 2 (Teach and practise)

Starter

Rehearse: Count from zero to 1000 and back again in hundreds. Invite children to pick starting numbers from the two-digit number cards and count on and back to just over 1000.

Main teaching activities

Recap what the class did on multiplication in Lesson 1 and demonstrate again the idea of arrays from the previous lesson's Review. Begin by explaining as you draw:

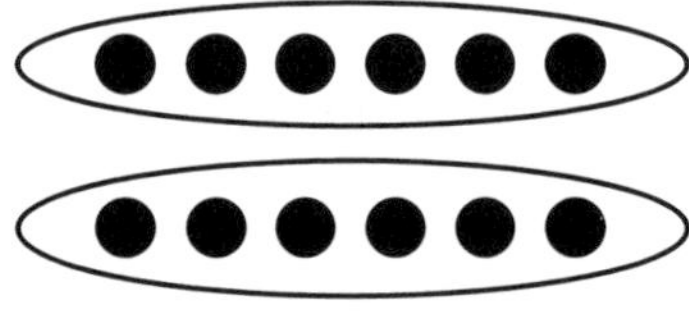

6 × 2

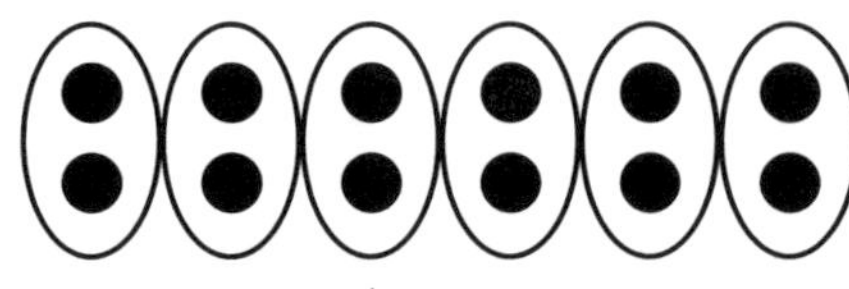

and 2 × 6

Go through a few examples from the two-, five- and ten-times tables, for example, four times five or five lots of four.

5 × 4, or four lots of five, which equals 20

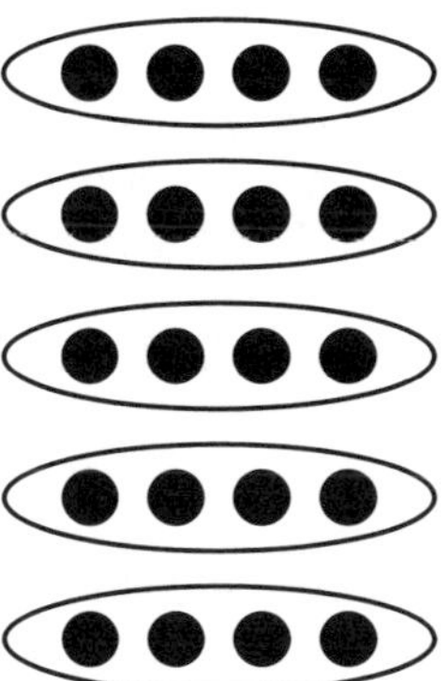

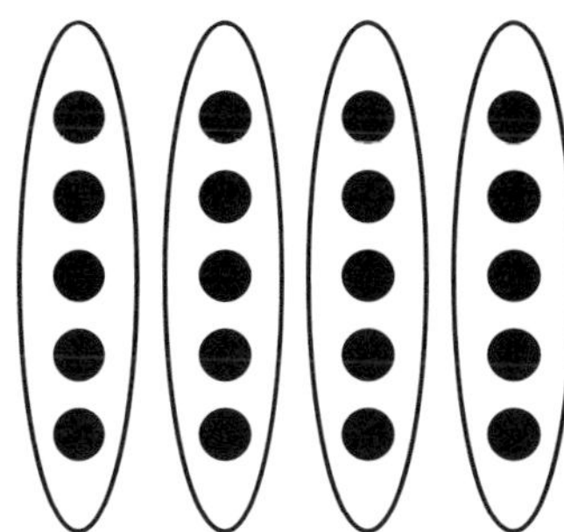

4 × 5, or five lots of four, which also equals 20

Draw an array on the board and ask the children what the two calculations would be, for example: ● ● ● ● ● / ● ● ● ● ●

Group work: Tell the children that they will be working in pairs to interpret arrays. Show them 'Array for maths !' and demonstrate how to draw the two arrays for each question.

Differentiation

Less confident learners: This group uses the support version of 'Array for maths !' to focus on arrays that need looping and labelling.
More confident learners: This group uses the extension version focusing on arrays to loop and label and drawing arrays for calculations, stating the 'opposite' multiplication.

Review

Ask the children how what they now know can help them to multiply 5 × 9, or five lots of 9. Work towards an answer similar to 'we can answer that because we know what nine lots of 5 is from our counting on in multiples and nine lots of 5 is the same answer as five lots of 9.' Put a few more examples on the board.

Lesson 3 (Review, teach and practise)

Starter

Recall: Practise saying the two- and ten-times tables. Then give out 'Function machine game' sheets. Ask the children to write random numbers up to 10 on the input side and write ×10 in the middle. When you say *Go!* they write the answer on the output side. Ask children who are struggling to write two or three input numbers. Repeat with a different set of input numbers, then do the same for the two-times table.

Main teaching activities

Whole class: Ask the children what the opposite operation to addition is. Draw an arrow diagram on the board to jog the children's memories. Now ask: *What do you think the opposite of multiplication is? If multiplication is repeated addition, what do you think division is? Look at this example: five lots of 2 is 2 + 2 + 2 + 2 + 2 which is 10, so 10 divided by 2 must be 10 - 2 - 2 - 2 - 2 - 2.* Demonstrate this using a number line. Repeat with more examples.

Paired work: Give the children the 'Jumping up and down' photocopiable sheet to complete in pairs.

Differentiation

Less confident learners: Provide the support version of 'Jumping up and down' that guides the child through multiplication and division by 2, using repeated addition and subtraction.
More confident learners: The extension version of the sheet invites the children to draw their own number lines.

Review

Ask questions such as: *Why is multiplication like addition? Why is division like subtraction? What do we mean by three lots of 2? Can you draw that as an array? What about two lots of 3?* Make the progression from here into missing number sentences, for example, 2 × ? = 12, ? × 7 = 21, 15 ÷ ? = 5. Ask the children to explain how they get their answers, reinforcing as appropriate the links between multiplication and division.

Lesson 4 (Teach and practise)

Starter

Refine: Ask the children to count in fives from 0 to 50 and back. Next ask them to count in fives from any given number and to tell you what they notice. Say: *Just as you did with the two- and ten-times tables, you are now going to practise five-times table multiplications.* Ask them to count in 5s from 0 to 50, putting up their fingers as they do. Ask them to stop at the sixth finger and ask them how many lots of 5 make 30. Write the number sentence 5 × 6 = 30. Repeat this so that all the facts are mentioned and write them up so that the sequence from 5 × 1 = 5 to 5 × 10 = 50 is listed.

Main teaching activities

Whole class: Recap on all that the children have learned so far about multiplication and division. Explain that today they will be focusing on division by grouping. Explain this as repeated subtraction as in Lesson 3 but change the language to *take away one group of...* Using the ITP Grouping, explain that there are 20 goldfish and they need to be put in bowls, 2 in each and that you need to find out how many bowls are needed. Click on two fish and jump from 0 to 2 on the number line, then click on another two and jump to 4. Continue to do this until all 20 are clicked on, then count the jumps and conclude that 10 bowls are needed. Write the number sentence 20 ÷ 2 = 10. Repeat for 26 goldfish and 5 bowls, writing the number sentence: 26 ÷ 5 = 5, remainder 1. Discuss the one left over and what that means - an extra bowl. Repeat with similar scenarios using crosses on the board. For these discuss how they can check (multiplication or repeated addition).

Group work: Give small groups of children up to 50 Multilink cubes or similar and ask them to group these into twos. Work out how many groups there are and then write the number sentence just as you did in class. Ask them to repeat this for groups of five and then ten.

Differentiation

Less confident learners: Give these children different numbers of cubes up to 20 and ask them to group each into twos, writing the number sentence as the others.

More confident learners: These children should be asked to group in threes and fours, as well as the other groupings, and record their findings.

Review

Take feedback from the activity, inviting children to come to the front of the class to demonstrate their work on the board, drawing boxes or crosses to represent their cubes. Together work out if they are correct by doing the reverse process (multiplication).

Lesson 5 (Teach, apply and evaluate)

Starter

Recall: Repeat the starter from Lesson 3 but add the five-times table.

Main teaching activities

Whole class: Recap on what the children did in Lesson 4, asking them to explain clearly what grouping is all about, how the answer to a grouping question can be checked using multiplication and what a remainder is. You may need to remind them by modelling using the ITP Grouping. Say: *You will be practising this skill again today, using number lines!* Demonstrate by writing a two-digit number. Ask the children to choose one between 10 and 30 (for example, 23) and then ask them to choose a divisor of 2, 5 or 10. Write the number sentence on the board, for example, 23 ÷ 5 = ? Use the ITP Grouping and add 23 stars to it. Click on five stars and jump from 0 to 5, continue in this until all groups of 5 are clicked on and 'jumped', then demonstrate the answer 23 ÷ 5 = 4 remainder 3.

Group work: The children should be given a pile of number cards from 10 to 30. They pick a card and draw that number of crosses and also draw a number line from 0 to 30. They then group their crosses firstly into twos, then fives and tens. For each, they make the jumps as you demonstrated and finally write the appropriate number sentence.

Differentiation

Less confident learners: Give these children cards to 20 and ask them to group each into 2s, writing the number sentence as the others.

More confident learners: These children should be given cards from 30 to 50 and asked to group in threes and fours as well as twos, fives and tens, and then record their work.

Review

Take feedback from the activity, inviting children to come to the front of the class to demonstrate their work on the board. Together, work out if they are correct by doing the reverse process. Finish by writing some missing number division sentences on the board and ask the children to explain their methods for solving them. Reinforce checking by multiplication as it arises.

Lessons 6-7

Preparation

Copy 'Problem solving practice' onto acetate. Make an A3 copy of 'Flip-flap for 20' and 'How to solve a problem'.

You will need

Photocopiable pages
'Make me a problem' (page 184).
CD resources
'Flip-flap for 20', '0-100 number cards' for each child, an A3 copy of 'How to solve a problem' (see General resources); 'Problem-solving practice', 'Problems, problems, problems' and 'Make me a problem', core, support and extension versions.
Equipment
Multilink cubes or other counting equipment; counters; scissors; paper clips.

Learning objectives

Starter

- Derive and recall all addition and subtraction facts for each number to at least 10, and all pairs with totals to 20.
- Derive and recall multiplication facts for the 2, 5 and 10 times-tables.

Main teaching activities

2006

- Identify and record the information or calculation needed to solve a puzzle or problem; carry out the steps or calculations and check the solution in the context of the problem.
- Represent repeated addition and arrays as multiplication, and sharing and repeated subtraction (grouping) as division; use practical and informal written methods and related vocabulary to support multiplication and division, including calculations with remainders.

1999

- Use known number facts and place value to carry out simple multiplications and divisions.
- Use mental addition and subtraction, simple multiplication and division, to solve simple word problems using one or two steps.
- Choose and use appropriate operations and efficient calculation strategies (eg mental, mental with jottings) to solve problems.

Vocabulary

double, halve, share, share equally, multiply, divide, partition, recombine

Lesson 6 (Review and apply)

Starter

Rehearse and recall: Give the children each a copy of 'Flip-flap for 20' and ask them to count the ladybirds. Fold back the top two rows and the bottom row of your A3 'Flip-flap for 20'. Hold it so you can see ten ladybirds and the children can see ten. Ask: *If you can see ten ladybirds, how many can I see? If I fold it so you can see five ladybirds* (fold back all but the far right edge), *how many can I see?* Repeat for several numbers.

Main teaching activities

Whole class: Explain that the next two lessons will be about solving real-life problems using the skills the children have learned from Lessons 1-5. Quickly recap on the meanings and methods of multiplication and division. Show the 'Problem solving practice' acetate problems one at a time on the OHP. For each one, ask: *What things do we need to do in order to answer this problem?* Stick the 'How to solve a problem' poster on the wall. Work through each problem on the acetate, asking questions as you go.
Paired work: Ask the children to work with a partner on the 'Problems, problems, problems' sheet, jotting on it to show their workings, perhaps using dice or number cards to generate more numbers.

Differentiation

Less confident learners: Use the support version of 'Problems, problems, problems' with less demanding numbers.
More confident learners: Use the extension version of 'Problems, problems, problems 3' with more demanding numbers.

Review

Invite a few children to explain how they solved one of the problems.

Compare their methods. Ask questions such as: *What did you need to know before you could start to work out the answer? Which bits of the problem are important? What clue words helped?*

Lesson 7 (Apply and evaluate)

Starter

Recall, refine and reason: Using the 'Flip-flap for 20' from Lesson 6, recap that starter and then move on by saying: *Each ladybird now represents 2; you can see 4, that represents 8. What do you need to do to work that out?* Encourage the children to think towards doubling or multiplying by 2. Continue to show different numbers of ladybirds and ask them to tell you how many they represent, then ask them to show what five ladybirds would represent (they show 10), nine ladybirds (18), and so on.

Main teaching activities

Whole class: Recap the work the children did in the last session with examples, including the concepts of multiplication and division. Go through the problem-solving steps again.

Write up two numbers and a multiplication sign. Ask the children to make up a problem using these and then to solve it. Repeat a few times with divisions included as well. Ask the children to explain how they solved each calculation.

Paired work: Say: *Today you will be working with a partner making up your own problems for us to answer during our review time.* Go through a few examples using any of the 'Make me a problem' sheets.

Differentiation

Less confident learners: This group uses the support version of 'Make me a problem' and focuses on multiplying and dividing by 2. If writing is a problem, ask them to say their problems for you or a teaching assistant to scribe for them.

More confident learners: This group uses the extension version and has more challenging numbers to work with.

Review

Take feedback from the activity. Invite pairs of children to ask one of their problems and, as a class, answer it. Use all the ways you have been thinking about to answer. Include remainders as appropriate.

Lessons 8-10

Preparation

Cut out the 'Spider charts for multiplying' and 'Spider charts for dividing', enlarge and copy onto A3 paper. Copy 'Dartboard doubles gameboard' onto card and laminate; cut out the spinners and provide paper clips. Copy 'Halve or double?' onto acetate.

You will need

Photocopiable pages

An acetate of 'Halve or double?' (page 185), laminated copy of the 'Functioning machine' activity (page 186) for each child.

CD resources

'Halve or double again', support and extension versions; '0-100 number cards', 'Spider charts for multiplying' and 'Spider charts for dividing' for each child, an A3 copy of 'How to solve a problem', a copy of 'Dartboard doubles spinner', 'Dartboard doubles game' and 'Dartboard doubles gameboard' for each group (see

Learning objectives

Starter

- Derive and recall multiplication facts for the 2, 5 and 10 times-tables and the related division facts; recognise multiples of 2, 5 and 10.
- Read and write two-digit and three-digit numbers in figures and words.

Main teaching activities

2006

- Identify and record the information or calculation needed to solve a puzzle or problem; carry out the steps or calculations and check the solution in the context of the problem.
- Use the symbols +, –, ×, ÷ and = to record and interpret number sentences involving all four operations; calculate the value of an unknown in a number sentence (eg □ ÷ 2 = 6, 30 - □ = 24).
- Understand that halving is the inverse of doubling and derive and recall doubles of all numbers to 20, and the corresponding halves.

1999

- Use mental addition and subtraction, simple multiplication and division, to solve simple word problems using one or two steps.
- Explain how the problem was solved.
- Choose and use appropriate operations and efficient calculation strategies (eg mental, mental with jottings) to solve problems.

Vocabulary

double, halve, share, share equally, multiply, divide, partition, recombine,

General resources), laminated 'Functioning machine', support version; number cards 1–9 for each child and 0–20 for each more able learner (from '0–100 number cards'), two A3 copies of the 'Functioning machine' for each group.

Equipment

Multilink cubes or other counting equipment; counters; scissors; paper clips; a large class 100 square; an individual 100 square for each child.

one-, two- or three-digit number, place, place value, represents, double, near double, total, addition, sum

Lesson 8 (Review and practise)

Starter

Recall and refine: Count in twos from zero to ten and back. Ask the children to close their eyes as they count and imagine jumping up and down a number line. Show them the spider chart for multiplying by 2. Point randomly to numbers around the outside. The children should call out the answer when the number is multiplied. Now show the spider chart for dividing by 2: *What would you multiply 2 by to get the numbers around the outside? If I point to 18, what would you call out? That's right, 9.* Draw their attention to the fact that finding out what you would multiply 2 by to get 18 is one way of working out 18 divided by 2. Repeat for facts for the five- and ten-times tables.

Main teaching activities

Whole class: Tell the children that they will be working on mental calculation strategies in the next two lessons, including doubling and halving, partitioning numbers and multiplying and dividing by 10. Ask them what 'doubling' and 'halving' mean. Explain that they are the same as 'multiplying by 2' and 'dividing by 2'.

Call out a few numbers up to ten for the children to double, writing the answers on their whiteboards. Call out even numbers to 20 for halving. Move on to multiples of 10 to 100.

Group work: Tell the children that they will be working in groups of two to four to practise doubling and halving. Model the 'Dartboard doubles' game and provide the resources.

Differentiation

Less confident learners: These children should use numbers to 10 or 20 and counting apparatus.
More confident learners: Write extra numbers on the blank cards provided, such as 24, 22, 32 and 40. Don't use numbers with a unit digit of 5 or above.

Review

Can the children double and halve all the numbers they worked with? Did they manage to halve 30, 50, 70 and 90, and if so, how? Explain that there is an easy way: numbers that have an odd number of ten can be partitioned into 10 and the rest of the tens. They all know half of 10 (5), and the other number is even and therefore easy to halve.

Lesson 9 (Teach and apply)

Starter

Refresh and reason: Give each pair of children A4 copies of the spider charts. In each pair, one child should ask multiplication and division questions (as you have done in Lesson 6) and the other child should answer them. After a couple of goes, they should swap roles. Ask several children to share their questions. End with a few key questions, such as: *If I write 2 × 6 = 12 on the board, what else do we know? How can we use our multiplication knowledge to help us divide?* Repeat this idea for five- and ten-times tables.

Main teaching activities

Whole class: Tell the children that in this lesson they will be solving word problems using the strategies from Lesson 6. Recap these strategies, then use the 'How to solve a problem' poster to recap the problem-solving process. Project the 'Halve or double?' acetate and talk through the problems together.

Group work: Tell the children that they may work individually or with a partner to complete the 'Halve or double again' activity sheet. Model how to make up problems like the example provided, using the information on this sheet.

Differentiation

Less confident learners: Provide the support version of 'Halve or double again' with smaller numbers.
More confident learners: Provide the extension version of 'Halve or double again 3' with much larger numbers.

Review

Invite children from each group to ask one of their questions for the rest of the class to try to answer. Ask what strategies they used, and watch and assess the children's responses.

Lesson 10 (Teach, practise and evaluate)

Starter

Read and rehearse: Practise reading two-digit and three-digit numbers. Ask the children to set out their number cards in order from 0 to 9. While they are getting ready, ask the class simple things like: *Show me four... seven... one more than 8... one less than 4... three more than 9...; double it.* Now ask the children to put the number card for 3 in front of them, then make the 3 into 53, then make 253. Ask them to swap the 2 and the 5. Ask one of the less confident children to read the digits, then invite any child to read the actual number. Repeat this several times.

Main teaching activities

Whole class: Remind the children that 9 can be added to numbers quite easily because it is so close to 10. Use a large 100 square to demonstrate how to add 9 by adding 10 (jump down a row) and then adjusting the answer by taking away 1. Show this for single-digit numbers, then for numbers to 20. Give each child a 100 square so that they can copy what you do. Once they have understood the idea, move on to demonstrate how to add 11 by adding 10 and then one more.
Group work: Demonstrate the 'Functioning machine' activity. Hand out the 'Functioning machine' photocopiable sheet and ask the children to play the game in groups.

Differentiation

Less confident learners: This group can use the support version of the 'Functioning machine' with starting numbers provided. Provide a large 100 square to help them.
More confident learners: Ask the children to write starting numbers from 50 to 100.

Review

Talk about using a similar strategy for subtracting 9, then 11. Write a few numbers on the board from which the children can subtract 9 and 11 by subtracting 10 and adjusting. They can use their 100 squares for this. Finally, write four calculations on the board, such as:

36 + 9 = ?   12 + 3 + 5 = ?   47 - 11 = ?   10 + 1 + 23 = ?

Ask the children which of the strategies they have thought about over the last two lessons is best for answering each of these. Question the children you need to assess by asking, for example: *Why did you choose this strategy? Why is it the best one?*

Lessons 11-15

Preparation

Cut a selection of food into halves and quarters. Copy the shapes on the 'Shapes to fold' sheet onto A3 paper for each pair of children. The recording sheet can be A3 or A4. If any children need help cutting out their shapes, do it for them before the lesson.

You will need

Photocopiable pages
'Clock faces' (page 187).
CD resources
'Shapes to fold', 'Empty 100 square', '0-100 number cards', 'Clocks', 'Feed Cedrick instructions' and 'Cedrick's hungry - please

Learning objectives

Starter

- Add/subtract 9 or 11: add/subtract 10 and adjust by 1.
- Order two-digit numbers and position them on a number line.
- Derive and recall all pairs of numbers with totals to 20.

Main teaching activities

2006
- Find one half, one quarter and three quarters of shapes and sets of objects.

1999
- Begin to recognise and find one half and one quarter of shapes and small numbers of objects.
- Begin to recognise that two halves or four quarters make one whole and that two quarters and one half are equivalent.

feed him!' (see General resources); 'Fraction strips 1', 'Feed Cedrick spinners', 'Pennies game 1 and Pennies game recording sheet', support and extension versions, ITP Fractions.

Equipment

Food for cutting into fractions (eg pizza, apple, chocolate bar), Plasticine, empty 100 square, strips of paper the length of A4, A3 paper (one piece per pair), glue, clock faces, counters, spinners, pendulum (three Unifix cubes on string or anything that will swing), pennies, plastic cups or beakers.

Vocabulary

part, equal parts, fraction, one whole, one half, two halves, one quarter, two... three... four quarters

Lesson 11 (Review, teach and practise)

Starter

Rehearse, read and reason: Demonstrate adding and subtracting 9 and 11 on a class 100 square by adding/subtracting 10 and adjusting. Ask the children to put their finger on a number on their 100 squares, then add or subtract 9 or 11, telling you what number they get to and how they got there. Repeat several times.

Main teaching activities

Whole class: Explain that the children will be learning about fractions. Ask: *Who has heard the word 'fraction'? Can anyone tell me what it means?* Use your food examples to show 'one half' and 'one quarter'. Demonstrate that the fractions are equal, that two halves fit back together to make a whole, and that four quarters do the same.

Give everyone a piece of Plasticine. Ask them to roll it into a worm shape and then break it into halves, then quarters. Make the point that half of a half is the same as a quarter. Say: *Compare your worm with your neighbour's. Is your half the same as theirs? Does that mean that it isn't a half? Why can all the half worms be different sizes? It's because half sizes are different if the whole lengths are different.*

Paired work: Model the 'Shapes to fold' activity by cutting out and folding the shapes. As you do this, ask: *What shape is this? How many parts will I have if I fold it in half? How many ways can I fold this shape in half? Who can fold this shape in half for me? Can anyone show us another way to fold it in half?* Give an activity sheet of shapes to each pair of children. Ask them to fold these in as many ways as they can to make equal halves. Give the children the recording sheet to fill in.

Review

Compare the ways the children found to fold their shapes in half. Invite a few children, particularly any whom you wish to assess, to demonstrate any new ways.

Lesson 12 (Teach and apply)

Starter

Read and rehearse: Give each pair a laminated 'Empty 100 square'. Display the 'Empty 100 square' acetate on the OHP. Use number cards to select random numbers to 100. Model a few numbers first. Ask the children to work in pairs, plotting random numbers that you give them on their 100 squares and writing each number in the correct place. After a few, check and write them on the acetate. Repeat.

Main teaching activities

Whole class: Recap the work the children did in Lesson 11. Show them 'Fraction strips 1' and ask them to tell you what they can see. Aim for: five strips, one whole, one cut into half with one half shaded, three cut into quarters with one quarter shaded on one of these, two quarters shaded in the second and three in the third. Discuss how the fraction strips are made, ensuring that you talk about equal parts and direct them to the equivalence of one half and two quarters. Give each child three strips of paper and ask them to keep one whole and then to fold the second into half and the third into quarters. Discuss how they did this: folding in half to make half and folding the half to make quarters, and that a quarter is half of a half. Discuss equivalences: $^2/_2 = 1$, $^4/_4 = 1$, $^2/_4 = {}^1/_2$. Reinforce this by demonstrating the ITP Fractions.

Paired work: The children use these strips plus others to build their own fraction wall. Ask them to stick their strips onto A3 paper and then colour a whole, 1/2, 1/4, 2/4 and 3/4 and to label each.

Differentiation

Less confident learners: Provide adult support to help these children if necessary.
More confident learners: These children could explore other folds and see if they can make eighths, thirds, fifths, and so on.

Review

Ask the children to tell each other and then the class what they did; take feedback from anyone who explored further. What fractions did they make? Draw out the important aspects of this lesson: fractions are wholes divided into equal parts, the bottom number tells you how many parts, the top tells you how many you need, for example, 3/4 divided into 4 and 3 parts needed. Write these symbols on the board: < > = and ask the children to use them to make number sentences. For example: 1/2 = 2/4, 1/2 > 1/4, 1/2 < 3/4.

Lesson 13 (Teach and apply)

Starter

Read, rehearse and refresh: Repeat the starter from Lesson 12, but when you plot a number, ask these questions: *Which number is 1/10 more/ less? Add/subtract 9/11, is it odd or even, round it to the nearest 10.* This rehearses other skills.

Main teaching activities

Whole class: Recap the work the children did in Lessons 11 and 12. Then, show the first clock on 'Clocks' and ask the children to tell you what they can see: a clock. Discuss the hour numbers, the minutes, how many minutes there are from hour number to hour number, how many minutes in an hour. Write 60 minutes = 1 hour on the board. Show the next clock and ask what has happened: One half of it has been shaded. Ask how many minutes that is, and write 1/2 hour = 30 minutes on the board. Discuss the fact that two half an hours make an hour, 30 + 30 = 60. Repeat for the other clocks, writing 1/4 hour = 15 minutes and 3/4 hour = 45 minutes.
Paired work: The children use 'Clock faces' to make up a poster. They cut out four faces, stick a whole one on A3 paper and label 1 whole = 60 minutes, then cut one face into halves, stick it on the paper and label 1/2 = 30 minutes, cut another into 1/4, stick it down and label 1/4 = 15 minutes and the fourth cut three quarters, stick it down and label 3/4 = 45 minutes. Encourage further exploration of other fractions, such as 1/3 = 20 minutes.

Differentiation

Less confident learners: Provide adult support to help these children create their clock poster.
More confident learners: These children can explore some of the other fractions of a clock.

Review

Ask the children to tell each other and then you what they did; take feedback from anyone who explored further, what fractions did they make? Recap the important things about fractions: that wholes are divided into equal parts, that the bottom number tells you how many parts, and the top tells you how many you need, for example, three quarters are a whole divided into four, and there are three parts needed. Write these symbols on the board: < > =. Ask the children to use them to make number sentences. For example, 1/2 = 2/4, 30 minutes = 1/2 an hour, 1/2 > 1/4, 30 minutes > 15 minutes, 1/2 < 3/4, 30 minutes < 45 minutes.

Lesson 14 (Teach and practise)

Starter

Refine: Repeat the activity in Lesson 11 for consolidation and then ask them to try this again but this time, visualising the 100 square in their heads.

Main teaching activities

Whole class: Focus on fractions of numbers. Demonstrate a half of different numbers with counters on the OHP by sharing (one by one) into two groups. Next, make the link to the halving strategy they were working on earlier in the unit. For example, share four counters into two groups and say: *If you* *halve the number four, you get two, and two lots of two give four again.* Repeat for six counters, three in each group. *If you halve six, you will get three, and two lots of three give six again.* Demonstrate quarters, linking this with the Plasticine worm work in Lesson 11, emphasising that $^1/_4$ is $^1/_2$ of $^1/_2$.

Paired work: Tell the children that they will be playing a game to help them practise halving and quartering numbers. Demonstrate the game 'Feed Cedrick'. Instructions and resources are on the CD. Encourage the strategy of halving and halving again for quarters. You could set a counter limit - for example, the first child to collect 20 counters is the winner.

Differentiation

Less confident learners: These children should use the support version of 'Feed Cedrick' using the spinners designed for them, which concentrate on halves.
More confident learners: These children should use the extension version, using spinners that encourage them to think about other fractions.

Review

Ask some quick-fire half and quarter questions, for example: *half of eight, a quarter of eight, half of 12, a quarter of 12, half of 14, can you find a quarter of 14 that is a whole number?* Target appropriately, giving extra time to those children who need it. Ask the children to write their answers on their whiteboards. Assess their answers to identify those who are still unsure about work involving halves and quarters.

Lesson 15 (Practise and evaluate)

Starter

Recall: Use the pendulum to practise number bonds for all numbers to 20. For example, for 15, swing the pendulum one way and call out 3, swing it the other and the children call out 12.

Main teaching activities

Whole class: Focus on fractions of numbers but this time using pennies. Recap the work done in the last four lessons, assessing the children's understanding of the concept of fractions. Call out numbers and ask them to write what a half, a quarter, and three quarters of this number are, on their whiteboards.

Paired work: Tell the children that they will be playing another game to help them practise halving and quartering numbers. Demonstrate the game 'Pennies game 1'. Instructions and recording sheet are on the CD.

Differentiation

Less confident learners: These children should play the support version of the game, which concentrates on halving.
More confident learners: These children should play the extension version of the game. Encourage them to find out if they can find other fractions, particularly those they found in Lesson 14, and to record these on their recording sheet.

Review

Ask some quick-fire half, quarter and three-quarter questions as in Lesson 14. Next, ask the children to think of all the things they have done over the last few lessons to help them learn about fractions. Ask them to tell a partner what they now know that they didn't before and then to feed back to the rest of the class.

Name ______________________ Date ______________________

Things to multiply

You will need a tray of small things to use for counting.

For each multiplication, put the right number of things in the right number of rows.

Draw what you have done in the box.

Write the answer, then write the addition sum, as shown below.

<table>
<tr>
<td>2 × 3 = [6]

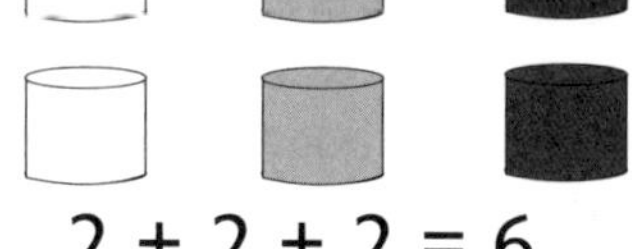
2 + 2 + 2 = 6</td>
<td>2 × 8 = [16]

2 + 2 + 2 + 2 + 2 + 2 + 2 + 2 = 16</td>
</tr>
<tr>
<td>2 × 4 = [ ]</td>
<td>2 × 6 = [ ]</td>
</tr>
<tr>
<td>10 × 2 = [ ]</td>
<td>10 × 4 = [ ]</td>
</tr>
</table>

Now see if you can work these out by counting in twos, tens or fives.

2 × 7 = 2 + 2 + 2 + 2 + 2 + 2 +2 = 14

2 × 9 = ______________________

10 × 6 = ______________________

10 × 9 = ______________________

5 × 6 = ______________________

Name ______________________ Date ______________________

Jumping up and down

Fill the number lines to show each multiplication and its division opposite.

Count the number of arrows for the answer.

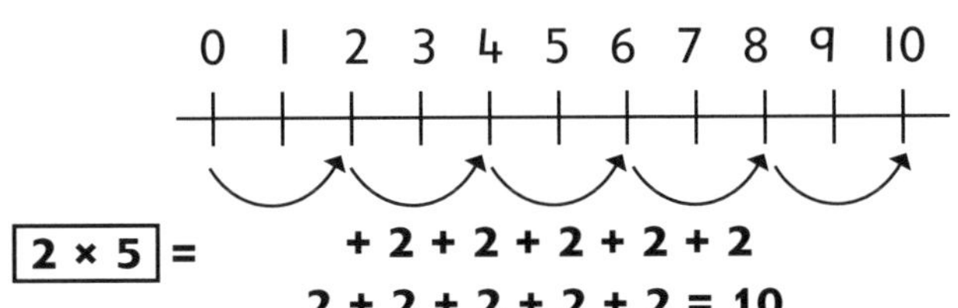

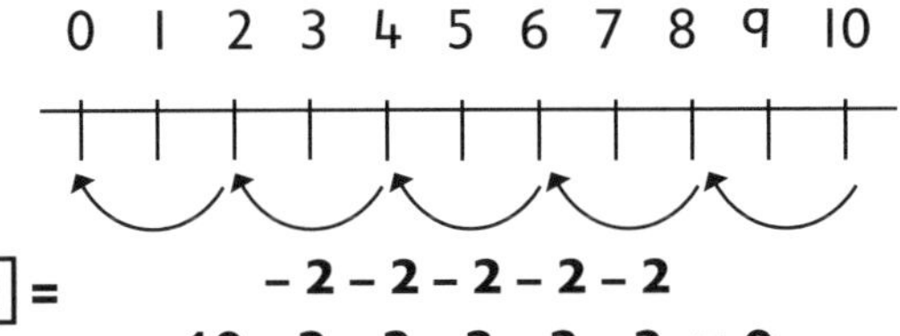

2 × 5 = **+ 2 + 2 + 2 + 2 + 2**
2 + 2 + 2 + 2 + 2 = 10

10 ÷ 2 = **– 2 – 2 – 2 – 2 – 2**
10 – 2 – 2 – 2 – 2 – 2 = 0

0 1 2 3 4 5 6 7 8 9 10 11 12 13 14 15 16 17 18 19 20

2 × 7 ______________________

____

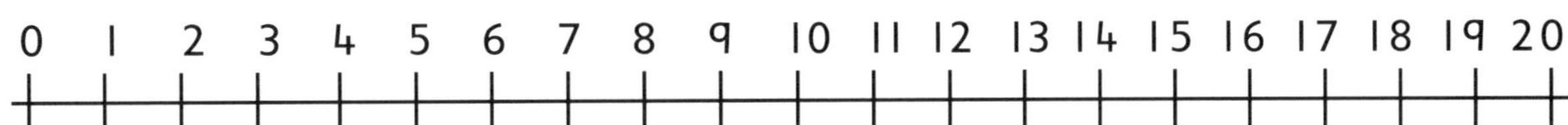

14 ÷ 2 ______________________

____

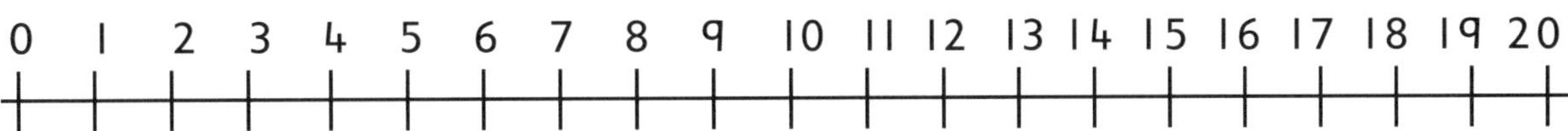

5 × 3 ______________________

____

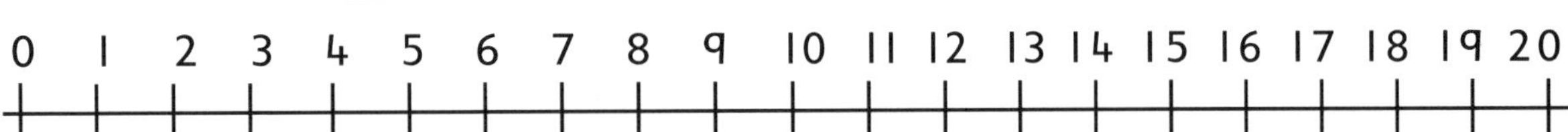

20 ÷ 5 ______________________

____

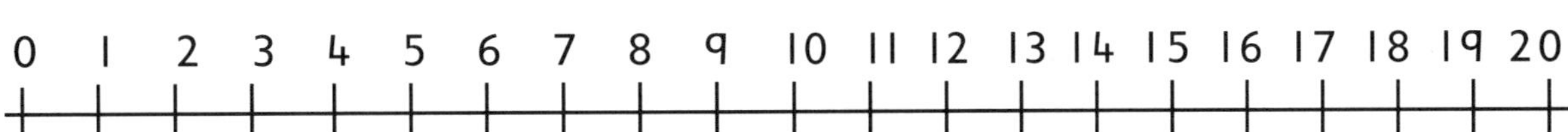

5 × 4 ______________________

____

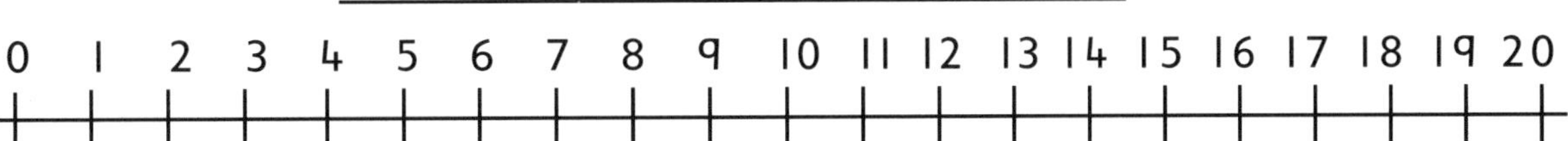

12 ÷ 2 ______________________

____

Name ______________________ Date ______________

Make me a problem!

Pick two numbers to make a multiplication problem.

3	5	10	2
12	7	9	4
6	15	8	20

Here is an example:

I have 5 teddies, my sister has 3 times as many. How many does she have?

Now you try.

Problem 1 ______________________

____

Problem 2 ______________________

____

Problem 3 ______________________

____

Now pick a number from each pentagon and make a division problem.

Here is an example:

I have 20 balls and want to put them in bags of 5 each. How many bags will I need?

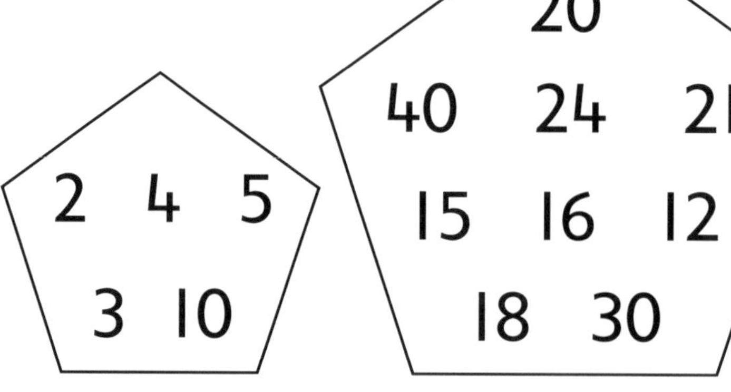

Problem 1 ______________________

____

Problem 2 ______________________

____

Name ____________________ Date ____________________

Halve or double?

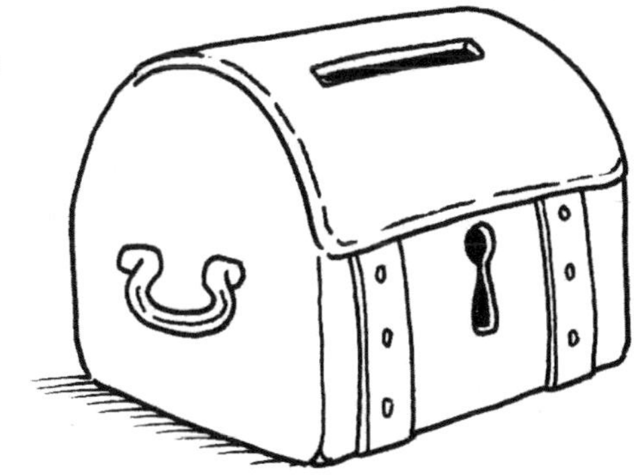

I looked in my money box and saw lots of coins.

I had fourteen 1p pieces.

I had the same amount of money in 2p pieces.

How many 2p pieces did I have? ☐

Sue had 40 marbles. Peter had half that number.

How many marbles did Peter have? ☐

Lizzie had 16 birthday cards.

Her friend Tom had double that amount.

How many birthday cards did Tom have? ☐

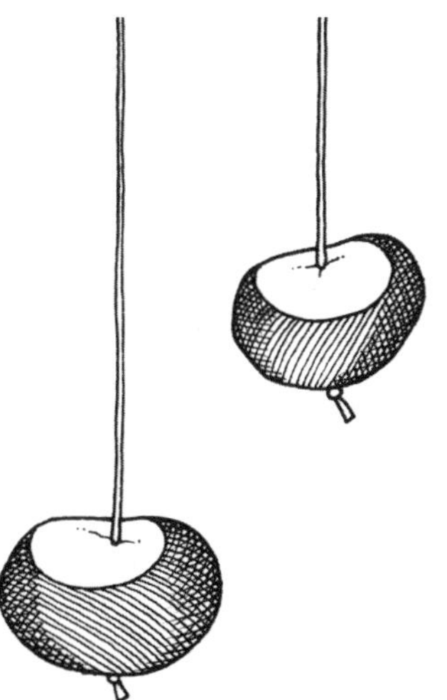

Laurie had 50 centimetres of string.

Laura had half that amount.

How long was Laura's piece of string? ☐ cm

Name ______________________ Date ______________________

Functioning machine

How quickly can you work out +9? +11?

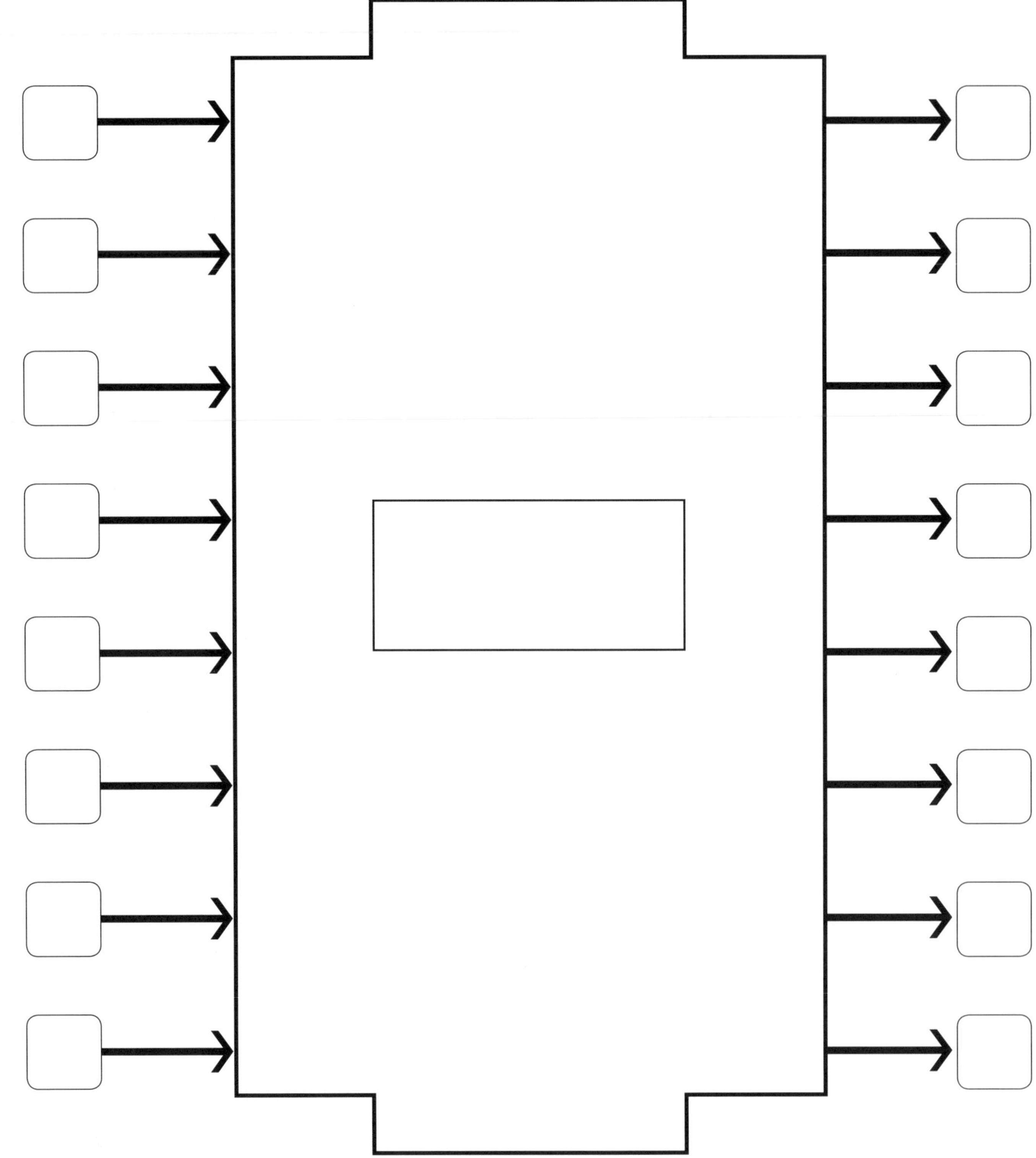

Name ______________________ Date ______________

Clock faces

Unit 2 3 weeks

Securing number facts, relationships and calculating

Lesson	Strands	Starter	Main teaching activities
1. Review, teach and apply	Use/apply	Mental calculations strategies: addition through partitioning, bridge through 10 and adjust, number pairs to 10 and multiples of 10 to 100, subtraction by counting up from the smaller to the larger number.	• Identify and record the information or calculation needed to solve a puzzle or problem; carry out the steps or calculations and check the solution in the context of the problem. • Solve problems involving addition, subtraction, multiplication or division in contexts of numbers, measures or pounds and pence.
2. Review, teach and apply	Use/apply	As for Lesson 1	As for Lesson 1
3. Review, teach and practise	Calculate	Read and write two-digit and three-digit numbers in figures and words.	Represent repeated addition and arrays as multiplication, and sharing and repeated subtraction (grouping) as division; use practical and informal written methods and related vocabulary to support multiplication and division, including calculations with remainders.
4. Teach and practise	Calculate	Derive and recall multiplication facts for the 2, 5 and 10 times-tables and the related division facts.	As for Lesson 3
5. Teach, practise and evaluate	Calculate	**Derive all pairs of numbers with totals to 20.**	As for Lesson 3
6. Review, teach and apply	Use/apply Calculate	**Derive and recall all addition and subtraction facts for each number to at least 10, all pairs with totals to 20 and all pairs of multiples of 10 with totals up to 100.**	• Represent repeated addition and arrays as multiplication, and sharing and repeated subtraction (grouping) as division; use practical and informal written methods and related vocabulary to support multiplication and division, including calculations with remainders. • Solve problems involving addition, subtraction, multiplication or division in contexts of numbers, measures or pounds and pence.
7. Apply and evaluate	Use/apply Calculate	As for Lesson 6	As for Lesson 6
8. Review, teach and practise	Use/apply Calculate	Read and write two-digit and three-digit numbers in figures and words; describe and extend number sequences and recognise odd and even numbers.	• Identify and record the information or calculation needed to solve a puzzle or problem; carry out the steps or calculations and check the solution in the context of the problem. **• Use the symbols +, -, ×, ÷ and = to record and interpret number sentences involving all four operations; calculate the value of an unknown in a number sentence (eg □ ÷ 2 = 6, 30 - □ = 24).**
9. Teach, practise and evaluate	Use/apply Calculate	Understand that halving is the inverse of doubling and derive and recall doubles of all numbers to 20, and the corresponding halves.	As for Lesson 8
10. Review, practise and evaluate	Use/apply Knowledge	As for Lesson 9	• Identify and record the information or calculation needed to solve a puzzle or problem; carry out the steps or calculations and check the solution in the context of the problem. • Understand that halving is the inverse of doubling and derive and recall doubles of all numbers to 20, and the corresponding halves.
11. Review, practise and evaluate	Use/apply Knowledge	As for Lesson 8	• Identify and record the information or calculation needed to solve a puzzle or problem; carry out the steps or calculations and check the solution in the context of the problem. • Derive and recall multiplication facts for the 2. 5 and 10 times-tables and the related division facts; recognise multiples of 2, 5 and 10.
12. Review, teach and practise	Counting	As for Lesson 4	Find one half, one quarter and three quarters of shapes and sets of objects.
13. Practise	Counting	As for Lesson 4	As for Lesson 12
14. Practise	Counting	As for Lesson 4	As for Lesson 12
15. Apply and evaluate	Counting	As for Lesson 3	As for Lesson 12

Speaking and listening objectives

- Listen to talk by an adult, remember some specific points and identify what they have learned.
- Adopt appropriate roles in small or large groups and consider alternative courses of action.

Introduction

This block contains 15 lessons, the first two of which focus upon open-ended problems that incorporate a variety of mental calculation strategies and encourage the thinking skills of enquiry and reasoning. During the next seven lessons, the focus is on multiplication and division. At the beginning of this sequence, there is direct teaching of these two operations, reinforcing, consolidating and progressing the children's knowledge. The last six lessons involve using and applying. The first of these (Lesson 10) is directly focused on doubling and halving, linked to multiplication and division. The following two lessons discretely involve recall of facts. The last four days focus on understanding fractions and their relationship to each other. The children are encouraged to find a half, a quarter and three quarters of amounts and then to use this skill to make up word problems for others to solve. Threaded throughout the block are elements of the using and applying objectives and also those from speaking and listening.

Using and applying mathematics

- Identify and record the information or calculation needed to solve a puzzle or problem; carry out the steps or calculations and check the solution in the context of the problem.

Lessons 1-2

You will need

Photocopiable pages
'Dicey problems' (page 201), one per pair or small group.
CD resources
'More problems', 'Extra money problems'. Interactive resource 'Money'.
Equipment
Counters, dice.

Learning objectives

Starter

- Mental calculations strategies: addition through partitioning, adding 10 and adjusting, number pairs to 10 and multiples of 10 to 100, subtraction though counting on.

Main teaching activities

2006

- Identify and record the information or calculation needed to solve a puzzle or problem; carry out the steps or calculations and check the solution in the context of the problem.
- Solve problems involving addition, subtraction, multiplication or division in contexts of numbers, measures or pounds and pence.

1999

- Use mental addition and subtraction to solve simple word problems involving numbers in 'real life', money or measures, using one or two steps. Explain how the problem was solved.
- Choose and use appropriate number operations and efficient calculation strategies to solve problems.

Vocabulary

problem, solve, calculate, calculation, answer, method, explain, predict, pattern, order

Lesson 1 (Review, teach and apply)

Starter

Refresh and read: Write a variety of calculations on the board for the children to answer on their whiteboards. Make these up according to the different calculation strategies mentioned in the objective, for example, 27 + 15 (partitioning), 24 + 9 (add 10 and adjust), 13 + 7 (pairs to 10) and 35 - 26 (counting on). For each, discuss and evaluate the methods used.

Main teaching activities

Whole class: Say: *Over the next two lessons you will be solving 'open-ended' problems.* Explain what you mean: problems with different answers or the same answer but different ways of answering. Show the problem from 'Extra money problems' on the CD: *I bought 5 gobstoppers at 15p each. I paid the exact amount. Which coins could I have given the shopkeeper?*

Discuss what the question is asking and ask the children to talk to a partner about what they think they need to do. Take feedback, then ask for suggestions as to how they might go about the task. Remind them of the work they did in multiplication in Unit 1, of the five-times tables facts they have been learning and about partitioning. Ask: *How can these help us?* Establish that they can partition 15 into 10 and 5 and then multiply each by 5, using their knowledge of tables' facts. Using the Interactive resource Money, explore ways of making 75p. Ask such questions as: *What are the fewest coins that can be given? How many possible answers do you think there are? If we wanted 2/3/4/10 gobstoppers, how much would that cost? How do you know?*

Explore the second problem, discussing the differences between this and the first, for example, no multiplication calculation. Then discuss the similarities, such as money, addition.

Group work: The children should work in mixed-ability groups of three or four to answer the investigative style problems on 'More problems'. Discuss the idea of finding all possibilities and being systematic.

Differentiation

Check that the less confident learners are taking an active part in the group discussions, and that the more confident children are not dominating proceedings.

Review

Take feedback from the activity, discuss the different possibilities. Invite children to demonstrate some of their ideas on the board using the interactive resource 'Money'. Ask: *How do you know that you have all the possible amounts using a £1 coin? Are there any other ways of doing this using a 50p piece?*

Lesson 2 (Review, teach and apply)

Starter

Refresh and read: As for Lesson 1.

Main teaching activities

Whole class: Explain that in today's lesson the children will be solving 'open-ended' problems again. Ask: *Can you remember what open-ended means?* Recap on the work they did in the last lesson and then move on to a slightly different investigation. Say: *In how many ways can you make 12? Write down as many different ways as you can on your whiteboards. Use addition, subtraction, multiplication and division.*

Encourage the more confident children to use more than one operation, for example, half of 20 plus 2, 3 × 2 and double it, 15 take away 5 add 2. Ask the children to find ways to record their work.

Group work: The children should work in pairs or small groups on 'Dicey problems'. Give them a plastic cup of counters and three dice. The aim of this activity is to collect the most counters. The first child throws the three dice and tries to get the highest answer possible by this rule: add two dice and subtract the third, for example, if 5, 3 and 6 are thrown, the 6 and 5 are added and the 3 taken away. Ask the children to record their answers in a way similar to this: 6 + 5 - 3 = 8.

After they have played this for about five minutes, change the rules slightly, for example, multiply two dice and subtract the third, or double one and add the others.

Differentiation

As for Lesson 1.

Review

Take feedback, asking the children to tell you how they made their highest scores. Write some totals up and ask: *Is there another way to make this? How could you include division? What about multiplication?* Order the numbers you have written on a number line and use this opportunity to rehearse <, >, = by writing the appropriate number sentences.

Lessons 3-5

Preparation

Photocopy 'Multiplication and division vocabulary' onto card and cut out the words. Photocopy the 'Home we go!' gameboard onto card and laminate for each group of three children. Make a pack of 0-30 number cards for each group. Make an A3 copy of 'Flip-flap for 20'.

You will need

Photocopiable pages
'Array for maths!' (page 202) and 'Group that!' (page 203) for each child.

CD resources
0-100 number cards for each group, 'Spider charts for multiplying' and 'Spider charts for dividing', 'Multiplication and division vocabulary' cards, an A3 copy of 'Flip-flap for 20', 'Home we go!' gameboard and instructions for each group (see General resources); 'Array for maths!' and 'Group that!', support and extension versions.

Equipment
Multilink or cubes; counters; number lines; a pendulum.

Learning objectives

Starter

- Read and write two-digit and three-digit numbers in figures and words.
- Derive and recall multiplication facts for the 2, 5 and 10 times-tables and the related division facts.
- Derive all pairs of numbers with a total of 20.

Main teaching activities

2006

- Represent repeated addition and arrays as multiplication, and sharing and repeated subtraction (grouping) as division; use practical and informal written methods and related vocabulary to support multiplication and division, including calculations with remainders.

1999

- Understand the operation of multiplication as repeated addition or as describing an array, and begin to understand division as grouping (repeated subtraction) or sharing.
- Use and begin to read the related vocabulary.

Vocabulary

lots of, groups of, times, multiply, multiplied by, multiple of, repeated addition, array, row, column, equal groups of, repeated subtraction, divide, divided by

Lesson 3 (Review, teach and practise)

Starter

Refine, read and rehearse: Ask the children to write single-digit and two-digit numbers on their whiteboards. Show them number cards and ask them to write these as words. Then say: *Write 2. Make it say 22. Now add 10.* (32) *Change the 2 to a 7. What number do you have now?* (37) *Add 3.* (40) *Take away two tens.* (20) *Add 100.* (120) *Double the tens number.* (140) *Add 9. What number do you have now?* (149) *Write the number in words.* Repeat several times.

Main teaching activities

Whole class: This week the children will be learning about multiplication and division. Revise the meaning of 'multiply' and 'divide', and ask for related vocabulary. Use the vocabulary cards to reinforce the words. Sort the words into two groups: multiplication and division. Say: *Today we will be concentrating on the words 'repeated addition', 'repeated subtraction', 'arrays' and 'groups'.* Write the number 6 on the board. Ask someone to draw an array of six dots. You may need to demonstrate. Ask the class how the array can be recorded as a number sentence: 2 + 2 + 2 = 6.

Explain that this repeated addition can be written as 2 × 3 = 6 (three groups of two). Link this to the two-times table by counting 2, 4, 6 on fingers. Ask whether there is another way of making an array. Link this to the three-times table by counting 3, 6... using fingers. Repeat with two arrays for 10 (5 × 2 and 2 × 5). Ask the children to draw arrays of 8 on their whiteboards and write number sentences. Ask those that do this quickly to try 12. Can they find more than two arrays?

Paired work: Ask the children to work in pairs to make arrays and derive two number sentences from each array. Model the example from the 'Array for maths!' activity sheet.

Review

Invite one pair to draw and explain one of their arrays. Use their work to introduce division in terms of grouping or repeated subtraction. (Note: an example of division by grouping is: *I have eight sweets and I put them in bags with two in each.* An example of division by sharing is: *I have eight sweets and I share them equally with my friend.*) Explain that because division is the opposite of multiplication and multiplication is repeated addition, division must be repeated subtraction. If the children's example is 3 × 4, explain that if four groups of 3 are 12, then to divide you can take away four groups of 3 from 12. Draw the groups on the board. Record this as 12 ÷ 3 = 4. Use an array to show that if 2 × 5 = 10 then 10 ÷ 2 = 5.

Differentiation

Less confident learners: Provide the support version of 'Array for maths!' with lower numbers. If possible, ask a teaching assistant to work with these children. Let them make the arrays with counters before drawing them.
More confident learners: Provide the extension version that asks for three different arrays for 24.

Lesson 4 (Teach and practise)

Starter

Recall: Practise saying the two-, five- and ten-times tables, then use the class spider charts to ask for random facts. Count in multiples of 2, 5 and 10 using fingers, saying 'Stop' at certain points and asking the children how many lots of 2 or 10 make that number. For example: *2, 4, 6, 8, 10, 12, Stop! How many fingers are you holding up? So how many twos make 12?*

Main teaching activities

Whole class: Recap on arrays and the link to division. Start with the example from the Review of Lesson 1, using cubes or similar objects to demonstrate. Say: *I have 12 cubes and I am going to divide them into groups of 4. Here's one group of 4. Salman, you hold them. Here's another. Sue, you hold these. And here is another, which I will hold. How many groups of 4 do I have? Yes, three. So 12 divided by 4 is 3, which we can record as 12 ÷ 4 = 3.* Repeat with other numbers and divisors, such as 12 ÷ 3 = 4, 12 ÷ 2 = 6 and 12 ÷ 6 = 2. Use the children in your demonstrations and ask questions: *What am I dividing by? How many are there in each group? How many groups have I taken away? How can I record that?* Demonstrate by recording, for example: 12 ÷ 4.
Individual work: Ask the children to practise dividing by grouping. Distribute the 'Group that!' photocopiable sheet and check that they understand what to do.

Review

Ask one child from each group to show the class an example of their work. Take an example such as 12 ÷ 2 and explain that we can also say this as 'How many twos make 12?' and that our times-table knowledge can help us to work out divisions. Show a few examples, such as: 8 divided by 2 is four groups (8 - 2 - 2 - 2 - 2). *How many twos make 8?* Answer is 4 (2 + 2 + 2 + 2). Draw the groupings on the board, then count up in twos using your fingers.

Differentiation

Less confident learners: Provide the support version of 'Group that!' with numbers to 12.
More confident learners: Provide the extension version where the children have to draw the arrays.

Lesson 5 (Teach, practise and evaluate)

Starter

Rehearse and recall: Use the A3 copy of 'Flip-flap for 20'. Show some ladybirds and ask the children to write on their whiteboards how many more they need to make 20. Ask more confident children to write this as a calculation (such as 13 + 7 = 20). Give less confident children a 0–20 number line to help them. Repeat for most of the numbers to 20. Now use a pendulum: as it swings one way, you call out a number; as it swings the other way, the children call out its complement to make 20.

Main teaching activities

Whole class: Write 18 ÷ 2 on the board and ask: *How can we answer this? Let's work out 18 ÷ 2 by counting in twos together, using our fingers: 2, 4, 6... 18. How many twos is that? How many fingers?* (9) *Try 15 ÷ 3. What should we count in this time?* (threes) Ask similar questions for the children to answer on their whiteboards. Make the divisors the numbers they have counted in steps of: 2, 3, 4, 5 and 10.

Group work: Ask the children to practise this by playing a game in groups of three or four. Model the 'Home we go!' game.

Review

Play 'Home we go!' in two teams. Make sure everyone counts. Use this as an opportunity to bring in remainders very briefly. For example, with 11 ÷ 3, count in threes: 3, 6, 9, 12. 11 is higher than 9, but lower than 12. Draw 11 dots on the board and say: *We can get three groups of 3 from 11, but then we have two left over. So we can say that 11 ÷ 3 is 3 remainder 2.* (See figure below.) This is mainly for more confident children. Encourage the children to self-assess how they think their knowledge and understanding of multiplication and division have improved.

Differentiation

Less confident learners: Let these children use number lines, counters or pennies to help them group. Adult support would be helpful.
More confident learners: Encourage these children to record their work like this: '12 ÷ 3 is 4 groups of 3' and '15 ÷ 2 is 7 groups of 2 and 1 left over'.

Lesson 6-7

You will need

Photocopiable pages
'Party problems example' (page 204) and 'Party problems' (page 205).
CD resources
An A3 copy of 'How to solve a problem', 'Flip-flap for 10' for each child, plus one A3 copy, an OHT of the 'Party problems example', 'Party problems' core, support and extension versions.
Equipment
Items to count; counting apparatus.

Learning objectives

Starter

- Derive and recall all addition and subtraction facts for each number to at least 10, all pairs with totals to 20 and all pairs of multiples of 10 with totals up to 100.

Main teaching activities

2006

- Represent repeated addition and arrays as multiplication, and sharing and repeated subtraction (grouping) as division; use practical and informal written methods and related vocabulary to support multiplication and division, including calculations with remainders.
- Solve problems involving addition, subtraction, multiplication or division in contexts of numbers, measures or pounds and pence.

1999

- Use mental addition, and subtraction, simple multiplication and division, to solve simple word problems involving numbers in 'real life', money or measures, using one or two steps.
- Explain how a problem was solved orally and, where appropriate, in writing.
- Choose and use appropriate operations and efficient calculation strategies (eg mental, mental with jottings) to solve problems.

Vocabulary

lots of, groups of, times, multiply, multiplied by, multiple of, repeated addition, array, row, column, equal groups of, repeated subtraction, divide, divided by

Lesson 6 (Review, teach and apply)

Starter

Rehearse and reason: Remind the children how to use a 'flip-flap' for number pairs to 10. Fold your A3 'Flip-flap for 10' so that when you hold it up towards the children, they can see one snail. Say: *If this snail represents ten snails, how many will two snails represent?* (20) *How about three?* Ask the children to write the answers on their whiteboards. Each time, ask: *How many more do I need for 100?* Use a pendulum to practise number bonds of multiples of 10 to 100.

Main teaching activities

Whole class: Explain that this lesson is about solving 'real-life' problems,

using multiplication and division. Write the five stages of problem solving ('How to solve a problem') on the board. Show the 'How to solve a problem' poster and stick it on the wall as a constant reminder. Using the OHT of 'Party problems example', work through the exemplar problem. Ask questions as you go along, such as: *What is the question? What do we need to know to find the answer? How many packets of biscuits can you see? How many biscuits are in each one? What are four lots of 10? What else do we need to find out? How many biscuits are there altogether? How did you work out the last part?*

Group work: Ask the children to work with a partner from their group. Give out the 'Party problems' photocopiable sheet. Tell the children that they can jot down their workings on it.

Differentiation

Less confident learners: Provide the support version of 'Party problems' with smaller numbers. Make counting apparatus available if needed.

More confident learners: Provide the extension version of 'Party problems' with larger numbers. Talk through a problem similar to question 2 on the sheet, such as: *Sam needs 17 little cakes. The shop sells them in packs of 10. How many packs does he need?* Discuss the fact that he will have to buy a second pack.

Review

Invite a few children, particularly any you want to assess, to explain how they solved one of their problems. Discuss and compare methods. Ask questions such as: *How did you know what was being asked? What information did you need? Explain how you worked it out. How did you know if you were right? What did you do if there were some things left over?*

Lesson 7 (Apply and evaluate)

Starter

Rehearse, recall and reason: Repeat the Starters from Lessons 5 and 6, focusing on a mixture of any number to 20 and multiples of ten to 100.

Main teaching activities

Whole class: Recap on the problem-solving process the children worked on in Lesson 6. Run through the exemplar problem on the 'Party problems example' sheet again as a reminder. Work through it, using the steps on the problem-solving poster.

Paired work: Give the pairs the activity 'Problem-solving practice' to work through. Before they begin, tell them that they have to think carefully about each problem, because there are different operations to do.

Differentiation

If the less confident learners find the activity sheet difficult to read and understand, suggest that a confident reader reads the problems to the whole group. Then encourage the children to explain to each other what they have to do.

Review

Cover up your problem-solving poster and ask: *Who can tell me the steps you have to take when you try to answer a problem?* Invite a child to explain, using one of the problems they had during the session. Say: *For the last two lessons of this week we have been solving problems. Who can remember what we were doing for the first three lessons? What does 'grouping' mean?* (Taking away groups of numbers.) *How do we know what groups to take away?* (The number that we divide by/the number on the other side of the division sign.) *Who can tell us what this means: 21 ÷ 3? Who can show us how to group that on this picture?*

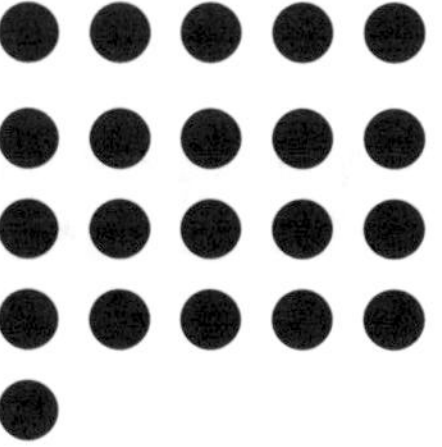

Lessons 8-9

You will need

CD resources
'0-100 number cards', 'Doubles and halves cards', (see General resources); a selection of about 15 to 20 cards from 'Missing number sentences' and 'Missing number sentences 2'; 'Missing number sentences recording sheet'.

Equipment
A dice; a class 100 square; individual 100 squares; a counting stick; counters; counting apparatus.

Learning objectives

Starter

- Read and write two-digit and three-digit numbers in figures and words; describe and extend number sequences; recognise odd and even numbers.
- Understand that halving is the inverse of doubling and derive and recall doubles of all numbers to 20 and the corresponding halves.

Main teaching activities

2006

- Identify and record the information or calculation needed to solve a puzzle or problem; carry out the steps or calculations and check the solution in the context of the problem.
- Use the symbols +, -, ×, ÷ and = to record and interpret number sentences involving all four operations; calculate the value of an unknown in a number sentence (eg □ ÷ 2 = 6, 30 - □ = 24).

1999

- Use the +, -, ×, ÷ and = signs to record mental calculations in a number sentence, and recognise the use of a symbol such as □ to stand for an unknown number.

Vocabulary

zero, one hundred, two hundred... one thousand, count on, count back, count on in ones/twos/tens, multiple of, sequence, continue, predict, pattern, rule

Lesson 8 (Review, teach and practise)

Starter

Read and refine: Use a class 100 square to count on and back in tens and ones. For example, find 36 and ask: *What is 10 more? ...10 less? ...1 more? ...4 less?* Now ask the children to imagine the class 100 square in their heads. Say a number, for example 23, and ask them to look at it in their minds: *Which number is below it on your 100 square?* (33) ... *above it?* (13) ... *two squares to the right?* (25)... *three to the left?* (20) Repeat several times with other numbers. If any children struggle with this, give them a 100 square to use.

Main teaching activities

Whole class: Explain that this and the next lesson will focus on counting backwards and forwards from zero in steps of 2, 3, 4, 5 and 10. Concentrate on 2, 5 and 10 today.

Using a counting stick, move your finger up and down, asking the children to count in jumps of 2, then 5, then 10. Make jumps along the stick, asking the children to predict what number you are pointing to and say how they know. Expect answers such as: *That is 35 because it is 7 jumps of 5* and encourage them to write the appropriate number sentence: 5 × 7 = 35. Repeat a few times with different starting numbers.

Write some missing number sentences on the board, for example, 5 × □ = 35 and ask the children how they can work this out: aim towards counting in fives to get to 35. Bring in the inverse operation: 35 ÷ 7 = 5.

Next, write up □ × 6 = 60 and ask them to tell you the missing number and how they knew, again bring in the inverse. Next write ○ × □ = 20 and ask the children to work with a partner to find out what the possible missing numbers could be. Encourage them to write the number sentences and their inverses. Repeat with different examples similar to these three.

Paired work: The children should work in ability groups for this game and use the cards from 'Missing number sentences'. They spread the cards face down on the table and pick two. They then try to make a missing number sentence using one of the numbers they have picked as the answer. If they can, they score two points, if they can only make one with the missing number at the end, they score one point. If they can't make one at all, they replace one of their cards and try again. Encourage them to include both multiplication and division sentences. Model the activity first. For example, if you pick 10 and 5, the sentence could be: 10 ÷ □ = 2, score: 2 points. If you pick 7 and 5, the sentence could be 5 × 7 = 35, score 1 point. The children should use the 'Missing number sentences recording sheet'to write their sentences and scores.

Differentiation
Less confident learners: Give this group cards to 20.
More confident learners: This group should have a range of cards up to 100.

Review
Take feedback from the game, asking volunteers to show some of their missing number sentences. Ask: *How would you work out the missing number in this number sentence? 24 ÷ □ = 6.* Say that during the next lesson the children will be thinking about counting in threes and fours.

Lesson 9 (Teach, practise and evaluate)

Starter
Refresh: Call out some numbers from 1 to 15 for the children to double, and some even numbers to 30 for the children to halve, writing on their whiteboards. Use the 40 'Doubles and halves cards' to play a 'Follow me' game. Let the children work in pairs, with at least two cards per pair.

Main teaching activities
Repeat the whole-class and group work from Lesson 8, but this time work on counting in threes and fours and use 'Missing number sentences 2' and record on the 'Missing number sentences recording sheet'.

Review
Adapt your Review from Lesson 8, ensuring that you evaluate the children's progress.

Lesson 10

You will need
CD resources
'Doubling game' (one for each pair), 'Doubling game scoreboard'.
Equipment
Number cards 0–9, dice, partitioning cards for less confident learners.

Learning objectives

Starter
- Understand that halving is the inverse of doubling and derive and recall doubles of all numbers to 20, and the corresponding halves.

Main teaching activities
2006
- Identify and record the information or calculation needed to solve a puzzle or problem; carry out the steps or calculations and check the solution in the context of the problem.
- Understand that halving is the inverse of doubling and derive and recall doubles of all numbers to 20, and the corresponding halves.

1999
- Derive quickly doubles of all whole numbers to at least 20 (eg 17 × 2), and the corresponding halves (eg 36 ÷ 2).

Vocabulary
double, halve, inverse

Lesson 10 (Review, practise and evaluate)

Starter

Refresh: As for Lesson 9.

Main teaching activities

Whole class: Discuss the skills used in the starter and ask the children to explain what they are doing when doubling: adding the same number twice, multiplying by 2. Repeat for halving: dividing by 2. Discuss the fact that doubling and halving are inverse operations and remind them of the inversion arrows they looked at in previous units:

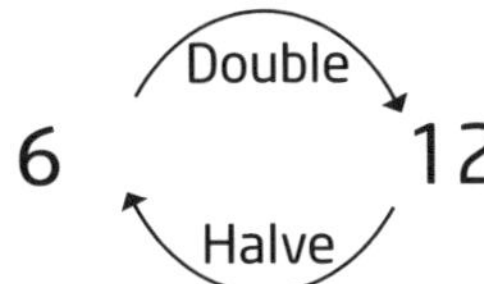

Ask the children to work with a partner to make up some inversion arrow diagrams like this for other numbers. Challenge them to make up larger numbers - for example, 36 and 72. Discuss strategies, encouraging them to look for knowledge they already have - for example, if doubling 36, they know that double 3 is 6, so double 30 is 60 and then they can add 12 by partitioning: 60 + 10 + 2 = 72.

Group work: The children should work in pairs within each group. Model the 'Doubling game' activity. The group needs a dice and a set of 0-9 number cards. The pairs should take it in turns to pick two number cards and make up the smallest two-digit number from these. Then they throw the dice. If they throw an even number, they double the number, using whatever strategy they wish. If they throw an odd number, they halve. If they are successful, they score a point. Say: *The first pair to score 12 is the winner.* There is a 'Doubling game scoreboard' to complete.

Differentiation

Less confident learners: These children should begin by picking single digits and then make teens numbers. For this, they should have a set of partitioning cards with the 1s numbers and also 10.

More confident learners: Encourage this group to make the highest numbers they can to double.

Review

Invite volunteers to demonstrate their strategies for doubling the two-digit numbers. Remind them to look for knowledge they already have, for example, if doubling 75, they know double 7 is 14, so double 70 is 140, and then they need to add 10. Ask: *You know that double 15 is 30. How could you use this to work out double 16? What about double 17?*

Lesson 11

Preparation

Copy and laminate the 'Lost in space gameboard'.

You will need

CD resources

0-50 number cards from '0-100 number cards' and 'Up the mountain' gameboard, a copy of 'Lost in space gameboard', 'Lost in space recording sheet' for each pair (see General resources).

Equipment

Counters.

Learning objectives

Starter

- Read and write two-digit and three-digit numbers in figures and words; describe and extend number sequences; recognise odd and even numbers.

Main teaching activities

2006

- Identify and record the information or calculation needed to solve a puzzle or problem; carry out the steps or calculations and check the solution in the context of the problem.
- Derive and recall multiplication facts for the 2, 5 and 10 times-tables and the related division facts; recognise multiples of 2, 5 and 10.

1999

- Begin to recognise two-digit multiples of 2, 5 or 10.

Vocabulary

two hundred... one thousand, count on, count back, count in ones/tens, odd, even, multiple of, sequence, continue, predict, count, tally, every other, how many times?

Lesson 11 (Review, practise and evaluate)

Starter

Reason: Divide the class into two teams. Display the 'Up the mountain' gameboard and attach a counter for each team. The teams take turns to pick a number card to 50 and say whether it is odd or even and how they know. If it is odd, move the team's counter one step up. The first team to reach the top wins.

Main teaching activities

Whole class: Recite the multiples of 2, 5 and 10 together. Draw three circles on the board and as the children say the numbers, write the multiples of 2 from 0 to 20 in one circle, of 5 from 0 to 50 in the second, and of 10 from 0 to 100 in the third. Ask the children to tell you about these numbers; focus on the units digits. Discuss those numbers that appear in more than one circle.

Paired work: Demonstrate the Lost in space game using the 'Lost in space gameboard' and the 'Lost in space recording sheet', then let the children play it.

Differentiation

Less confident learners: Provide cards for numbers to 20.
More confident learners: Provide cards for a selection of numbers to 100.

Review

Ask the children for examples of numbers that allowed them to move three spaces, six spaces and no spaces. Draw loops for multiples of '2 only', '5 only' and '2 and 5'. Ask which numbers will go in the loops. *Is 10 a multiple of 2? Let's count in twos to check. Can we write 10 in our '2 only' loop? Why not? What about 20 or 30? Why not?* (A multiple of 10 is also a multiple of 5 and 2.) Evaluate the children's knowledge and understanding of multiples.

Lessons 12-15

Preparation

Make A3 copies of 'Spider charts for multiplying' and 'Spider charts for dividing'; copy and laminate 'Small spider charts' and cut out at least two charts per child; copy and laminate the 'Spin a fraction cards', cut out the spinners. Copy 'Fraction strips' onto acetate and cut out. Make one copy of 'Pennies game 2', and 'Pennies recording sheet' for each child, according to ability. Copy 'Fraction number line' to A3 and laminate it; copy and laminate the 'Fraction cards'. Make some sets of the 'Spin a fraction' cards. Prepare five Multilink towers: 1) two red, one yellow and one green; 2) three red, two yellow and one green; 3) four red, two yellow and two green; 4) five red, two yellow and three green; 5) six red, three yellow and three green.

You will need

CD resources
'0-100 number cards', 'Spider charts for multiplying' and 'Spider charts for dividing', 'Small spider charts', Fraction number line and cards instructions', 'Fraction

Learning objectives

Starter

- Derive and recall multiplication facts for the 2, 5 and 10 times-tables and the related division facts.
- Read and write two-digit and three-digit numbers in figures and words.

Main teaching activities

2006

- Find one half, one quarter and three quarters of shapes and sets of objects.

1999

- Begin to recognise and find one half and one quarter of shapes and small numbers of objects.
- Begin to recognise that two halves or four quarters make one whole and that two quarters and one half are equal.

Vocabulary

part, equal parts, fraction, one whole, one half, two halves, one quarter, two... three ... four quarters

Lesson 12 (Review, teach and practise)

Starter

Refine and rehearse: Count in twos from zero to 20 and back. Ask the children to close their eyes as they count and imagine jumping up and down a number line. Stop them part-way along their line (say, at 14) and ask how many jumps they have made. Repeat a few times, then move on to counting in tens. Show the children the spider chart for multiplying by 2. Recap on how it is used. Now show the spider chart for dividing by 2 and ask: *What*

number line', 'Fraction cards' 'Fraction spinner', 'Spin a fraction', 'Number spinner', 'Pennies game 2', 'Pennies game 2: recording sheet 1', '2' or '3' (see General resources); 'Penny fractions', 'Fraction problems', 'My fraction problems', ITP Fractions.

Equipment

Paper clips; Multilink cubes; counters; pennies; A4 paper.

would you multiply 2 by to get the numbers around the outside? If I pointed to 18, what would you say? (9) Point to random numbers. Now say: *When I point to a number, tell me what that number is divided by 2. If I pointed to 18, what would you say?* (9) *What do you notice?* Emphasise that finding what you multiply 2 by to get 18 is a way of finding 18 ÷ 2. Repeat with the ten-times table and then the five-times table.

Main teaching activities

Whole class: Explain: *The next four lessons are about fractions. Who can tell me some thing about fractions?* Write down the children's statements on the board. Look for (and if necessary, prompt) these statements: 'a fraction is part of a whole thing'; 'half is when you divide something into two equal parts'; 'a quarter is when you divide something into four equal parts'. Spend time focusing on the following relationships: two halves and four quarters make a whole, two quarters are the same as one half, therefore one quarter is half of a half, three quarters is a half plus one quarter. Use the ITP Fractions as a tool to demonstrate this. Bring up three strips and leave the first whole, make the second into halves and the third into quarters. Ask: *How many quarters are the same as a whole?* Click on each quarter to show the children. Ask: *How many quarters are the same as a half?* Again, click on these to show them. Discuss three quarters as being the same as two quarters plus one quarter or one half and one quarter. Ask the children to draw their own strips on their whiteboards to show some of these relationships.

Focus on fractions of amounts. Show 4p, saying that this is the whole amount and point to the whole strip. Ask how many would be in each half, then each quarter. Blu-Tack the pennies onto the ITP in the correct places. Repeat for 8 pennies, then 12 and 16. Now try ten pennies. Ask: *What happens? Why?* Five pennies cannot be halved again and to make a quarter, they need to be. Ask the children to tell you another number that can only be divided into halves.

Paired work: Give each pair a copy of 'Penny fractions', a collection of pennies or, if not available, counters and a pack of about 15 number cards to 30. Ask them to select a card, put that number of counters on the whole strip and then work out how many half the number is and then a quarter. Demonstrate this, explaining that they won't always be able to make the fractions as they saw earlier. They should complete the recording sheet as they go along.

Differentiation

Less confident learners: These children should use number cards to 20.

More confident learners: These children could use random, even number cards to 100. You may like to encourage them to try to find other fractions.

Review

Take feedback from the activity, writing number sentences to complement what they say. For example, $^1/_2$ of 14 = 7. Recap why five pennies cannot be halved again to make a quarter. Ask: *Can you think of a number that can only be divided into quarters and not into halves? Can you explain why this is impossible?*

Lesson 13 (Practise)

Starter

Recall: Give the children their own small spider charts. They should work with a partner. One child does what you did in the Lesson 12 Starter (which you may need to model) and the other responds. After a couple of turns, they swap roles.

Main teaching activities

Whole class: Recap all the points of the last lesson with amounts of pennies or counters. For example, whole = 24, $^1/_2$ of 24 = 12, $^1/_4$ of 24 = 6, $^2/_4$ of 24 = 12, $^3/_4$ of 24 = $^1/_2$ + $^1/_4$ = 12 + 6 = 18.

Group work: Encourage the children to practise finding fractions of numbers by playing the Spin a fraction game. Let them use the 'Fraction spinner' and 'Spin a fraction' cards. Ask them to record their work.

Review

Show the Multilink towers and plain paper. Make statements, asking the children to tell you whether they are true or false. Each time, ask them to explain their response. First, take a sheet of paper and fold it once, but not in half. Say: *I have folded this sheet of paper in half. True or false?* Here are some other statements you can make: *I am folding this paper into four equal pieces, so I have folded it in half.* (F) 1. *One quarter of this tower is yellow.* (T) *Three quarters are a mixture of red and green.* (T) 2. *One quarter of this tower is green.* (F) *One half is yellow.* (F) 3. *One quarter of this tower is green.* (T) *Half is red.* (T) 4. *One quarter of this tower is red.* (F) *Half is made up from the yellow and green cubes.* (T) 5. *The red and yellow cubes make up three quarters of this tower.* (T) *The green makes up one half.* (F)

Differentiation

Less confident learners: These children can use the number spinner and find halves only.

Lesson 14 (Practise)

Starter

Recall: Repeat the whole class and paired spider chart activities from Lessons 12 and 13.

Main teaching activities

Whole class: Ask the children to tell you all they can about fractions. Compare this with what they said at the start of Lesson 12. Are they more confident? Explain that they are going to continue to practise working out halves and quarters and looking for patterns, but this time with a game.

Paired work: Model the 'Pennies game 2' using the instructions on the CD page. Let the children play version 1 in pairs, taking pennies from a pile of up to 40.

Review

Discuss the game. Did any children notice which numbers could be divided into halves and quarters? Look for the answer: multiples of 4. Show the children the 'Fraction number line' cards and instructions, and ask them to place some of the fraction cards correctly on the line. Discuss where each card should go and what clues the number line provides.

Differentiation

Less confident learners: These children can play version 2, taking pennies from a pile of up to 20.

More confident learners: These children can take pennies from a pile of up to 80 and record their findings on version 3 of the recording sheet.

Lesson 15 (Apply and evaluate)

Starter

Refine: Repeat the Starter from Lesson 3.

Main teaching activities

Whole class: Begin by asking the children to tell you all they can about fractions. Say that today, they will be using this knowledge to solve problems. Work through the problems on 'Fraction problems', one at a time and very clearly, questioning appropriately. For example: *How can we find half? What is an easy way of finding a quarter? What do we know that helps us find three quarters?*

Paired work: The children's task involves them selecting numbers from 'My fraction problems' and making up problems for another pair to solve. Model an example and then give them between five and ten minutes to make up as many as they can. After their time is up, they should swap problems with another pair working on the same sheet and try to solve them. They could then move on to make their own numbers up.

Review

Go through some examples of the children's problems. Ask them to self-assess their confidence in finding halves and then quarters and finally three quarters of amounts.

Differentiation

Less confident learners: These children work with numbers to 20 and find a half.

More confident learners: These children work with higher numbers and a half, a quarter and three quarters.

Name ____________________ Date ____________________

Dicey problems

Take it in turns to throw three dice.

Try to get the highest answer possible by this rule:

Add two dice and subtract the third.

Collect that number of counters.
Record your results below.
The player with the most counters at the end is the winner!

For example:

If you throw 5, 3 and 6, add the 6 and 5 and take away the 3.
Record your answer like this:
6 + 5 – 3 = 8.
Collect eight counters.

Dice thrown	Calculation
5, 3, 6	6 + 5 – 3 = 8

Name ______________________ Date ________________

Array for maths!

You will need a container of small counters.

Take the number of counters that is written in the box.
Make up an array. Draw under the number in the box.
Then draw the other array that goes with it.

Write the two number sentences for the two arrays like this:

10 (2 rows of 5 dots; 5 rows of 2 dots) 2 × 5 = 10 5 × 2 = 10	12 (3 rows of 4 dots; 4 rows of 3 dots) × = 12 × = 12
15 × = 15 × = 15	18 × = 18 × = 18
12 not the same as before! × = 12 × = 12	18 not the same as before! × = 18 × = 18
24 × = 24 × = 24	24 not the same as before! × = 24 × = 24

Now choose some more numbers up to 30.

Use them to make your own arrays on the back of this sheet.

Name ______________________ Date ______________

Group that!

For each of these:

- Look at the number that the dots need to be divided by.
- Group the dots.
- Work out how many groups there are.
- Complete the number sentence.

Here is an example:

8 ÷ 2

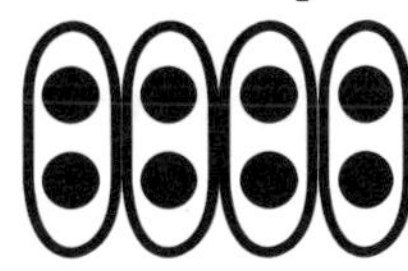

4 groups of 2

8 ÷ 2 = 4

8 ÷ 4 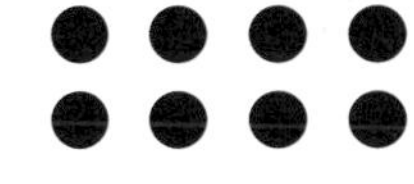 groups of [ ]	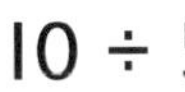 10 ÷ 5 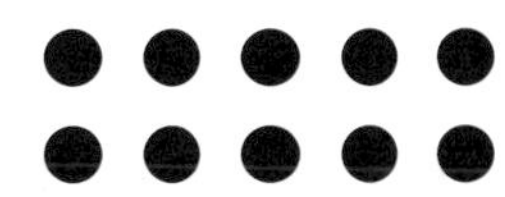 groups of [ ]
12 ÷ 4 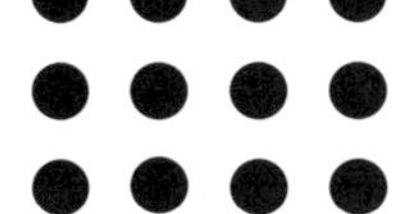 groups of [ ]	20 ÷ 4 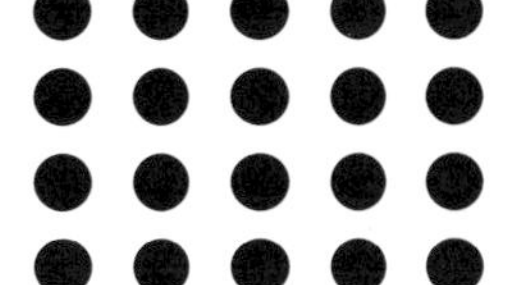 groups of [ ]
18 ÷ 6 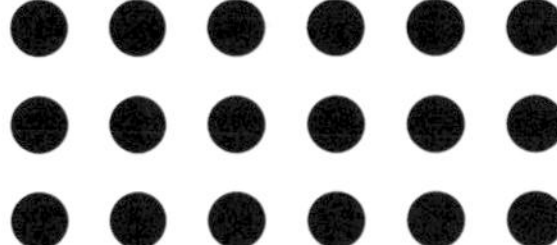 groups of [ ]	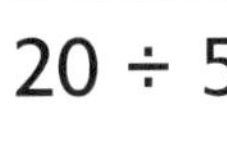 20 ÷ 5  groups of [ ]

On the back of this sheet, make up some for a friend to do.

Name ______________________ Date ______________________

Party problems example

There are 10 biscuits in each packet and 3 more biscuits.

How many biscuits are there altogether? ______ biscuits

Name ______________________ Date ______________

Party problems

Sam and Lizzie are having a party.

Help them solve some of their problems.

1. Lizzie has 6 packets of biscuits with 10 biscuits in each packet and 6 more.
How many biscuits does she have altogether?

[ ] biscuits

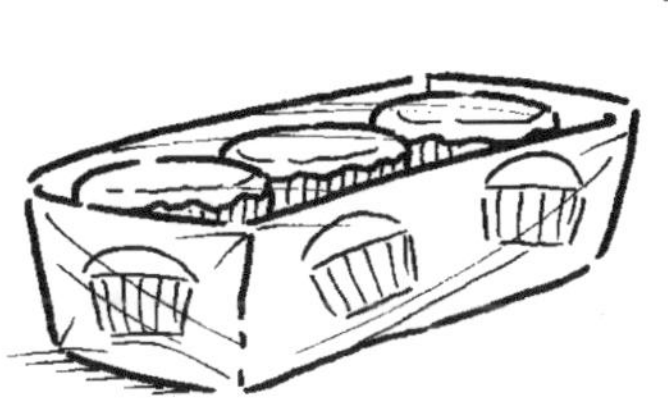

2. Sam needs 18 little cakes.
The shop sells them in packs of 3.
How many packs does he need? [ ] packs

3. Lizzie needs 14 cans of cola.
The shop sells cola in packs of 4 cans.
How many packs does she need? [ ] packs

How many cans will she have left over? [ ] cans

4. There are 25 children at the party.
For the party games, they get into teams of 5.
How many teams are there at the party?

[ ] teams

When you have answered these, make up some more party problems like them.

Make sure you can answer them first, then give them to your friend to solve.

Unit 3 3 weeks

Securing number facts, relationships and calculating

Lesson	Strands	Starter	Main teaching activities
1. Review, teach and practise	Use/apply	Add/subtract 9 or 11: add/subtract 10 and adjust by 1.	Present solutions to puzzles and problems in an organised way; explain decisions, methods and results in pictorial, spoken or written form, using mathematical language and number sentences.
2. Teach and practise	Use/apply	As for Lesson 1	As for Lesson 1
3. Apply and evaluate	Use/apply	Read and write two-digit and three-digit numbers in figures and words.	As for Lesson 1
4. Review and practise	Use/apply Calculate	As for Lesson 3	• Represent repeated addition and arrays as multiplication, and sharing and repeated subtraction (grouping) as division; use practical and informal written methods and related vocabulary to support multiplication and division, including calculations with remainders. • Identify and record the information or calculation needed to solve a puzzle or problem; carry out the steps or calculations and check the solution in the context of the problem. • Present solutions to puzzles and problems in an organised way; explain decisions, methods and results in pictorial, spoken or written form, using mathematical language and number sentences.
5. Teach and practise	Use/apply	As for Lesson 3	As for Lesson 4
6. Review, teach and practise	Use/apply	Derive and recall multiplication facts for the 2, 5 and 10 times-tables and the related division facts; recognise multiples of 2, 5 and 10.	As for Lesson 4
7. Teach and practise	Use/apply	As for Lesson 6	Represent repeated addition and arrays as multiplication, and sharing and repeated subtraction (grouping) as division; use practical and informal written methods and related vocabulary to support multiplication and division, including calculations with remainders.
8. Apply and evaluate	Use/apply	Describe and extend number sequences.	• Represent repeated addition and arrays as multiplication, and sharing and repeated subtraction (grouping) as division; use practical and informal written methods and related vocabulary to support multiplication and division, including calculations with remainders. • Solve problems involving addition, subtraction, multiplication or division in contexts of numbers, measures or pounds and pence.
9. Review and practise	Calculate	**Visualise common 2D shapes and 3D solids; sort, make and describe shapes, referring to their properties.**	**Use the symbols +, -, ×, ÷ and = to record and interpret number sentences involving all four operations; calculate the value of an unknown in a number sentence (eg □ ÷ 2 = 6, 30 - □ = 24).**
10. Review, practise and evaluate	Use/apply Knowledge	As for Lesson 9	• Identify and record the information or calculation needed to solve a puzzle or problem; carry out the steps or calculations and check the solution in the context of the problem. • Understand that halving is the inverse of doubling and derive and recall doubles of all numbers to 20, and the corresponding halves.
11. Review, teach and practise	Use/apply Counting	Understand that subtraction is the inverse of addition and vice versa and use this to derive and record related addition and subtraction number sentences.	• Identify and record the information or calculation needed to solve a puzzle or problem; carry out the steps or calculations and check the solution in the context of the problem. • Find one half, one quarter and three quarters of shapes and sets of objects.
12. Teach and practise	Use/apply Counting	As for Lesson 11	Find one half, one quarter and three quarters of shapes and sets of objects.
13. Teach and practise	Counting	Derive and recall multiplication facts for the 5 times-tables.	As for Lesson 12
14. Teach and apply	Use/apply Counting	Understand that halving is the inverse of doubling and derive and recall doubles of all numbers to 20, and the corresponding halves.	• Find one half, one quarter and three quarters of shapes and sets of objects. • Solve problems involving addition, subtraction, multiplication or division in contexts of numbers, measures or pounds and pence.
15. Apply and evaluate	Use/apply Counting	As for Lesson 14	As for Lesson 14

Speaking and listening objective

- Adopt appropriate roles in small or large groups and consider alternative courses of action.

Introduction

This block contains 15 lessons, the first three of which focus upon open-ended problems that encourage the thinking skills of enquiry and reasoning. In Lessons 4-8, the focus is on multiplication and division. At the beginning of this sequence, multiplication and division are considered as inverse operations. There are opportunities to link with multiplication and division facts and missing number sentences. Division focuses on grouping and sharing with remainders. The last two lessons of this group (Lessons 7-8) involve using and applying through problem solving. Lessons 9-10 directly focus on subtraction through counting on and addition using doubles and near doubles. The last five lessons focus on understanding fractions and their relationship to each other. The children are encouraged to make links to doubling and halving and time and then use their knowledge to solve word problems. Threaded throughout the block are elements of the using and applying objectives and also those from speaking and listening.

Using and applying mathematics

- Identify and record the information or calculation needed to solve a puzzle or problem; carry out the steps or calculations and check the solution in the context of the problem.

Lessons 1-3

Preparation

If necessary, photocopy onto card and laminate enough copies of 'Count it!' (gameboard, instructions and cards) for each group of four children. Make an A3 copy of the gameboard. Make a set of regular shape templates for each pair of children. Display an A3 copy of 'Number words'. Make an A3 'Count it!' gameboard. Prepare an OHT with the headings: Dice 1, Dice 2, Total, How many more do you need to make 12?, Number sentences.

You will need

CD resources

'0-100 number cards', 'Count it!' instructions, cards and gameboard for each group, plus an A3 gameboard, an A3 copy of 'Number words', 'Star number' (see General resources).

Equipment

A class 100 square; individual 100 squares (if needed); coins; counters; an OHP; two dice for each pair.

Learning objectives

Starter

- Add/subtract 9 or 11: add/subtract 10 and adjust by 1.
- Read and write two-digit and three-digit numbers in figures and words.

Main teaching activities

2006

- Present solutions to puzzles and problems in an organised way; explain decisions, methods and results in pictorial, spoken or written form, using mathematical language and number sentences.

1999

- Explain how a problem was solved orally and, where appropriate, in writing.
- Describe and extend simple number sequences
- Count on in steps of 3, 4 or 5 to at least 30, from and back to zero, then from and back to any given small number.
- Solve mathematical problems or puzzles, recognise simple patterns and relationships, generalise and predict.

Vocabulary

problem, solve, calculate, calculation, answer, method, explain, predict, pattern, order, zero, one hundred, two hundred... one thousand, count on, count back, count on in ones/twos/tens, multiple of, sequence, continue, predict, pattern, rule, odd, even

Lesson 1 (Review, teach and practise)

Starter

Rehearse, read and refine: Use a class 100 square to count together on and back in tens and ones: *Find 27. What is 10 more? What is 1 less?* Repeat. Now ask the children to imagine a 100 square. Say a number and ask them to look at it in their minds; ask them which number is below it, above it, one more, ten less and so on. Repeat. Now ask: *How can you add 9 onto 14 easily in your head?* (By adding 10 and taking away 1.) Ask them to add 9 to various two-digit numbers in this way, visualising the 100 square and writing on their whiteboards. Repeat for adding 11. Give any children who struggle a 100 square.

Main teaching activities

Whole class: Explain that the next three lessons involve solving puzzles and investigations and that today's focuses on counting in steps of 3, 4 and 5. Pick a single-digit number card and ask the children to count forwards and then backwards from it, first in threes, then in fours and finally in fives. Repeat a few times, including a few two-digit starting numbers (up to 30). Say a starting number, then move your finger along a counting stick, asking the children to count in threes, fours or fives. Ask the children to predict what number you will point to and why. Write some counting sequences on the board. Ask the children whether each sequence has a pattern they can use to check that the numbers are correct. For example:
5 8 11 14 17 __ __ __ ... (alternate odd/even numbers)
6 __ 16 21 26 31 __ __ ... (alternate final digits the same)
47 43 39 35 31 27 __ __ 15 __ 7 ... (groups of five numbers ending 7 3 9 5 1, all odd).
Group work: Put the children into mixed-ability groups of four. Model the 'Count it!' game using the instructions.

Differentiation

Less confident learners: Provide a 100 square as a visual aid.
More confident learners: Give this group the cards that ask them to count on in threes and fours.

Review

Play the 'Count it!' game as a class, using an A3 gameboard. Write the counting that you do on the board. Focus on any patterns you have looked at earlier in the lesson. Count the money together at the end, beginning with the highest-value coins.

Lesson 2 (Teach and practise)

Starter

Rehearse, read and refine: Repeat the Starter activity from Lesson 1. Encourage the children to visualise the 100 square. After some practice at adding 1, 10, 9 and 11, move on to taking away 1, 10 and 9 with the help of a 100 square.

Main teaching activities

Whole class: You will need the OHT you have prepared earlier (with the headings Dice 1, Dice 2, Total, How many more do you need to make 12?, Number sentences), a marker pen and two dice.

The aim is to find ways of making 12 by adding the two numbers thrown with the dice and working out what the third number (to make 12) must be. Invite various children to come to the front, throw two dice and write the numbers on the acetate as an addition with a symbol to represent the third. Ask: *What do these numbers total? How did you work that out? What do we need to add on to make 12? How did you work that out?* Use their suggestions to complete the number sentence. Write the numbers on the board in a different order and ask whether this makes a difference to the total. Make sure that the children understand that it does not. Repeat with several more pairs of numbers and write appropriate missing number sentences for them to complete.
Paired work: Ask the children to work in pairs, finding as many other combinations to make 12 as they can. Give each pair two dice and a whiteboard and pen for recording. Tell the children to record their results in a table in the same way that you did (you can leave the OHT displayed for their reference).

Differentiation

Less confident learners: Give these children 12 counters each. They can match the counters with the numbers on the dice and count how many are left over.
More confident learners: These children can use their own methods to make 12 in as many ways as possible by adding three numbers. Also encourage them to think of ways to make 12 using subtraction, such as 20 - 4 - 4 or 24 - 20 + 8.

Review

Discuss the children's findings. Invite some pairs from the main and less confident groups to explain their answers. Invite some pairs from the more confident group to explain how they worked out the totals.

Lesson 3 (Apply and evaluate)

Starter

Rehearse, read and refine: Ask the children to write a two-digit number on their whiteboards. Give them instructions to follow, such as: *Write 18, add 2, double your number, subtract 10, add 3, add 8, swap the digits round, what is your number?* Repeat with more numbers. Ask the children to write some two-digit numbers in words, encouraging them to look at the 'Number words' poster for clues.

Main teaching activities

Whole class: This lesson is about making numbers in different ways. Write '10' on the board and ask the children to suggest some ways of making 10. Target the less confident children to answer first, when the easier methods have not yet been suggested. Encourage additions and subtractions, mixtures of both (such as 20 – 19 + 9), multiplications (5 × 2), divisions (20 ÷ 2) and fractions ($^1/_4$ of 40). Write another number on the board; ask the children to work with a partner and come up with as many ways of making the number as they can, writing on their whiteboards. Take feedback, and find out which pair has the most unusual way.

Paired work: Give each pair some number cards to 50 and the 'Star number' activity sheet for recording.

Differentiation

Less confident learners: Give these children number cards to 20.

More confident learners: Give these children number cards to 100.

Review

Ask a pair from each ability group to give an example of their work, writing all the ways they found on the board. Ask the class to vote for the most interesting method, and then to think of another unusual way of making a number such as 15, 50 or 75. Review the various strategies that have been used over the last three lessons and ask the children to assess their confidence in using them.

Lessons 4–8

Preparation

Photocopy 'Multiplication and division vocabulary' onto card and cut out the words. Photocopy the 'Home we go!' gameboard onto card and laminate for each group of three children. Make a pack of 0–30 number cards for each group. Make an A3 copy of 'How to solve a problem' (see General resources).

You will need

Photocopiable pages

'Array for maths 2' (page 218), 'Fruity problems' (page 219).

CD resources

'Multiplications and division vocabulary', 'Home we go!', 'How to solve a problem' (see General resources); 'Array for maths 2' and 'Fruity problems' support and extension versions, core version of 'Table facts', ITP Grouping.

Equipment

Counters, counting apparatus.

Learning objectives

Starter

- Read and write two-digit and three-digit numbers in figures and words.
- Derive and recall multiplication facts for the 2, 5 and 10 times-tables and the related division facts; recognise multiples of 2, 5 and 10.
- Describe and extend number sequences.

Main teaching activities

2006

- Represent repeated addition and arrays as multiplication, and sharing and repeated subtraction (grouping) as division; use practical and informal written methods and related vocabulary to support multiplication and division, including calculations with remainders.
- Solve problems involving addition, subtraction, multiplication or division in contexts of numbers, measures or pounds and pence.
- Identify and record the information or calculation needed to solve a puzzle or problem; carry out the steps or calculations and check the solution in the context of the problem.
- Present solutions to puzzles and problems in an organised way; explain decisions, methods and results in pictorial, spoken or written form, using mathematical language and number sentences.

1999

- Understand the operation of multiplication as repeated addition or as describing an array, and begin to understand division as grouping (repeated subtraction) or sharing.
- Use and begin to read the related vocabulary.

- Use ×, ÷ and = signs to record mental calculations in a number sentence.
- Use mental addition and subtraction, simple multiplication and division, to solve simple word problems involving numbers in 'real life', money or measures, using one or two steps.
- Explain how a problem was solved orally and, where appropriate, in writing.
- Choose and use appropriate operations and efficient calculation strategies (eg mental, mental with jottings) to solve problems.
- Use known number facts and place value to carry out mentally simple multiplications and divisions.

Vocabulary

lots of, groups of, times, multiply, multiplied by, multiple of, repeated addition, array, row, column, equal groups of, repeated subtraction, divide, divided by, remainder

Lesson 4 (Review and practise)

Starter

Rehearse, read and refine: Ask the children to write single-digit and two-digit numbers on their whiteboards. Show them number cards and ask them to write these as words. Then say: *Write 2. Make it say 22. Now add 10.* (32) *Change the 2 to a 7. What number do you have now?* (37) *Add 3.* (40) *Take away two tens.* (20) *Add 100.* (120) *Double the tens number.* (140) *Add 9. What number do you have now?* (149) *Write the number in words.* Repeat several times with different start digits.

Main teaching activities

Whole class: Explain that over the next few lessons the children will be learning more about multiplication and division. Revise the meaning of 'multiply' and 'divide', and ask for related vocabulary. Use the vocabulary cards and sort them into two groups: multiplication and division. Say*: Today we will be focusing on division and multiplication as opposite operations.* Explain this by linking to work they have done on this for addition and subtraction as inverse operations, and demonstrate using a number line. Follow this by demonstrating using arrays. Draw an array of 8 dots on the board and ask volunteers to loop dots to show the possible multiplications, that is, 2 × 4 and 4 × 2. Draw it again and demonstrate 8 divided into 2 and then 4 and write the division sentences: 8 ÷ 2 = 4 and 8 ÷ 4 = 2. As part of this, write the repeated additions and subtractions. Ask them to draw as many different arrays as they can for 12 and to write the appropriate multiplications. Take feedback and then go through each to show the division.

Paired work: Ask the children to work in pairs to make arrays and derive four number sentences from each: 2 multiplications and 2 subtractions. Model the example from the 'Array for maths 2' photocopiable sheet.

Differentiation

Less confident learners: Provide the support version of 'Array for maths 2' with lower numbers. If possible, ask a teaching assistant to work with these children. Let them make the arrays with counters before drawing them.

More confident learners: Provide the extension version that asks for different arrays for 24 and 36.

Review

Invite pairs to draw and explain one of their arrays. Discuss what is helpful in order to do this quickly. Establish that knowledge of their tables facts will help. Go through a couple of examples. If you take 12, a multiplication could be 2 × 6, another could be 6 × 2 because they both total 12, the divisions would be the opposite: 12 ÷ 2 = 6, 12 ÷ 6 = 2.

Lesson 5 (Teach and practise)

Starter

Refine, read and rehearse: As for Lesson 4.

Main teaching activities

Whole class: Repeat the inversion aspect of Lesson 4 in detail. Then discuss how multiplication facts can help as in the Review for Lesson 4, using plenty of examples. Write 8 on the board, and ask the children to use their times tables knowledge to make up as many sentences as they can with 8 as the answer. Ask them to draw an array to explain one of their sentences. Ask them to make up division facts in the same way.

Paired work: The children should work through 'Table facts', which gives them a number and asks them to think of multiplication and division facts to go with it and to draw arrays to show their thinking. Encourage them to think of facts to do with their two-, five- and ten-times tables.

Differentiation

Less confident learners: This group should focus on two-times table facts.

More confident learners: Encourage this group to think about three- and four-times tables as well as two-, five- and ten-times tables.

Review

Invite pairs to explain their work. Write □ × □ = 30 on the board and ask them to think of as many ways as they can to complete the missing number sentence. Then write this: 30 ÷ □ = □ and ask the children to use the previous task to help them make up as many division sentences as they can. Reiterate the fact that multiplication and division are opposite operations and that you can often use one to help solve the other.

Lesson 6 (Review, teach and practise)

Starter

Recall and refresh: Call out random numbers and ask the children to write down those that are multiples of 2. Repeat for 5 and 10. Next, call out other numbers and ask them to write down as many multiplication and division facts for these as they can think of.

Main teaching activities

Whole class: Say that today they will be focusing on division. Find out what they can remember about this area of maths. Focus on the two aspects: grouping and sharing. Briefly explain the difference, using two word problems as follows:

- *I have 16 sweets and I want to share them equally between my 4 friends. How many will they each get?*
- *I have 16 sweets and want to put them in bags of 4, how many bags do I need?*

Focus on grouping for the rest of this lesson. Use the ITP Grouping to model this concept. Link to repeated subtraction. Initially begin with multiples of 2, 4 or 5 and then choose numbers that will produce a remainder.

Group work: Ask the children to practise this concept by playing 'Home we go!' Model the game according to the instructions outlined for this lesson.

Differentiation

Less confident learners: Let these children use number lines, counters or pennies to help them group. Adult support would be helpful.

More confident learners: Encourage these children to record their work like this: 16 ÷ 3 is 5 remainder 1.

Review

Play 'Home we go!' in two teams. Make sure everyone counts. Recap the main points of this lesson: division can be grouping which is repeated subtraction and there can be remainders.

Lesson 7 (Teach and practise)

Starter

Recall and refresh: As for Lesson 6.

Main teaching activities

Whole class: Say that today they will be focusing on division by sharing. Make up some word problems to explain, for example:

- *Sam has 18 cars; he shares them between himself and his friend. How many do they each get?*
- *Sam, Adam, Jenny, Peter and Jane are having a picnic. Peter has brought 20 biscuits to share equally with Jane. How many will they each have?*

Demonstrate these problems physically, using counters or similar apparatus. Ask some problems that will give a remainder, for example: *Sally has 20 dolls; she shares them between herself and two friends. How many do they each get?* Discuss the meaning of a remainder and link to the previous session when they found remainders while grouping.

Group work: Ask the children to practise this concept by playing 'Home we go!' again, but this time counting out the number on the card in counters and sharing the counters into the number on the board. Again, they move according to the remainder.

Differentiation

Less confident learners: These children should use number cards to 30. Let them also use number lines, counters or pennies to help them group.

More confident learners: Encourage these children to record their work like this: 16 ÷ 3 is 5 remainder 1.

Review

Go through a few examples from the game, writing them as number sentences. Compare the two methods of division. Ask them to explain how their knowledge of table facts can help them.

Lesson 8 (Apply and evaluate)

Starter

Recall and refresh: Call out different numbers and ask the children to write down the number that is 1 or 10 more or less. Progress to numbers that are 100 more/less.

Main teaching activities

Whole class: Explain that the children will be using all they have done over the last few lessons to solve problems. Recap on what they have learned and then recap the problem-solving process, displaying the 'How to solve a problem' poster. Discuss this using the following example: *Andrew, Katie, Tom and Steph have been given 26 sweets. Katie shares them out equally. How many will be left over?* Ask: *What do they need to find out, what is the relevant information, what do they need to do, roughly how many do they think will be left?* Ask a similar problem and then explain the paired work involved in 'Fruity problems'.

Paired work: The children should work through 'Fruity problems'.

Differentiation

Less confident learners: These children should use the support version of 'Fruity problems', which encourages the use of two- and ten-times tables.

More confident learners: These children should use the extension version, which encourages use of different times tables.

Review

Cover up the 'How to solve a problem' poster and ask: *Who can tell me the steps you have to take when you try to answer a problem?* Invite a child to explain using one of the problems they had during the session. Finally, discuss the main points they need to remember about multiplication and division. Bring out the following points: Multiplication is repeated addition, can be solved by arrays, is the inverse of division, multiplication facts are useful to solve it. Division is repeated subtraction, grouping, sharing and arrays can be used to solve it, is the inverse of multiplication, multiplication facts are useful.

Lessons 9-10

Preparation

If necessary, make and laminate a copy of the 'Lost in space gameboard' and 'Lost in space recording sheet' for each group of three or four. Make OHTs of the 'Lost in space gameboard'.

You will need

CD resources
'Lost in space game board', 'Lost in space recording sheet', 'Near doubles' game and cards; '0-100 number cards' (see General resources).
Equipment
Plasticine.

Learning objectives

Starter

- Visualise common 2D shapes and 3D solids; identify shapes from pictures of them in different positions and orientations; sort, make and describe shapes, referring to their properties.

Main teaching activities

2006

- Use the symbols +, –, ×, ÷ and = to record and interpret number sentences involving all four operations; calculate the value of an unknown in a number sentence (eg □ ÷ 2 = 6, 30 - □ = 24).
- Understand that halving is the inverse of doubling and derive and recall doubles of all numbers to 20, and the corresponding halves.

1999

- Use the +, –, ×, ÷ and = signs to record mental calculations in a number sentence, and recognise the use of a symbol such as □ to stand for an unknown number.
- Derive quickly doubles of all whole numbers to at least 20 (eg 17 × 2), and the corresponding halves (eg 36 ÷ 2).

Vocabulary

add, addition, more, plus, make, sum, total, altogether, score, tens boundary, difference, subtract, subtraction, take away Double, halve, inverse

Lesson 9 (Review and practise)

Starter

Refresh and reason: Give the children a lump of Plasticine each and remind them of the work they did making 3D shapes in Block B. Ask them to name as many different 3D shapes as they can. Ask them to make one 3D shape with the Plasticine. When they have all done this, ask them to stand up if their shape has certain properties. For example: *Does your shape have six faces?... at least one triangle face?... no edges?... a square face?* Ask them to explain to a partner how they know and how this relates to the properties of the shape they have made. Bring in as many different properties as you can. Ask the children to make another shape from the Plasticine. Repeat this a few times.

Main teaching activities

Whole class: Ask the children what is meant by 'finding the difference' between two numbers. Write some two-digit numbers up to 50 on the board. Ask the children to calculate the differences between pairs of these numbers using a number line.
Group work: Ask the children to practise the subtraction strategy of finding the difference by counting up. Give them the 'Lost in space' gameboard and explain the rules for this lesson, keeping the number range 1 to 50.

Differentiation

Less confident learners: The children can use number cards 1 to 12.
More confident learners: The children can use number cards to 100.

Review

Divide the class into three teams. Play 'Lost in space' again together, using an OHT. During the game, choose children to demonstrate how to count along a number line on the board for their team. Ask these children: *What is the first thing you do? What is the next multiple of 10? How many units do you need to get to the next multiple of 10? What do you do next? How do you find the answer?*

Lesson 10 (Review, practise and evaluate)

Starter

Reason: As for Lesson 9.

Main teaching activities

Whole class: Say that today the children will use doubles to help them with addition. Write some single-digit numbers, two-digit numbers to 20 and multiples of 10 to 100 on the board and ask the children to double them, writing the answers on their whiteboards to show you.

Write 30 + 40 on the board. Ask the children how doubling could help them to add these numbers. Look for the strategy: 30 + 40 = 30 + 30 + 10 = double 30 + 10. Repeat with these additions: 20 + 21, 7 + 8, 50 + 60, 20 + 31. In each case, record the reasoning used.

Group work: Model the group work. The children need to spread a set of 'Near doubles game cards' face up on the table, then find two numbers that come next to each other (such as 12 and 13), then add them together using the 'near doubles' method. Ask them to work out and record the additions as you did in the main teaching session: 12 + 13 = 12 + 12 + 1 = 25.

Differentiation

Less confident learners: Give this group the near doubles cards with numbers to 20.

More confident learners: Challenge this group to use all the near doubles cards.

Review

Write some missing number addition sentences on the board, such as: 20 + ◯ = 41; 15 + ◯ = 29; 7 + ◯ = 13. Ask the children to work out which 'near double' number would go in each box to make the number sentence correct (21, 14, 6). Each time, ask the children to explain how they found the answer; target children whom you wish to assess. Look for speed and confidence in answering.

Lessons 11-15

Preparation

Copy 'Fraction strips 2' onto acetate and cut out. Copy 'Fraction number line and cards' onto A3 paper and laminate, then cut out the cards. Remove the hands from one of the card clocks and copy it onto acetate. Cut out three card circles the same size as the clock; keep one whole, halve the second and quarter the third. Adapt the 'Number spinners' and 'Fraction spinners'. Make five Multilink towers: 1) five red, five green; 2) three red, three yellow, three blue, three green; 3) six red, three yellow, three green; 4) four red, four yellow, four blue, four green; 5) eight red, four yellow, four green.

If necessary: make an A3 poster of 'How to solve a problem'; copy the 'Dartboard doubles' game onto card, then laminate the gameboard and cut out the spinners and cards. Make an OHT of 'Fraction problems'. Make enough copies of 'Fraction cards' to cut out three or four cards for each pair of children.

Learning objectives

Starter

- Understand that subtraction is the inverse of addition and vice versa and use this to derive and record related addition and subtraction number sentences.
- Derive and recall multiplication facts for the 5 times-table.
- Understand that halving is the inverse of doubling and derive and recall doubles of all numbers to 20, and the corresponding halves.

Main teaching activities

2006

- Find one half, one quarter and three quarters of shapes and sets of objects.
- Identify and record the information or calculation needed to solve a puzzle or problem; carry out the steps or calculations and check the solution in the context of the problem.
- Solve problems involving addition, subtraction, multiplication or division in contexts of numbers, measures or pounds and pence.

1999

- Begin to recognise and find one half and one quarter of shapes and small numbers of objects.
- Begin to recognise that two halves or four quarters make one whole and that two quarters and one half are equivalent.
- Choose and use appropriate operations and efficient calculation strategies to solve problems.

Vocabulary

part, equal parts, fraction, one whole, one half, two halves, one quarter, two... three... four quarters, calculate, calculation, mental calculation, jotting, answer, correct, number sentence, sign, operation, symbol

You will need

Photocopiable pages
'Clock fractions' (page 220) - A3 copy and one per child, 'Fraction problems 2' (page 221).
CD resources
An A3 copy of 'How to solve a problem', 'Dartboard doubles', game, spinner and gameboard, 'Fraction cards', '0-100 number cards', 'Fraction strips 2', 'Spin a fraction', 'Fraction number line and cards', 'Addition and subtraction cards', 'Pennies game' and 'Recording sheet 3', 'Spider charts for multiplying and dividing by 5' (see General resources); 'Fraction problems 2' support and extension versions.
Equipment
Multilink cubes; counters; pennies; card clocks; counting equipment.

Lesson 11 (Review, teach and practise)

Starter

Recall and reason: Show some of the addition cards from 'Addition and subtraction cards' and ask the children to write the corresponding subtraction on their whiteboards and to explain their answer.

Main teaching activities

Whole class: This week's lessons are about using fractions. Ask: *Who can tell me something about a fraction?* Write down responses on the board. As in Block E, Unit 2, aim for these statements (prompting if necessary): *A fraction is part of a whole thing. Half is when you divide something into two equal parts. 4 is half of 8. A quarter is when you divide something into four equal pieces. Two halves make a whole. Four quarters make a whole. A quarter is half of a half.* Remind the children that finding a fraction such as a half or a quarter is the same as dividing, because you are taking a whole number of things and sharing them out equally.

Ask whether the children remember the fraction strips and what they demonstrate (see Unit 1). Use the 'Fraction strips 2' OHT to demonstrate that one whole is equal to two halves and four quarters, two quarters is equal to one half, and three quarters is equal to one half and one quarter. Put 12 counters on the whole strip. Give another 12 to a volunteer to put correctly on the halves strip (six in each section) and 12 to another volunteer to put on the quarters strip. Ask how many would go in each section if you had 16, 20 and 24 counters; then what would happen if you had 14 counters and then 15, and why. Agree that only even numbers can be halved, and that the half can only be halved again (to make quarters) if it is even.

Group work: Ask the children to practise finding fractions of numbers by playing the 'Pennies game 2'. Ask whether they remember the game. Briefly model the instructions using up to 50 pennies. This time, they need to use 'Recording sheet 3', which asks them to identify whether the number of pennies they picked is odd or even.

Differentiation

Less confident learners: Work with this group and encourage them to find quarters as well as halves, using up to 30 counters.
More confident learners: This group could use number cards to generate numbers from 30 to 100.

Review

Use the Multilink towers to make true and false statements. Ask the children to respond by holding their thumbs up/down or writing T/F on their whiteboards, and to explain their decisions. Reinforce the fact that any number that can be halved is even. Make statements such as:

1. *Half of this tower is green.* (T) *You can find a quarter of 10 cubes.* (F) *Why not?*
2. *Half of this tower is red.* (F) *The red and the green make up half.* (T) *If I add the yellow to the red and green, I will have $^3/_4$.* (T)
3. *Half of this tower is yellow.* (F) *A quarter is green.* (T) *The green and the yellow make half.* (T)

Ask the children to work in pairs to make some true and false statements for towers 4 and 5. Work through some with the class.

Lesson 12 (Teach and practise)

Starter

Recall and reason: Show some of the subtraction cards from 'Addition and subtraction cards' and ask the children to write the corresponding addition on their whiteboards and explain how they know. Next, ask them to make up two corresponding sentences of their own.

Main teaching activities

Whole class: Ask the children to tell you the 'fraction facts' they learned yesterday. Say that today they will be linking fractions with time. Ask: *Can anyone tell me when we use fractions to talk about time?* (Quarter past, half past and quarter to.) Show the clock OHT and say: *This is a whole clock. How many minutes are there all the way round it? So how many minutes* *are there in an hour?* Cover half the clock with the half card circle. *How much of the clock can you see now? How much of it can't you see? How many minutes are showing? How did you work that out? Did anyone halve 60? If I put this other half on the clock, how much is covered now?* Take off the card halves and cover the first quarter (from 12 to 3), and ask similar questions. Invite children to come to the front to cover different quarters: 3 to 6, 6 to 9, 9 to 12 and other quarters such as 2 to 5. Ask for a volunteer to cover three quarters.

Paired work: Using an A3 copy of 'Clock fractions', make and label some halves and quarters of the clock faces. Give each pair a copy of the sheet. Encourage the children to make halves and quarters in various ways. (Keep the second copy for Lesson 3.)

Differentiation

Less confident learners: Provide pre-cut half and quarter circle shapes. Ask the children to find up to four different ways of making half and then a quarter.

More confident learners: Ask this group to find three-quarters as well as halves and quarters.

Review

Ask a few pairs to show some of the ways they covered fractions of their clocks. Covering from 4 to 10, ask: *How do we know this is half?* Cover from 2 to 5, then 8 to 11. *What fraction is covered here? And here? How do you know? Are two quarters the same as a half?* Show the children the fraction number line and ask them to place some of the fraction cards on the line. Discuss where each card should go, and what clues are on the number line.

Lesson 13 (Teach and practise)

Starter

Recall and refresh: Practise recall of five-times table facts by counting in multiples with fingers, then using the ×5 spider chart.

Main teaching activities

Whole class: The children will need a card clock each. Ask them to find twelve o'clock. Now ask them to move the minute hand around in fractions of an hour, and tell you the new time. For example: *Move clockwise a quarter of an hour, clockwise half an hour, anticlockwise a quarter of an hour.* If necessary, remind them to move the hour hand as well. Spend five minutes or so doing this.

Group work: Remind the children of the task in Lesson 12. Give them the second copy of 'Clock fractions'. Ask them to find different ways of making half and three-quarters, using quarter pieces only. The halves should be different from those made the day before.

Differentiation

Less confident learners: Ask these children to make quarters and halves, using the quarter piece.

More confident learners: Encourage this group to look for other fractions, perhaps thirds or twelfths.

Review

Play 'Spin a fraction' as a class team game. Adapt the 'Number spinner' to give six larger even numbers to 50 and the fraction spinner to include $^3/_4$. When $^3/_4$ comes up, ask the children how they can find this amount. If necessary, prompt them by saying: *If we know $^1/_4$ is... then $^3/_4$ is three times...*

Lesson 14 (Teach and apply)

Starter

Rehearse and recall: Call out some numbers in the ranges specified by the learning objectives (see above) and ask the children to double and halve them, writing on their whiteboards. Play 'Dartboard doubles', adapting the instructions so the whole class can play in two or three teams.

Main teaching activities

Whole class: The next two lessons are about solving problems that involve fractions. Ask: *What do we need to do when we are working out the answer to a problem?* Write the children's responses on the board. Display the 'How to solve a problem' poster as a reminder. Work through the problems on the OHT of 'Fraction problems 2' together, inviting children to come to the OHP and underline the relevant information in each problem. Talk about the strategies that can be used to solve these problems, such as: partitioning

and halving or quartering each number, then recombining; putting counters into two or four groups. Discuss which strategy is the most efficient for each problem, and why.
Paired work: Ask the children to work in pairs to complete 'Fraction problems 2'.

Differentiation
Less confident learners: Provide the support version of 'Fraction problems 2'. Give help with reading. Let the children use counting equipment.
More confident learners: Provide the extension version of 'Fraction problems 2'.

Review
Invite some pairs from each group to explain how they solved one of their problems. Include those children whom you wish to assess. Ask questions such as: *How did you find a quarter? What would three quarters of that number be?*

Lesson 15 (Apply and evaluate)

Starter
Rehearse, recall and reason: Repeat the Starter from Lesson 14, but use numbers to 20. Ask the children to double and double again, and to halve and halve again where appropriate.

Main teaching activities
Whole class: Explain that today the children will make up their own problems for the rest of the class to solve. Write some information on the board, such as: 20 apples, Granny Smith. Make up a problem from these: *Granny Smith picked 20 apples from her apple tree. She needed a quarter of these to make apple sauce, and she gave the rest to me. How many did she use for her sauce?* Show the problem on the board, using simple pictures, words and numbers. Ask the children to solve it.

Ask the children to turn to a partner and together make up a similar problem, using the same information. Give them a few minutes, then take feedback. Write some more information on the board and repeat the process.
Paired work: Give each pair of children three or four fraction cards; ask them to make up one problem for each card.

Differentiation
Less confident learners: Provide cards with numbers to 20, quarters and halves.
More confident learners: Provide cards with higher numbers. Write information (with numbers to 100) on the blank cards for these children to use.

Review
Invite pairs from each ability group to describe one of their problems and invite the other children to solve it. Include those children whom you wish to assess. As they begin to solve the problems, ask: *What do you need to know? How are you going to use this information? What do you need to know before you can work it out?*

Name ______________________ Date ________________

Array for maths 2

You will need a container of small counters.

Take the number of counters that is written in the box.

Make up an array. Draw your array under the number.

Write the four array 'sums' like this:

16		16 must be different!	
●●●●●●●● ●●●●●●●●			
2 × 8 = 16	16 ÷ 8 = 2	× =	÷ =
8 × 2 = 16	16 ÷ 2 = 8	× =	÷ =

Now you try.

20		20 must be different!	
× =	÷ =	× =	÷ =
× =	÷ =	× =	÷ =
24		**24 must be different!**	
× =	÷ =	× =	÷ =
× =	÷ =	× =	÷ =

Now make up some more arrays and number sentences for 24 on the other side of this sheet.

Securing number facts, relationships and calculating

BLOCK E

Name ______________________ Date ______________

Fruity problems

Sally and Sanjeev have been asked to solve some problems for their teacher. They are having difficulty. Can you help them?

1. Mrs Smith has 34 apples in a basket. 5 children come along and take out 4 apples each.
How many apples does she have left?

[   ] apples

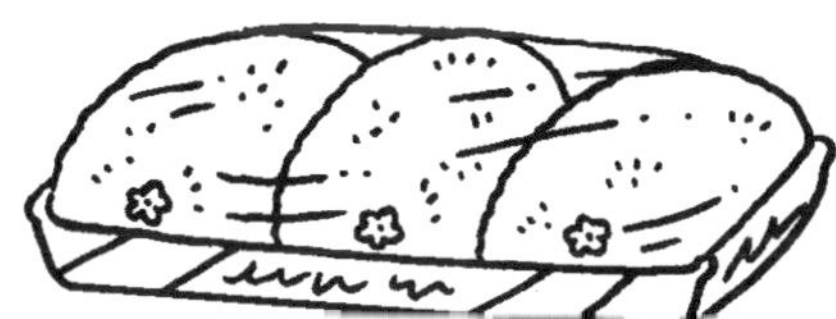

2. Mrs Smith needs 24 kiwi fruit for a salad. The shop sells them in packs of 3.
How many packs does she need to buy?

[   ] packs

3. Mrs Smith needs 75 plums to make into jam. The shop sells plums in packs of 10.

How many packs does she need to buy?

[   ] packs

How many plums will she have left over?

[   ] plums

4. There are 30 children in Mrs Smith's class. She wants to buy them each an apple for every day they are in school this week.
How many apples will she need?

[   ] apples

Make up some more fruity problems like these.

Make sure you can answer them first, then give them to your friend to solve.

Name ______________________ Date ________________

Clock fractions

Cut out the two circles at the bottom of the page.

Colour the fractions you make on the clocks.
Fill in the sentence to say what the fraction is.

I've covered ____ of my clock.

I've covered ____ of my clock.

I've covered ____ of my clock.

I've covered ____ of my clock.

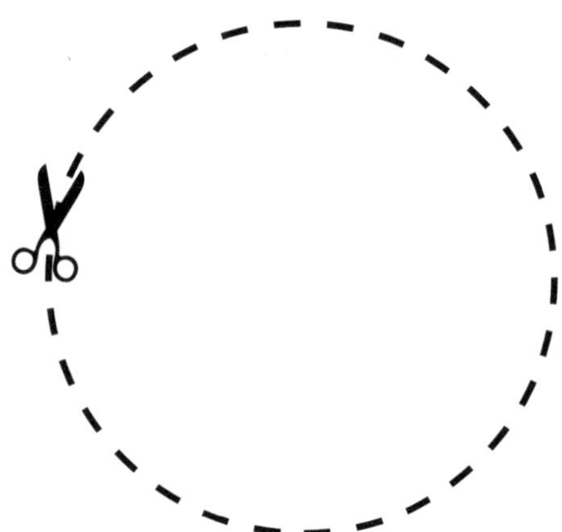

Cut this one in half.

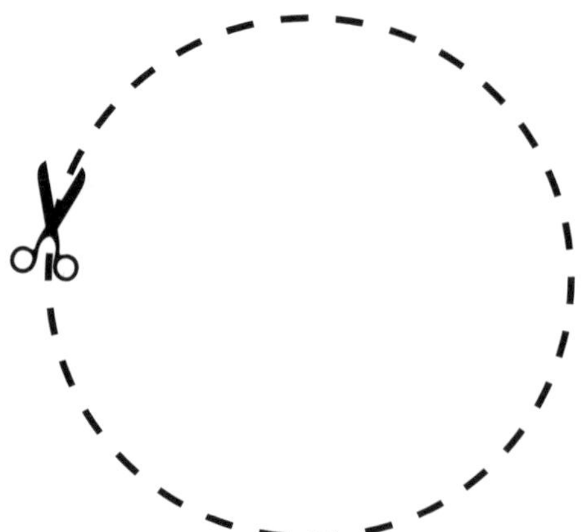

Cut this one into quarters.

Name ____________________ Date ____________________

Fraction problems 2

I had a car collection. There were 30 cars in it.
I gave half of my collection to my best friend.

How many cars did I have left?

How I worked it out:

____

My teacher was baking biscuits for our class.
There are 20 children in our class.
She baked a biscuit for each child.
A quarter of our class were missing when she brought them in.

How many biscuits did she have left over?

How I worked it out:

____

Juan counted his toy farm animals. He had 50.
He gave half of them to his little sister.

How many animals did he have left?

How I worked it out:

____

Sakina had 14 pairs of shoes.
She wanted to give a quarter of them away.

Could she? Why or why not?

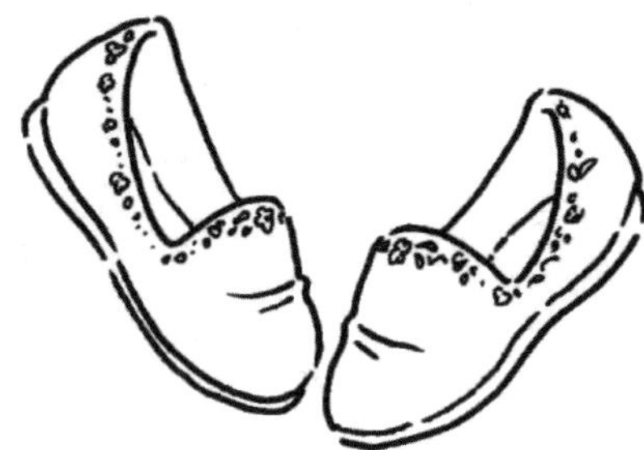

How I worked it out: __________

____

Marcia bought a packet of sweets.
There were 40 in the packet.
She gave a quarter to her mum.

How many did they each have?

____

How I worked it out: ______________________________

Pupil name ____________________ Class name ____________________

Year 2 End-of-year objectives	✓	Comments
Count up to 100 objects by grouping them and counting in tens, fives or twos; explain what each digit in a two-digit number represents, including numbers where 0 is a place holder; partition two-digit numbers in different ways, including into multiples of 10 and 1.		
Add or subtract mentally a one-digit number or a multiple of 10 to or from any two-digit number; use practical and informal written methods to add and subtract two-digit numbers.		
Use the symbols +, –, ×, ÷ and = to record and interpret number sentences involving all four operations; calculate the value of an unknown in a number sentence (eg □ ÷ 2 = 6, 30 - □ = 24).		
Derive and recall all addition and subtraction facts for each number to at least 10, all pairs with totals to 20 and all pairs of multiples of 10 with totals up to 100.		
Visualise common 2D shapes and 3D solids; identify shapes from pictures of them in different positions and orientations; sort, make and describe shapes, referring to their properties.		
Use units of time (seconds, minutes, hours, days) and know the relationships between them; read the time to the quarter hour; identify time intervals, including those that cross the hour.		

Teacher name ____________ Class name ____________

Year 2 End-of-year objectives																								
Count up to 100 objects by grouping them and counting in tens, fives or twos; explain what each digit in a two-digit number represents, including numbers where 0 is a place holder; partition two-digit numbers in different ways, including into multiples of 10 and 1.																								
Add or subtract mentally a one-digit number or a multiple of 10 to or from any two-digit number; use practical and informal written methods to add and subtract two-digit numbers.																								
Use the symbols +, –, ×, ÷ and = to record and interpret number sentences involving all four operations; calculate the value of an unknown in a number sentence (eg □ ÷ 2 = 6 , 30 - □ = 24).																								
Derive and recall all addition and subtraction facts for each number to at least 10, all pairs with totals to 20 and all pairs of multiples of 10 with totals up to 100.																								
Visualise common 2D shapes and 3D solids; identify shapes from pictures of them in different positions and orientations; sort, make and describe shapes, referring to their properties.																								
Use units of time (seconds, minutes, hours, days) and know the relationships between them; read the time to the quarter hour; identify time intervals, including those that cross the hour.																								

Consolidation of level 2, and start on level 3

SCHOLASTIC

Also available in this series:

MATHS

ISBN 978-0439-94546-2

ISBN 978-0439-94547-9

ISBN 978-0439-94548-6

ISBN 978-0439-94549-3

ISBN 978-0439-94550-9

ISBN 978-0439-94551-6

ISBN 978-0439-94521-9

ISBN 978-0439-94522-6

ISBN 978-0439-94523-3

ISBN 978-0439-94524-0

ISBN 978-0439-94525-7

ISBN 978-0439-94526-4

To find out more, call: 0845 603 9091
or visit our website www.scholastic.co.uk